A NETWORKED SELF AND PLATFORMS, STORIES, CONNECTIONS

We tell stories about who we are. Through telling these stories, we connect with others and affirm our own sense of self. Spaces—be they online or offline; private or public; physical, augmented or virtual; or of a hybrid nature—present the performative realms upon which our stories unfold. This volume focuses on how digital platforms support, enhance, or confine the networked self. Contributors examine a range of issues relating to storytelling, platforms, and the self, including the live-reporting of events, the curation of information, emerging modalities of journalism, collaboratively formed memories, and the instant historification of the present.

Zizi Papacharissi is Professor and Head of the Communication Department and Professor of Political Science at the University of Illinois-Chicago, and University Scholar at the University of Illinois System. Her work focuses on the social and political consequences of online media. She has published nine books, including *Affective Publics, A Private Sphere, A Networked Self: Identity, Community, and Culture on Social Network Sites* (Routledge, 2010) and over 60 journal articles, book chapters and reviews. She is the founding and current editor of the open access journal *Social Media and Society*.

A Networked Self

Each volume in this series develops and pursues a distinct theme focused on the concept of the Networked Self. The five volumes cover the broad range of socio-cultural, political, economic, and sociotechnical issues that shape and are shaped by the (networked) self in late modernity—what we have come to describe as the anthropocene.

> *A Networked Self: Identity, Community and Culture on Social Network Sites*
> *A Networked Self and Platforms, Stories, Connections*
> *A Networked Self and Love*
> *A Networked Self and Birth, Life, Death*
> *A Networked Self and Human Augmentics, Artificial Intelligence, Sentience*

Growing upon the initial volume, *A Networked Self: Identity, Community and Culture on Social Network Sites*, published in 2010, the five volumes will form a picture of the way digital media shape contemporary notions of identity.

A NETWORKED SELF AND PLATFORMS, STORIES, CONNECTIONS

Edited by Zizi Papacharissi

Routledge
Taylor & Francis Group

NEW YORK AND LONDON

First published 2018
by Routledge
711 Third Avenue, New York, NY 10017

and by Routledge
2 Park Square, Milton Park, Abingdon, Oxon OX14 4RN

Routledge is an imprint of the Taylor & Francis Group, an informa business

© 2018 Taylor & Francis

Library of Congress Cataloging-in-Publication Data
Names: Papacharissi, Zizi, editor.
Title: A networked self and platforms, stories, connections / edited by
    Zizi Papacharissi.
Description: New York : Routledge, 2018. | Series: A networked self
Identifiers: LCCN 2017055434 | ISBN 9781138722675 (hardback) |
    ISBN 9781138722682 (pbk.)
Subjects: LCSH: Social networks. | Interpersonal relations.
Classification: LCC HM741 .N455 2018 | DDC 302.3—dc23
LC record available at https://lccn.loc.gov/2017055434

ISBN: 978-1-138-72267-5 (hbk)
ISBN: 978-1-138-72268-2 (pbk)
ISBN: 978-1-315-19343-4 (ebk)

Typeset in Bembo
by Apex CoVantage, LLC

MIX
Paper from
responsible sources
FSC
www.fsc.org   FSC® C013056

Printed and bound in Great Britain by
TJ International Ltd, Padstow, Cornwall

For my students, who tell inspiring stories

CONTENTS

FIGURES

CONTRIBUTORS

Taina Bucher is Associate Professor in the Department of Media, Cognition, and Communication at the University of Copenhagen, Denmark. She teaches in the Communication and IT program, which blends communication theory with programming skills and design research. Her research focuses on social media, and the power of algorithms in everyday life, at the intersection of software studies, STS, and media theory. She is the author of *IF . . . THEN: Algorithmic Power and Politics* (Oxford University Press, 2018) and her work on software and sociality has appeared in journals such as *New Media & Society, Information, Communication & Society, Television & New Media, Computational Culture,* and *Culture Machine.*

Matt Carlson is Associate Professor of Communication at Saint Louis University. He is author of *Journalistic Authority: Legitimating News in the Digital Era* (Columbia University Press, 2017) and *On the Condition of Anonymity: Unnamed Sources and the Battle for Journalism* (University of Illinois Press, 2012), and co-editor of *Boundaries of Journalism* (Routledge, 2015) and *Journalists, Sources, and Credibility* (Routledge, 2010). In addition, he is the author of over forty journal articles and book chapters. His research examines the discursive struggles through which journalism comes to be defined and legitimated as a cultural practice in the digital news environment.

Kathleen M. Cumiskey is Chairperson and Associate Professor in the Department of Psychology at the College of Staten Island, City University of New York (CUNY) and faculty member of the PhD in Critical Social-Personality Psychology Program at the CUNY Graduate Center. She is co-author (with Larissa Hjorth) of *Haunting Hands: Mobile Media Practices and Loss* (Oxford University Press, 2017) and co-editor of *Mobile Media Practices, Presence and Politics: The Challenges of Being Seamlessly Mobile* (with Larissa Hjorth, Routledge, 2013). Her work centers on the affective role that mobile media play in shaping our lives and the intimacy generated between users and their devices. Her work has been featured in important anthologies like *The Handbook of Psychology of Communication Technology* (Wiley, 2015) and *The Routledge Companion to Mobile Media* (Routledge, 2014) and in journals like *Feminist Media Studies*. She also serves on the editorial board of *Mobile Media and Communication*.

Stefanie Duguay is Assistant Professor of Data and Networked Publics in the Department of Communication Studies at Concordia University in Montreal, Canada. Her research focuses on the influence of digital media technologies in everyday life, with particular attention to sexual and gender identity and social media. This has included studies of lesbian, gay, bisexual, trans and queer (LGBTQ) people's use of social media, dating apps, and multiple platforms for everyday activism. Stefanie's research has been published in *New Media & Society*, *Social Media + Society*, *Information, Communication & Society*, *Disability & Society*, and other international, peer-reviewed journals.

Jason Farman is Associate Professor in the Department of American Studies at the University of Maryland, College Park. He is also Director of the Design Cultures & Creativity Program and a faculty member with the Human-Computer Interaction Lab. He is author of the book *Mobile Interface Theory* (winner of the 2012 Book of the Year Award from the Association of Internet Researchers). He is the editor of the books *The Mobile Story* (2014) and *Foundations of Mobile Media Studies* (2016). He has published scholarly articles on such topics as mobile technologies, the history of technology, digital maps and cultural geography, locative and site-specific art, videogames, digital storytelling, performance art, social media, and surveillance. His most recent book is titled *Delayed Response: The Art of Waiting from the Ancient to the Instant World* (Yale University Press, 2018).

Aristea Fotopoulou is Senior Lecturer (Assistant Professor) Media and Communications at the University of Brighton, where she leads the MA Digital Media, Culture & Society. Her research focuses on social transformations that relate to digital media and data technologies, such as self-tracking, wearables, and AI. She is the author of *Feminist Activism and Digital Networks: Between Empowerment and Vulnerability* (Springer, 2017) and serves as Chair of the European Communication Research & Education Association (ECREA) Digital Culture and Communication Section. She is currently writing a book on feminist data studies.

Larissa Hjorth is a digital ethnographer, artist, distinguished professor and director of the Design & Creative Practice ECP platform at RMIT University. Hjorth studies the sociocultural dimensions of mobile media and play practices in the Asia-Pacific region with an emphasis on interdisciplinary, collaborative, and cross-cultural approaches. She has published a dozen co-authored books, edited over a dozen handbooks/companions and has over forty journal articles. With Professor Heather Horst, she co-founded the Digital Ethnography Research Centre (DERC: http://digital-ethnography.com/). She has been a CI on three ARC Discoveries and two ARC Linkages. Her books include *Haunting Hands* (with Cumiskey, 2017), *Screen Ecologies* (with Pink, Sharp & Williams, 2016), *Digital Ethnography* (Pink et al., 2016), *Mobile Media in the Asia-Pacific* (2009), *Games & Gaming* (2010), *Online@AsiaPacific* (with Arnold 2013), *Understanding Social Media* (with Hinton, 2013), and *Gaming in Locative, Social and Mobile Media* (with Richardson, 2014). Previously, she was Deputy Dean, R&I, in the School of Media & Communication (2013–2016).

Philip Howard is a professor and writer. He teaches at Oxford University and is Professorial Fellow at Balliol College. He writes about information politics and international affairs, and is the author of eight books, including *The Managed Citizen* (CUP, 2005), *Digital Origins of Dictatorship and Democracy* (Oxford University Press, 2010), and *Pax Technica: How the Internet of Things May Set Us Free or Lock Us Up* (Yale University Press, 2015). He has won multiple "best book" awards, and his research and commentary writing has been featured in the *New York Times*, *Washington Post*, and many international media outlets. *Foreign Policy* magazine named him a "Global Thinker" for 2018 and the National Democratic Institute awarded him their "Democracy Prize" for pioneering the social science of fake news.

Anastasia Kavada is Senior Lecturer at the Westminster School of Media, Arts & Design at the University of Westminster. She is Co-leader of the MA in Media, Campaigning and Social Change and Deputy Director of the Communication and Media Research Institute (CAMRI). Her research focuses on social movements and campaigning groups, investigating the links between digital media and decentralized organizing practices, participatory decision-making, and the development of solidarity among participants in collective action. Anastasia's research has appeared in a variety of edited books and academic journals, including *Media, Culture & Society* and *Information, Communication & Society*.

Daniel Kreiss is Associate Professor in the School of Media and Journalism and Adjunct Associate Professor in the Department of Communication at the University of North Carolina at Chapel Hill. His research explores the impact of technological change on the public sphere and political practice. In *Taking Our Country Back: The Crafting of Networked Politics from Howard Dean to Barack Obama* (Oxford University Press, 2012), he presents the history of new media and Democratic Party political campaigning over the last decade. *Prototype Politics: Technology-Intensive Campaigning and the Data of Democracy* (Oxford University Press, 2016) charts the emergence of a data-driven, personalized, and socially embedded form of campaigning and explains differences in technological adoption between the two U.S. political parties. He is an affiliated fellow of the Information Society Project at Yale Law School and received a PhD in Communication from Stanford University.

Risto Kunelius is Professor of Journalism at the Faculty of Communication Sciences, University of Tampere, Finland. His work has focused on journalism and political power, professionalism and public sphere as well as on coverage of global issues (climate change, surveillance, free speech). Recent books include *Media and Global Climate Knowledge: Journalism and the IPCC* (Palgrave, 2017) and on surveillance and journalism (*Journalism and the NSA Revelations: Privacy, Security, and the Press*, Reuters Institute/I.B.Tauris, 2017).

Seth C. Lewis is the Shirley Papé Chair in Emerging Media in the School of Journalism and Communication at the University of Oregon, and is an affiliated fellow of the Information Society Project at Yale Law School. His research in journalism studies has examined the emergence of social media, audience metrics, user participation, open-source software, and big data in news production, and his present work examines the implications of algorithms and automation for understandings of news. He also has co-developed conceptual models for interpreting the boundary work of journalism as well as the interplay of social actors and technological actants in media organizations. Lewis has published some fifty journal articles and book chapters, and is a two-time winner of the International Communication Association's award for Outstanding Article of the Year in Journalism Studies. With Matt Carlson, he edited *Boundaries of Journalism: Professionalism, Practices and Participation* (Routledge, 2015).

Thomas Poell is Senior Lecturer in New Media & Digital Culture and Program Director of the Research Master Media Studies at the University of Amsterdam. His research focuses on digital platforms and the transformation of public communication around the globe. He has published widely on social media and popular protest in Canada, Egypt, Tunisia, India, and China, as well as on the role of these media in the development of new forms of journalism. His co-authored and co-edited books include *Global Cultures of Contestation* (Palgrave/McMillan, 2017), *The Sage Handbook of Social Media* (Sage, 2018), and *The Platform Society* (Oxford University Press, 2018).

Erika Polson is Associate Professor in the Department of Media, Film, and Journalism Studies at the University of Denver. She is the author of *Privileged Mobilities: Geo-Social Media, Professional Migration, and a New Global Middle Class* (Peter Lang, 2016), and is co-editor of *The Routledge Companion to Media and Class* (forthcoming, 2019). Her work has appeared in journals such as *New Media and Society*, *Media, Culture, and Society*, *International Journal of Communication*, *European Journal* *of Cultural Studies*, and *Communication, Culture & Critique*, and her research on street-based WiFi in Cuba is forthcoming in the Routledge collection, *Location Technologies in International Contexts* (Wilken, Goggin & Horst, 2018).

Sudha Rajagopalan is Assistant Professor in East European Studies at the University of Amsterdam. She also serves on the steering committee of the peer-reviewed, international journal *Digital Icons: Studies in Russian, Eurasian and Central European New Media*. A historian and cultural studies scholar, her book *Indian Films in Soviet Cinemas: The Culture of Moviegoing after Stalin* (Indiana University Press, Bloomington, 2009) was a pioneering, ethnohistorical study of Soviet movie reception. Rajagopalan's recent publications have been on participatory practices within Russian digital media cultures. Her work engages with debates on new public spheres, citizenship, affect and emotion, celebrity, identity work and memory, and can be seen in publications such as *Celebrity Studies, Transformative Works and Culture*, and *International Journal of Cultural Studies*, among others.

Adrienne Russell is Mary Laird Wood Professor of Communication at the University of Washington. Her research and teaching focus on the digital-age evolution of activist communication and journalism and include study of activists, technologists, media publics, and others who shape information products and spaces. She is author most recently of the books *Journalism as Activism: Recoding Media Power* and *Networked: A Contemporary History of News in Transition*, and is co-editor of *Journalism and the NSA Revelations: Privacy, Security and the Press*.

Samantha Shorey is a PhD candidate in the Department of Communication at the University of Washington and a researcher at the Tactile and Tactical Design Lab in the Department of Human Centered Design and Engineering. Her research explores gender and material practices in media making and technology innovation cultures.

Karin Wahl-Jorgensen is Professor in the Cardiff School of Journalism, Media and Cultural Studies at Cardiff University, Wales, and also serves as Director of Research Environment and Development in the school. Her research focuses on journalism and citizenship, and she has authored or edited nine books, including *Emotions, Media Politics* (Polity, forthcoming), *Digital Citizenship in a Datafied Society* (with Arne Hintz and Lina Dencik, Polity, forthcoming), *Disasters and the Media* (with Mervi Pantti and Simon Cottle, Peter Lang, 2012), and *Handbook of Journalism Studies* (co-edited with Thomas Hanitzsch, Routledge, 2009). She has published close to 100 journal articles and book chapters. She has received funding from agencies including the European Commission, the Economic and Social Research Council, and the Arts and Humanities Research Council, as well as from organizations including the BBC Trust and the whistleblowing charity

Public Concern at Work. She is a frequent media commentator and contributor to *The Conversation*.

Samuel Woolley is Research Director of the Digital Intelligence Lab at the Institute for the Future and a doctoral candidate (ABD) in the Communication Department at the University of Washington. He is a co-founder, and former Director of Research, at the Computational Propaganda Project at the Oxford Internet Institute, University of Oxford. He holds a fellowship with the Tech Policy Lab at UW Schools of Law and Information and is a former research fellow at Google Jigsaw and the Center for Media Data and Society at Central European University. His work is focused at the intersection of automation, persuasion, and social life.

ACKNOWLEDGMENTS

Let me use this space to acknowledge the support of Jamie Foster, my whiz of a research assistant and presently working toward her PhD on something that will undoubtedly be thoughtful, fun, and provocative. Erica Wetter, here's to your guts and foresight, and not thinking me crazy when you asked for a single sequel to the first *A Networked Self*, and I said how about four sequel volumes instead? Mia Moran, I know you will bring many more inspired projects to fruition with your insight.

The rest of you rascals, you know who you are. You are in my heart. I have thanked you personally, many times. I will probably continue to do so. Cheers.

1

INTRODUCTION

Zizi Papacharissi

We tell stories about who we are, and through telling these stories, we connect with others and affirm our own sense of self. For human beings, this is our modus operandi. It is how we survive—through expression and social connection. We vary in those behaviors, as some people may be more outgoing in certain situations and others more introverted in different contexts. Still, we adjust, we reconsider, and we evolve. So more than a mode of daily survival, storytelling for human beings is a way of understanding who we are and imagining who we would like to be. Media have always helped along with this process. From the ancient days of carving our daily experiences in caves, to drawings, to developing languages so as to communicate, to then developing many platforms for telling, printing, publishing, broadcasting, podcasting, and sharing our stories, it has all been about expression and connection. Sometimes we succeed in telling great stories that inspire and other times we fail in telling stories that disconnect us. Still, most often, we tell stories that are *always in the making*: always being revised, always soluble. The technologies are there to help us along and to network us, but it is our stories that identify us, connect us, or further tear us apart.

This is a volume about how we tell stories in the contemporary networked digital environment. We tell a variety of stories in our everyday lives, but I focus on storytelling that enables us to sustain our sense of self: to help us make sense of the world surrounding us and find our place(s) in it. This volume is part of a series of books that build on the concept of the *Networked Self*. In earlier work, serving as the prequel to this volume, I drew inspiration from this quote: "Attention shapes the self, and is in turn shaped by it" (Csikszentmihalyi, 1990, p. 13). I wanted to focus the volume on the self, and the sense of self attained (and imagined) via social media. Csikszentmihalyi (1990) was writing about flow at the time. He explains that happiness is not a constant state, but rather a fleeting emotion we experience when we find ourselves at our most creative. That is typically attained when we are immersed in activities optimally, in ways that afford us great mental and emotional satisfaction. He is careful to locate this in the realm of creativity, which extends beyond the work realm to include a number of creative pursuits. I was very interested at the time in how social media can help connect us to our lifeworlds in ways that optimize flow, and I relied on the knowledge of gifted researchers, leaders in work on social media, to help me respond to questions revolving around identity, community, and culture, as those took form online and offline.

I thus made the argument that the self, in late modern societies, is expressed as a fluid abstraction, *always in solution*,[1] reified through the individual's association with a reality that may be equally flexible. The process of self-presentation and representation becomes an ever-evolving cycle through which individual identity is presented, compared, adjusted, or defended against a constellation of social, cultural, economic, or political realities. Goffman (1959) had described this as an information game: "a potentially infinite cycle of concealment, discovery, false revelation, and rediscovery" (p. 13). This made me think of playful uses of social media. I imagined (and still do) expression on social media (and in everyday life) as a fun game, through which we leave traces of our stories in the places we inhabit and derive pleasure when others discover them, relate to them, and thus connect with us, all the while playing the same game themselves. This is a somewhat ego-centered approach and playful, I will admit. There are important consequences for communication being ego-driven in late modernity. Play also possesses an infrastructure that reflects, reproduces, and sometimes, albeit not often enough, reinvents geopolitical, sociocultural, and economic hierarchies. Play always has been that way: a wanted distraction that pays off in ways public and private, personal and commercial, from the days of agoras in Ancient Greece, arenas of the Roman Empire, medieval theater, and all types of playgrounds, material and imagined, adult and non-adult that have emerged and are yet to come.

Several scholars connect the cultural tendencies, which render the self more liquid (Bauman, 2000, 2004), reflexive (Giddens, 1991) and self-identity a process, to historical developments. A sense of self has always been developed across public and private, or hybrid terrain. These conventional boundaries are challenged through amplified networks of connections and overlapping or distinct milieus of interaction we traverse in late modernity, or, broadly speaking, in the anthropocene (e.g. Gergen, 1991; Latour, 2017). Technology is the playing ground of the anthropocene. It provides the stage for hybrid modalities of expression and connection, linking the individual, separately or simultaneously, with multiple audiences. Online social networks present recent sites of self-presentation and identity negotiation. The *Networked Self* five-volume anthology presents a collection of discussions on what it means to present the self while striving toward a sense of self in contemporary societies and cultures.

Stories and Platforms of a Networked Self

Technologies advance at a pace that invites us to reconsider and adjust the locus of our social habits. This is a distinction to be emphasized. Technology does not render us more or less social. But it does reorganize our social activities, and thus offers up new places for us to tell stories about who we are, who we would like to be, and how we might connect with others. It is true that over the past several years, the web has become increasingly platformized (Helmond, 2015) and accessible through interfaces that suggest an order for the experiences it affords (Galloway, 2012). A sense of community is thus frequently not organically developed, but suggested through the affordances and algorithmic architecture of platforms. Still, the advent of constantly re-developed technologies, technologies that are in permanently beta form (Neff & Stark, 2004), or always already new (Gitelman, 2006), introduces a modality of accelerated reflexivity, leading us to feel that our habitus, our social environment of comfort that is, is incessantly changing. Bourdieu (1987) understands the habitus as always already changing fluid environment, generated through the "durably instilled generative principle of regulated improvisations" (p. 78). It is a malleable collection of our social habits, practices, and norms that serves as a constant reference point: an ever-evolving social backdrop that helps us adapt to the new while also sustaining the familiar.

Easton and I (Papacharissi & Easton, 2014) originally used the term *habitus of the new* to talk about how the affordances of specific platforms interact with our habituated predispositions for sociality to insert an affect, that is, a mood or an atmosphere that evokes a feeling of ongoing, and sometimes relentless change. In the habitus of the new, our repertoire of storytelling practices is constantly reinvented. So, with Easton, we described the following expressive and connective modalities that become prominent as sociality emerges (and evolves) within the habitus of the new: (authorship as) disclosure, listening, and redaction. And so, as I articulate the meaning of this multipart anthology, I find myself moving away from language that focuses on presentations and representations of the self online. Instead, I see the scholarship presented in this anthology as work focused on the storytelling project of the self: using technology to help us make sense of who we are, who we have been, and who we can become.

In doing so, I understand storytelling as a process that involves disclosure, as much as it involves listening and redaction. Here, John Hartley's articulation of the *homo nuntius*, or the "messaging human," comes to mind. Hartley (2010) understands the *homo nuntius* as a contemporary species that expresses identity via and as message, and "produces individual identity out of social network interaction" (p. 305). In Hartley's words, "Individuals in the species *homo nuntius* don't just 'send' messages as an action ('message' as verb), they are a system of messages ('message' as noun); they are both constituted by and productive through messages, which are the process by means of which reason emerges (it is the product of a process, not an input)" (p. 19). In the habitus of the new, agency is claimed storytelling. Individuals attempt to reconcile the distance between structure and agency through authoring (disclosure), listening, and redacting messages about the self and others.

Spaces—be they online or offline; private or public; physical, augmented or virtual; or of a hybrid nature—present the performative realms through which one's sense of self is articulated, actualized, presented, and represented. In line with the central theme of this multivolume anthology, people tell stories about who they are in order to affirm their sense of self and become who they are and want to be. People tell these stories on spaces that function as platforms for performativity. This volume focuses on how these platforms support, enhance, or confine the networked self. In so doing, it focuses on three areas of interest:

1   Platforms and the politics of platforms.
2   Stories people tell about themselves on these platforms.
3   Stories people tell about themselves, others, and events they experience on these platforms.

The first area considers how the web has become increasingly platformized, moving from an architecture that supported organically formed communities to a structure comprising distinct or interconnected platforms. While these platforms support self-expression, connection, and communities, they do so within spaces prescribed and defined by algorithms. This first area of interest concerns the architecture of platforms as performative space for the networked self. The second area focuses on how the stories people share, in performing the networked self, are restricted, enhanced, and adorned by the affordances of these platforms. The third area of interest explores how stories we tell about ourselves, others, and events we experience on networked platforms. As such, the focus is on storytelling as it connects to live-reporting of events, curation of information, emerging modalities of journalism, collaboratively formed memories, and the instant historification of the present.

Kreiss sets the stage by synthesizing diverse literature on the long storytelling project of the self to draw attention away from the broad story of "disembedding," and reflexivity, and back to core existential constructs that define how we understand ourselves, and then tell stories that help advance this form of self-understanding. Relying on Castells's (2011) work on identity, he calls for scholars to focus on the "persistence of structuring identities" of what Castells calls "God, nation, family, and community" that "provide unbreakable, eternal codes" to stand against the global flows of power and information and "the individualization of identity." This call is timely, especially as globalization flows have only partially networked some publics, while mostly disconnecting others through fragmented narratives that negate agency and reproduce insecurity.

Human identity, as Carlson and Lewis reiterate, in exploring new storytelling, journalistic epistemologies, and platforms, is performed and networked. Most accounts of performance and identity focus on identity and connection, and skim over engagement with news as a performative representation of the self. Still, involvement with news and news storytelling suggest an important way of socio-culturally orienting oneself within the world. The two draw from Carey's (2009) work to illustrate how news storytelling provides ways of connecting with others and thus suggesting modalities of collective identity. Platform design, however, enables, identifies, and restricts ways in which individual and collective identity may be performed. This is not new. Performative spaces by nature suggest ways in which identity may be presented or represented. And they support performativity through multiple forms of sharing (John, 2017; Lingel, 2017), although, unmistakably, there is a certain digitality to the form sharing takes on: algorithmically enabled, yes, but also editable, remixable, and exploitable (Gunkel, 2016; Scholz, 2017).

There is a different texture to the publicness that users experience, as they perform the self online. The materiality of these performances is different. Poell, Rajagopalan, and Kavada engage this question directly, by examining what publicness truly means in the age of datafication. In the circular process through which user data are both systematically collected and simultaneously redirected back to users in the form of metrics, trending topics, and personalized content, publicness becomes both an act and a form of being. It becomes the performative imaginary against which independent or coordinated acts of expression and connection are developed, experienced, and reified. The feedback loop rendered as users are interpellated by algorithmic processes that have been set into motion by users' own performances of public acts sets the stage for potential performances.

Datafication is borne out of public and networked forms of participation in a digitally enabled public sphere. As Barney and colleagues (2016) remind us:

> Participation has become a tremendously valuable social, political, and economic resource . . . [naming] a particular instance of what Louis Althusser described as interpellation, the process whereby we become the subjects we are by responding to the hail of ideological formation that structure our social environments . . . Participation is one of the most prominent means by which individuals and publics (at least in the contemporary West) become subjects and inscribe themselves in the social order.
>
> *(pp. ix–x)*

Datafication is, therefore, the prevalent mode of algorithmically generated interpellation or interpolation [*sic*], as Cheney-Lippold (2017) argues in the recent *We Are Data*. And *we have always been data*, I would argue, in further extending this line of thinking. It is not my intention to gloss over the relevance of these processes, but rather, to place them in a historical continuum. The participatory condition has always empowered and enforced a sense of order; enabled independent forms of expression but also organized them within a social habitus; facilitated autonomous reactions and interpellated them at the same time. Data, digital and non-digital, make up the social fabric of collaboratively enabled interaction. Datafication, that is, the order of data, is set into motion by mechanisms that both *reproduce* and *remediate* those described by Foucault (1970) in the *Order of Things*.

From this premise, we can better appreciate the nuances of performative modalities that emerge through storytelling practices online. Woolley, Shorey, and Howard's foray into bots, that is, automated programs built in the style of real users, reveals how these software-driven social actors are both imbued with the intentions of their creators and capable of functioning as distinct entities. Bot proxies capture the tendencies and tensions of the participatory condition. They reflect the paradox of interactivity that has long puzzled their creators, something Andrejevic (2016) refers to as the pacification of interactivity, that is, the tendency for "active forms of participation online [to be] redoubled by increasingly passive ones, amounting to automated participation in data-driven control systems" (p. 204). As byproducts of datafication, bot proxies are, in the words of Woolley, Shorey, and Howard, "more than a mask for a user, but less than a fully independent sentient entity." Bots present a supporting cast for both the networked self and its aftermath. They are part of the infrastructure of the storytelling project of the networked self and the story itself. They are the product of the stories we tell about ourselves, and yet are also capable of reflexively producing their own stories.

What is the place of sentiment, then, within the algorithmically generated performative stage for the self? Wahl-Jorgensen examines how the emotional architecture of platforms is intentionally designed to facilitate certain forms of pro-social sentiment in some cases, while in others it unexpectedly and coincidentally produces emotive modalities of expression. She traces the ongoing negotiation of affective aspects of online media that lead to further commodification of emotional labor (see also Scholz, 2017) and introduces a commodified affect control structure that is ripe for monetization. As emotion becomes a central component of platform design, its centrality in weaving storytelling platforms and practices together is amplified. While sentiment has never been absent from the stories we tell about ourselves, the infrastructure of online platforms predisposes affective attunement in ways that nullify discursive responses to content. Simply put, emojis are not a story; rather, they are a layer to a story, a reaction to a story or perhaps even a way for social actors to feel their way into a story. What becomes of the storytelling project of the networked self once the performative palette is affectively constructed?

The texture and cohesion of those stories changes, and this is something that the next set of authors examines, by taking a closer look at the genres of stories people tell about themselves on online and mobile platforms. The ongoing interplay between commodification and autonomy defines how stories are told. Duguay combines platform, textual and visual analysis with interviews to examine how queer women employ Instagram to draw together individual and collective identity statements. The commodified nature of the platform together with its dominant heteronormative character tend to complicate self representation for queer women. Furthermore, queer women are able to claim, play with, and re-organize dominant strategies for microcelebrity in ways that permit them to harness the affordances of the platform and gain visibility.

Focusing exclusively on the affective infrastructure of the mobile technologies, Hjorth and Cumiskey talk about the ways in which sentiment-driven visual forms of communication "prick our skin, but also bruise us with an affective texture that haunts." They use the emergent genres such as "selfies at funeral" and "selfies-as-eulogies" to investigate signal relations between intimacy, mobile media, etiquette and affective witnessing. They suggest that rather than reproducing the divide between the mourner and those that witness, affective viral media shapes new types of witnesses–mourner interpellations. While these sustain what the two authors term *affective mobile spectres*, drawing in meaningful emotional investments that further support our understanding of our own life story, they are also susceptible to the economic realities of the mobile communication industry. Ultimately, Hjorth and Cumiskey wonder about the extent to which mobile enforced nostalgia facilitates coping or further complicates processes of letting go and accepting the mortality of the self, and the stories that are part of it.

Further exploring the stories people tell about themselves, others, and events they experience on these platforms, Bucher examines how people use the ordinary as a space through which they can discursively access power and claim voice. She uses the Reply Girls, a group of young women who rose to fame in YouTube for using their cleavage-baring thumbnails as way to drive and benefit from traffic, as a case study of subaltern storytelling in the realm of algorithms. By exploiting algorithmic architectures designed to elevate the sensational, the Reply Girls claim agency and render their stories authentic. Their narratives, built around desire and resistance, hail viewers by interpellating the algorithmic structure that enables *and* confines them.

The impasse generated by fluid structures that both liberate and order is central to the thinking of most authors who populate this volume. Fotopoulou follows up on questions regarding datafication, platformization, the quantified self, and algorithmically generated identities through the use of differently imagined vocabulary. She discusses the performative and material aspects of the self and the centrality of ritual through focusing on the imagination of data, sentiment, caring as privacy, forms of soft resistance to imposed data sharing, and finally, the subjectivity of data. Starting with the simple question of how self-tracking technologies predispose the stories we tell about who we are online, she draws from cultural texts to arrive at meaningful conclusions. Not all disclosure constitutes sharing, she points out, a point that has eluded us in our tendency to use the two terms interchangeably. Through rituals of performativity, automated, conscious, or subliminal, "data can be recycled and repurposed, to tell different stories about who we are, about the past and the future. The stories we tell about the data we collect, and the meanings we make by interpreting these data are performative re-enactments of our identities." She ultimately understands underlying trust in numbers as a signifier of new performative rituals, in which sharing personal data not only paves the path to social connection, but also reinforces a certain moral economy.

Polson moves us to different storytelling territory—that of the self-traveler. Through discourses produced and reproduced via social and mobile media, she traces how individual users position their own experiences as unique and exceptional while "connect[ing] their experiences to those of others through similar visual representations and emotional responses to travel." Here she draws on the history of travel as a "status asset" for aspirational middle classes, and investigates how strategies for storytelling online permit one to distinguish one-self through travel, even though the resulting representations of travel circulated bear a weary similarity. Of interest here is how networked modes of storytelling, motivated by a need for distinction inadvertently interpellate familiar status symbols as a storytelling strategy.

Russell and Kunelius further examine how tales of receding privacy in popular culture refocus the stories we tell about who we are and how we connect to others. Ambivalent about our ability to delineate between stories that may be shared and others that may be shared more privately in the contemporary era, we develop storytelling strategies that are the byproduct of growing cynicism, lingering anxiety, and growing insecurity. What is at stake here is the ability to safeguard our storytelling autonomy and maintain agency over how our public and private selves are linked, if at all. Popular novels offer a familiar habitus of storytelling that permits us to reimagine ways out of the performative cul-de-sacs we encounter in presenting the self within constantly surveilled architectures. In the context, they conclude, "as surveillance increases so too does everyday awareness and cultural resistance," inviting us to rely on our own abilities of rei-magining strategies for combating privacy.

This volume commenced with a look at the storytelling project of the self in the age of identity fundamentalism. Authors further articulated the perfor-mative realms upon which this networked storytelling project unfolds. Spaces confine, liberate, and modulate. It is only fitting that the volume concludes with Farman's contribution on what space really means when it is mostly ren-dered into place through mobile and digital media. He examines how space is produced, claimed, possessed, renegotiated, and vacated through storytell-ing. Our primary mode of self-expression, storytelling, is also our main mode of agency, and our key path to advocacy. Mobile and networked storytelling enable collaborative and polyvocal forms of experience sharing. The resulting stories may connect or diverge, creating, per Farman, "contested landscapes." Location conveys point of view and perspective, and it is only through occupying a storytelling position that is open, liquid, and mobile that space can be made for all stories to be voiced, and heard.

Three themes emerge as I read these chapters over and over again. I hope many more emerge for the readers of this volume. The first dominant theme, as articulated through the thoughts of the contributors, reaffirms that human beings tell stories about random, mundane, and grand things. These stories can easily traverse from the banal to the magnificent and back in the course of a minute, word, gif, or emoji. They are sometimes narcissistic in a charming and affable manner, other times self-centered in an affected and vainglorious way, and most often, both. They are serious and funny, authentic and put-on, playful and serious, sarcastic and empathetic. They are the different and contradictory things that make us who we are all at once. These expressions, that turn into stories, which then shape longer narratives, have one thing in common: they are traces we leave as we strive toward sense of self. Prosaic and imaginative, they become part of our storytelling project of who we are, have been, and would like to be.

Speaking of traces. The traces that we leave, pick up, and assemble, as we work through who we are through our everyday routines, are increasingly binary. The narrative infrastructure we construct is molded with and through data. Our sense of self is always soluble, but also constantly reified through data—datafied. This is the second core theme for all contributors to this volume, who explicate the complex ways in which the narrative architecture of platforms invites us to tell stories that carry a certain texture, tonality, and affect. The effect is subtle, but amplified over time, especially as storytelling practices that develop over one platform cross over to others, intentionally or not. It should not disturb us that our sense of self is datafied. When has it not been? We have always lived on and through data; what has changed is how we define, speak, and share data. Likewise, our performative platforms have always suggested a particular form, or order (if Foucault is your medicine of choice), to how we tell the stories that we think up. It is important that we understand that we order, master it, and are able to reimagine it. It is important for us to tell stories that help us imagine ourselves within and beyond the established order. Parenting, friendship, and literacy play a central part here, and this is something further visited in the next two volumes.

Finally, the platforms we tell and perform these stories on are networked but not connected. A final theme that emerges from the contributors to this volume is that the architecture of the spaces we use to rehearse, play with, and attune with our sense of self supports connection but does not guarantee it. This renders the narratives we produce connective, but not always connected. The challenge for us, as we move forward, will be to tell these stories in words, memes, gifs, and modes that connect us and identify us more often than they drive us apart. To perform the self in a way that is ego-driven but communally oriented. To strive toward a sense of self that is autonomous, without being absolutist. This is where this volume ends, and where the next one, on Love, begins.

Note

1 Here, I am alluding to Raymond Williams's work on structures of feeling. Human experiences and the stories we tell are always in solution: soluble.

References

Andrejevic, M. (2016). The pacification of interactivity. In D. Barney, G. Coleman, C. Ross, J. Sterne, T. Tembeck, N.K. Hayles, P. Krapp, R. Raley and S. Weber (Eds.), *The participatory condition in the digital age* (pp. 187–206). Minneapolis: University of Minnesota Press.

Barney, D., Coleman, G., Ross, C., Sterne, J., & Tembeck, T. (Eds.). (2016). *The participatory condition in the digital age.* Minneapolis and London: University of Minnesota Press. www.jstor.org/stable/10.5749/j.ctt1ggjkfg

Bauman, Z. (2000). *Liquid modernity.* Cambridge: Polity Press.

Bauman, Z. (2004). *Wasted lives: Modernity and its outcasts.* Oxford: Polity Press.

Bourdieu, P. (1987). *Distinctions: A social critique of the judgment of taste.* Cambridge, MA: Harvard University Press.

Carey, J.W. (2009). *Communication as culture.* New York: Routledge.

Castells, M. (2011). *The power of identity. Vol. 2: The information age—Economy, society, and culture.* Chichester: John Wiley & Sons.

Cheney-Lippold, J. (2017). *We are data: Algorithms and the making of our digital selves.* New York: New York University Press.

Csikszentmihalyi, M. (1990). *Flow: The psychology of optimal experience.* New York: Harper & Row.

Foucault, M. (1970). *The order of things: An archaeology of the human sciences.* New York: Pantheon Books.

Galloway, A.R. (2012). *The interface effect.* Cambridge: Polity Press.

Gergen, K.J. (1991). *The saturated self: Dilemmas of identity in contemporary life.* New York: Basic Books.

Giddens, A. (1991). *Modernity and self-identity: Self and society in the late modern age.* Palo Alto, CA: Stanford University Press.

Gitelman, L. (2006). *Always already new: Media, history, and the data of culture.* Cambridge, MA: MIT Press.

Goffman, E. (1959). *The presentation of self in everyday life.* New York: Anchor Books.

Gunkel, D.J. (2016). *Of remixology: Ethics and aesthetics after remix.* Cambridge, MA: MIT Press.

Hartley, D. (2010). *Understanding human need.* Bristol: Policy Press.

Helmond, A. (2015). The platformization of the web: Making web data platform ready. *Social Media and Society,* 1(2), 1–11.

John, N.A. (2017). *The age of sharing.* Cambridge: Polity Press.

Latour, B. (2017). *Facing gaia: Eight lectures on the new climate regime.* Hoboken, NJ: John Wiley & Sons.

Lingel, J. (2017). What Facebook can learn from Craigslist. *Slate*, July 3. www.slate.com/articles/technology/future_tense/2017/07/what_facebook_can_learn_from_craigslist.html

Papacharissi, Z. & Easton, E. (2014). In the habitus of the new: Agency, structure, and the social media habitus. In J. Hartley, A. Bruns, & J. Burgess (Eds.), *New media dynamics* (pp. 171–184). Chichester: Blackwell.

Neff, G. & Stark, D. (2004). Permanently beta. In P. H. Howard & S. Jones (Eds.), *Society online: The internet in context* (pp. 173–188). Thousand Oaks, CA: Sage.

Scholz, T. (2017). *Big data in organizations and the role of human resource management: A complex systems theory-based conceptualization*. New York: Peter Lang.

2

THE NETWORKED SELF IN THE AGE OF IDENTITY FUNDAMENTALISM

Daniel Kreiss

Over the latter half of the twentieth century, social theorists told a broad story of social "disembedding." Anthony Giddens (1991) famously charted the rise of modernity in the reshaping of local geographies in terms of distal social influences and reordered relations of time. For Giddens, the self of modernity is reflexivity constructed between the local and global; the individual crafts her identity and lifestyle amid diversity. While Giddens was writing long before the advent of social media, contemporary communication and media scholars have charted the rise of "cultures of connectivity," "networked sociality," and "connective action." Taken as a whole, these accounts generally are premised on the idea of individuated reflexive selves, where people actively construct their identities, and continually do so, in an era marked by the decline of traditions, institutions, and locales. To date, much of the emphasis in the communication and media studies literature might be termed an "actor-centric" self. This is a self that is generally free to pick and choose among available identities and cultural forms, often in private. In this view, the self quite literally constructs itself.

While this premise undoubtedly captures important aspects of the contemporary relationship between networked media and reflexive, flexible identities, how do we explain the surprising endurance, and even newfound importance, of nationalism, religious fundamentalism, and ethnicity in the context of social identity? For example, the persistence, and new public visibility, of white racial identity and its attendant American nationalism and Christian underpinnings were on full display during the 2016 election cycle, in both the campaign of Donald Trump and the attendant rise of the "alt-right." The alt-right is a diffuse, networked, and primarily online movement (Marwick & Lewis, 2017) premised on assertions of white identity as a legitimate basis for social affiliation and wielding political power. In "An Establishment Conservative's Guide to the Alt-Right,"

Allum Bokhari and Milo Yiannopoulos (2016), contributors to the flagship alt-right media site Breitbart, chronicle the origins of the alt-right movement and the development of its various strains:

> In short, they [the alt-right] want what every people fighting for self-determination in history have ever wanted, and what progressives are always telling us people should be allowed—unless those people are white. This hypocrisy is what has led so many Trump voters—groups who have in many cases not voted since the 1970s or 80s—to come out of the woodwork and stand up for their values and culture.

The various groups in the alt-right movement share a white nationalist ideology that conceptualizes race as the primary basis of social affiliation and differentiation and a legitimate means for making claims on political power. The alt-right rejects any attempt to change traditional, Christian morality by the left, and the progressive value of diversity, whether it is on sexual, gender, or racial and ethnic terms (Marwick & Lewis, 2017). The alt-right critiques what it sees as liberal attempts to jettison white Western civilization in favor of the cultural elevation of those oppressed in this history (such as African Americans). However, there is considerable debate in the literature, and more importantly within the alt-right itself, about its other key tenets and symbolic boundaries. Kreiss and Mason (2017), for instance, argue that while older white supremacist groups such as the neo-Nazis and the KKK received the lion's share of attention after the racial violence in Charlottesville during the summer of 2017, more common among the alt-right's key sites such as Breitbart is the argument for *equality* in the context of white self-determination. For example, Bokhari and Yiannopoulos argue that the primarily white, male, and middle-American "natural conservative" subset of the alt-right movement found on sites such as Breitbart reject the violence and inherent claims of white racial superiority espoused by the neo-Nazis (or "1488ers"). Instead, these individuals embrace self-determination for *all* racial and ethnic groups ("homogeneity" in terms of Haidt's (2012) values), see white identity as a legitimate and desirable basis for making political claims, and argue that America is historically a white nation, a legacy which they believe should be preserved.[1]

These explicit forms of white racial identity on display during the election cycle on sites such as Breitbart are surprising in light of the three decades-old literature cited above that generally posits that contemporary identities are more fluid and flexible than those of the past. This idea of identity fluidity and its construction from a range of available alternatives is premised on a number of factors, including the erosion of traditional forms of authority rooted in religion and place and the development of global information networks and social media platforms that place networked sociality at the heart of contemporary social relations (Van Dijck, 2013). For example, the idea of flexible selves and identities is a key tenet of contemporary sociological and especially media theory. In her influential work, Zizi Papacharissi (2014, p. 304) argues that

> the self, in late modern societies, is expressed as fluid abstraction, reified through the individual's association with a reality that may be equally flexible. The process of self-presentation becomes an ever-evolving cycle through which individual identity is presented, compared, adjusted, or defended against a constellation of social, cultural, economic, or political realities.

In this view, self-identity is something that is actively and reflexively constructed and reconstructed, particularly through the use of networked media. As Papacharissi argues, drawing on her previous work in *A Private Sphere*, our social lives are marked by "autonomy" and "fluidity" as "the individual engages socially through a private media environment located within the individual's personal and private space" (ibid., p. 306). Individuals find rootedness in the temporary senses of place they arrive at through their identity performances, even as they navigate the context collapse (Marwick & boyd, 2011) that happens when social media platforms bundle together many disparate types of relations and encounter economic, social, and political forces that bound self-construction and performances. Even still, the guiding concepts of contemporary identity in this tradition are flexibility, multiplicity, reflexivity, and play, especially when compared with the received identities of traditional societies.

Other theorists, however, have told a different story that helps shed light on new expressions and social formations of white nationalism. The sociologist Manuel Castells's *The Power of Identity* (2011 [1997], p. 11) argues that reflexive selves are the purview of *elites*: "reflexive life-planning becomes impossible, except for the elite inhabiting the timeless space of flows of global networks and their ancillary locales." Those left out of global information networks, or who perceive themselves being culturally or economically marginalized by them, retreat to the "defensive trenches" of nationalism, religiosity, and race and ethnicity, which are buffeting forces against the power and play of information and global networks, in addition to the withering of civil society (ibid., p. 33). Castells (ibid., p. 68) argued that these resultant "cultural communes" offer reactionary, defensive, and solidaristic identities organized around values coded by symbols of identification, and provide mooring for individuals excluded from or resistant to "the individualization of identity."

In light of the 2016 election, Castells (2011, p. 69) was perceptive in understanding that "God, nation, family, and community will provide unbreakable, eternal codes" that stand against global flows of power and information. This chapter details these contrasting theories on identity before providing an analysis of how Breitbart provides the supporting media for a contemporary white nationalist cultural commune that falls under the label of the alt-right. The site, founded in 2005 by Andrew Breitbart, a conservative media entrepreneur and provocateur, is the 44th most popular website in the United States according to Alexa, and received massive traffic during the election, with over 2.3 million followers on Facebook and 18 million homepage visitors a month (Grynbaum and Herrman, 2016). Even more, the site was highly influential. A team of researchers (Benkler et al, 2017) demonstrated that Breitbart significantly shaped online communication in the public sphere during the election, so much so that the site was much more central than *Fox News* to political discourse. And, the fact that Steve Bannon, a founding member of the board and executive chair of Breitbart, served as chief executive officer of the Trump campaign and the White House chief strategist during the first eight months of the Trump administration also speaks of its considerable influence.

As this chapter reveals, Breitbart advances the assertion of identity fundamentalism in an age of elite networked selves. Breitbart's various contributors reject contemporary pluralist, multicultural democracy, economic and institutional globalization, and cosmopolitanism in favor of an American democracy premised upon white, Christian American identity. In doing so, Breitbart provides a forum for ideas and identities that animate the alt-right, drawing in new audiences and reifying the identities of extant ones, helping people scared and anxious about a changing world and their diminished place in it to connect and assert political and economic claims on the basis of a shared identity. Given its influence and role, Breitbart offers an ideal opportunity to analyze the defensive trenches of contemporary identity, showing how older bases of collective symbolic identification and belonging not only persist in a changing world, but can also become stronger.

The Surprising Rootedness of Networked Identity

Scholars have grounded the concept of identity in the idea of social difference. Craig Calhoun (1994, pp. 9–10) argues that:

> We know of no people without names, no languages or cultures in which some manner of distinctions between self and other, we and they, are not made . . . Self-knowledge—always a construction no matter how much it feels like a discovery—is never altogether separable from claims to be known in specific ways by others.

In this formulation, identity is actively constructed by social actors over time and fundamentally premised on social *difference* (i.e. distinction). Identities distinguish between self and society, individuals and groups, in-groups and out-groups, and they are fundamentally public, ways of being known by others. People can also have multiple identities, encompassing citizenship status, religious affiliation, social groups, political party, and racial and ethnic groups, and so on.

Many social theorists have argued that a key feature of modernity is that identity is less rooted in received social groupings than in the past, such as handed down notions of religion and place. Instead, theorists posit that contemporary identity is the result of an active and self-reflexive process. Giddens (1991) saw the key condition of modernity in the erosion of received forms of identity rooted in place and faith. As tradition loses its hold, individuals navigate their own life choices in a process of "reflexively organized life planning": "Self-identity is not a distinctive trait possessed by the individual. It is *the self as reflexively understood by the person in terms of her/his biography.*" (Giddens, 1991, p. 53, emphasis in the original)

Giddens's (ibid., p. 32) key insight is that "in the context of post-traditional order, the self becomes a reflexive project." Taking the place of received selves, such as on the basis of terrestrial community and religious identity, are reflexive selves that are comparatively free to remake their identities in the context of their cultural surroundings. This idea has taken on new life and urgency in the age of the Internet and social media (Bauman, 2013; Van Dijck, 2013). While the idea of a continually remade "project self" did not originate with the Internet, scholars have argued that the growth of global information networks and social media has made the process of self-construction more widespread, expansive, fluid, and socially, culturally, and politically important (Bennett and Segerberg, 2013; Ratto and Boler, 2014). The informational and social networks that people are embedded in are both more diverse and more expansive when constituted through communications technology. As Papacharissi (2010, p. 17) argues, in late modern societies the locus of politics resides in the citizen's

> private sphere of contemplation, evaluation, and action, in which the self remains the point of reference. The citizen is alone, but not lonely or isolated. On the contrary, within the private sphere, the individual cultivates civic habits that enable him or her to connect with others on the basis of shared social, political, and cultural priorities.

Of course, fluidity has never been complete, as two decades of scholarship on networked media in the context of race and ethnicity have pointed out. Cultural theorist Lisa Nakamura (2013), for instance, pointed out that the idea of a de-raced Internet was always a fantasy, a fiction of whiteness as the absence of race. People could never escape from the racial and ethnic identities that shape their culture and bodies, nor did people of color ever necessarily desire to. Even still, the broad consensus in the literature is that individuals are able to seek out like-minded others in the private sphere, and build their own networks of political, social, and cultural affiliation.

Manuel Castells, in contrast, makes a structural argument regarding who gets to participate in the free flow and voluntaristic construction of identities in the network society. As noted above, for Castells it is only elites in the global information society that are able to construct their fluid selves. Most non-elite individuals only have *local* experiences and orientations, while power resides in *global* networks. For most people, life in the "network society" is characterized by a comparative powerlessness, as the local lives they live are structured by increasingly global forces. Meanwhile, civil society has become fractured and attenuates in power given that local associations and means of political representation are increasingly rendered powerless in the face of global networks. This, in turn, leads people to retreat into the defenses of nationalism, religion, and ethnicity. As Castells (2011, p. 11) argues:

> The search for meaning takes place then in the reconstruction of defensive identities around communal principles. Most of social action becomes organized in the opposition between unidentified flows and secluded identities . . . But, I propose the hypothesis that the constitution of subjects, at the heart of the process of social change, takes a different route to the one we knew during modernity, and late modernity: namely, *subjects, if and when constructed, are not built any longer on the basis of civil societies, which are in the process of disintegration, but as prolongation of communal resistance.*
>
> *(emphasis in the original)*

Castells presciently proposes that this communalism takes four forms: religious fundamentalism, nationalism, ethnic identity, and territorial identity. They are identities that are fundamentally *reactive* to shifts in global power and information, and offer independent and "autonomous" sources of meaning vis-à-vis global networks (ibid., p. 68). These "cultural communes" become havens for those "excluded from or resisting the individualization of identity attached to life in the global networks of power and wealth" (ibid.). In sum, Castells argues that these are identities carved out in reaction, and opposition, to globalization (which erodes territorial, national, and cultural sovereignty), flexible networks and identities (which foster economic precarity and make social groupings unclear), and breakdowns of traditional social and cultural roles found within family units and other social groupings. As Castells (ibid., pp. 68–70) argues, cultural communes

> are, at the outset, defensive identities that function as refuge and solidarity, to protect against a hostile, outside world. They are culturally constituted; that is, organized around a specific set of values whose meaning and sharing are marked by specific codes of self-identification: the community of believers, the icons of nationalism, the geography of locality . . .
>
> This negation of civil societies and political institutions where cultural communes emerge leads to the closing of the boundaries of the commune. In contrast to pluralistic, differentiated civil societies, cultural communes display little internal differentiation. Indeed, their strength, and their ability

to provide refuge, solace, certainty, and protection, comes precisely from their communal character, from their collective responsibility, canceling individual projects. Thus, in the first stage of reaction, the (re)construction of meaning by defensive identities breaks away from the institutions of society, and promises to rebuild from the bottom up, while retrenching themselves in a communal heaven.

Writing in the late 1990s, Castells sees these cultural communes take shape in "the dominance of symbolic politics in the space of media" (ibid., p. 73). His case studies document how groups such as the Zapatistas and the American militia movements utilize communications technologies, particularly the Internet, to craft their symbolic politics, which provide fertile ground for the sharing of conspiracy theories, support expression, and provide the basis for collective self-definition and action. In Castells's work, then, we see a clear alternative to the emphasis on individual self-reflexivity, often through networked media use, that characterizes accounts of digital "connective action" (Bennett & Segerberg, 2013). For Castells, the defensive work of symbolic and social retreats into older forms of *stabilizing* identity shape contemporary politics.

These were precisely the dynamics on display in the 2016 U.S. presidential election and, I would argue, that lay behind many of the overtly nationalistic, populist, and racially exclusionary forces now driving politics in contemporary Western democracies. The 2016 U.S. presidential election, as well as its predecessor in Brexit, revealed the continued importance of race, ethnicity, religion, nationalism, and territorial identification in the public life of advanced Western democracies.

For example, a trio of books written in advance of the presidential election— Cramer's (2016) *The Politics of Resentment*, Gest's (2016) *The New Minority*, and Hochschild's (2016) *Strangers in thir Own Land*—reveal the underlying dynamics of U.S. politics that help explain the outcome of the presidential race. In an ethnographic study, Cramer revealed the degree to which *rural* identity shapes people's perceptions of politics, from who has political power to who benefits from governmental action. Gest, in a comparative ethnography and survey of people in white working-class London and Youngstown, Ohio, shows how people's perceptions of their identity group's decline in status shapes their turn to radical, exclusionary politics designed to restore white cultural, social, and economic status. Hochschild's ethnographic study of Tea Party supporters in Louisiana reveals how white identity, partisanship, and religion shape perceptions of the un-deserving (black) and deserving (white) poor, and fueled the identity movement that carried Donald Trump to the presidency. Trump was the candidate who provided emotional release from the "feeling rules" that govern normative relations toward others (e.g. people of color, lesbians and gays, Muslims), and which the president's supporters chafed at (Hochschild, 2016).

I turn now to an analysis of the white nationalist website Breitbart to reveal what the identity media of a cultural commune looks like.

Breitbart and the Rise of the New White American Nationalism

What is Breitbart? There are few published academic studies of the site. Those that exist cover the highest profile controversies involving the early history of the site, including its undercover sting operations and selectively edited videos of ACORN, the progressive low-income housing organization, which ultimately led to the organization's demise, in addition to the site's exposé of supposedly racist comments made by former Department of Agriculture employee Shirley Sherrod (Shah and Yamagami, 2015). Both of these incidents received media coverage in hundreds of articles. Existing academic commentary situates Breitbart as a contemporary manifestation of Richard Hofstadter's (1966) influential critique of a "paranoid style" of American politics on the right, putting the site in line with Rush Limbaugh, Glenn Beck, and Bill O'Reilly, especially for its style of political outrage and combat (Berry & Sobieraj, 2013). Dreier and Martin (2010) called Andrew Breitbart an "opinion entrepreneur" for this role in the ACORN incident, particularly the way he was able to manufacture a controversy in national legacy media, and see the site generally as a faux outrage media outlet.

There is truth to these views. As a site, Breitbart is prone to disinformation, selective editing, faux outrage, and juvenile tactics of dishonest "gotcha" journalism. However, this is not the whole story. Media and journalism matter for their importance with respect to identity as much as information. An analysis of the articles published on Breitbart during and immediately after the election reveals the ideology of Breitbart's contributors, the stories they told themselves about American politics, and their collective political identity as a movement.

Breitbart packages a white nationalist ideology in a twenty-first-century media entertainment style. In doing so, Brietbart should be understood as a form of commercial identity media that helped give rise to, and supports, a defined white nationalist cultural commune, to use Castells's terms. As the following pages demonstrate, the various contributors to Breitbart reject *multiculturalism, globalization, and cosmopolitanism* in favor of white, nationalist, identity.[2] In accord with Castells's theory of identity, Breitbart turns from cultural and social pluralism and embraces homogeneity, enrolls individuals in a collective, defensive project to reclaim the symbolic borders of the nation against a tide of immigrants and Islam, and promotes and inculcates a coherent collective identity and ideology (Harris-Lacewell, 2010) that presumably offers a protected defensive space for its followers, while turning from individuated identity projects.

In other words, there is a coherent worldview and collective identity threaded through Breitbart's content, which revolves around the rejection of multicultural democracy, cosmopolitanism, and globalization. The first encodes a deep distrust of Islam, but also symbolically defines non-whites as aberrant and pluralism as a negative feature of American society and democracy. The rejection of cosmopolitanism is a critique of politicians and others who espouse an outlook, worldview, or style that extends beyond America's borders, in favor of an embrace of nostalgic and backward-looking constructions of Americans' cultural traditions. Finally, and related, the third is a critique of economic and institutional globalization in favor of a new American nationalism in economic and international affairs.

In identifying these elements of Breitbart's symbolic work as a forum in support of a cultural commune, the site cannot be reduced to populism as a style, rhetoric, or a set of governing ideas (Block and Negrine, 2017; Kazin, 1998; Panizza, 2005). The reality is, unfortunately, darker. Breitbart, and the broader alt-right movement of which it is an integral part, not only reject pluralism, but, like all populist movements, also advances claims for a singular "people" (Muller, 2016). Breitbart explicitly rejects pluralism in favor of an expressly white American identity. Breitbart offers a coherent ideology, a set of ideas for understanding politics, narrative tropes that help people situate and understand politics, and a collective identity of white American and Christian nationalism.

For example, perhaps the most common theme to emerge in articles published on Breitbart during the election was the general idea and refrain of "taking back our country." Trump himself tweeted after Brexit that "They took their country back, just like we will take America back" (Swoyer, 2016). Across these articles, Trump supporters were said to be taking their country back from a litany of explicit targets including: Democrats, the socialist left, Muslims, the media, people of color, women, immigrants, establishment Republicans, free traders, Wall Street, and Washington DC insiders. Throughout many of these articles, those "taking back their country" were characterized in terms of "middle America," "real America," "deplorables," and "fly over country." These groups were hailed by Breitbart for standing up, asserting themselves and their values, and rejecting those who would repudiate them.

With respect to multiculturalism, Breitbart authors explicitly rejected immigrant incorporation, particularly for Muslims, into democracy (Yiannopoulos, 2016a). Numerous Breitbart articles espoused the idea that Islam is incompatible with democracy, freedom of speech, and the peaceful and law-bound resolution of conflict (e.g. Yiannopoulos, 2016b). And, in others, there was a broader critique of contemporary immigrants for their failure to incorporate themselves into American democracy. For example, in an article entitled "The Emerging Trumpian Majority" that entwines both ideas, James Pinkerton (2016a) writes:

> Once upon a time, immigration to the U.S. was a positive civic ritual that affirmed American values; that is, foreigners would come here legally, get a job, learn English, and embrace American ways. And presto! They too were Americans. It's hard to think of anything healthier for a country's psyche than to see others come and adapt to its ways.

By contrast, today, the situation is much different; too many foreigners come here illegally, wangle [*sic*] their way onto public assistance, and then sit as unassimilated clumps at best, as terrorists at worse. No wonder the American people are angry. And the Republican Party, at least, is reflecting that anger.

Breitbart contributors also rejected cosmopolitanism in favor of U.S. cultural, economic, and institutional nationalism. In an article entitled "The ten ideologies of America," Breitbart writer Virgil (2016a, emphases in the original) defines cosmopolitanism as

> the view that we are all, everywhere, a part of a single world community, and that such things as nation-states, including the United States, only slow down the fulfillment of our true destiny—coming together in a global harmonic convergence . . . *Left* Cosmopolitanism means support for open borders, of course, and also for multiculturalism. As might be said, "Celebrate diversity—or else!" In addition, Left Cosmos love international organizations, such as the United Nations; to them, that's the future—one big New World Order. *Right* Cosmopolitans also support open borders. In addition, being good capitalists, they support free trade and anything else that multinational corporations might wish for. And since they are private-sector-loving corporatists, they avidly embrace pro-business international combines, such as the World Trade Organization.

Broadly, Breitbart contributors espouse an American nationalism, one that explicitly turns inward to the United States for its source of moral values and strength. At the same time, the rejection of cosmopolitanism is linked to the critique of elites, who are seen as looking down upon ordinary Americans and their values in favor of an other-directed, outward-oriented, cosmopolitan outlook. Cosmopolitanism here is in part a cultural critique, linked to a perceived style of being and carrying oneself in the world, in sharp distinction to "American" identity and values.

At the same time, as is clear in the quote above, there is an associated critique of globalism on Breitbart that assaults global financial flows and international financial capitalism and free trade in favor of protectionism. It also encompasses a distrust of international governing bodies such as the United Nations and alliances that are perceived to weaken American sovereignty. For example, in a piece published in August titled "The worldwide Trumpian majority: Lessons from Brexit, Britain, and the United States," James Pinkerton (2016b) writes:

> Indeed, we can step back and see that around the world, the dueling forces are globalism, on the one hand, and nationalism, on the other.

Globalism, as we have observed, is a curious combination of socialism and capitalism—that is, bureaucrats and bankers, working together to flatten national boundaries and, indeed, to flatten the nation-state itself . . .

As for nationalism, that's the credo of all others, whether we like them or not. Trump, Farage, and LePen are nationalists, but then so, too, are the Russians, Chinese, and Iranians. In other words, just about all the peoples of the world are instinctive nationalists; it's globalism that is the strange mutation, afflicting mostly the West.

Taken together, Breitbart offers a rather coherent and over-arching critique of contemporary currents in politics and the existing Democratic and Republican establishments. What is striking is the degree to which the positions in Breitbart commentary—which closely tracked Trump's own rhetoric during the campaign— tell a clear political story. Breitbart is, in part, about defining the symbolic border of the nation and protecting the white, Christian body politic in a way that is premised on *exclusion*. This is precisely the expectation of Castells's ideas regarding the homogeneity of cultural communes; Breitbart espouses a collective identity marked by a defensive retreat into white Christian and American nationalism.

Even more, many of Breitbart's contributors argue that the embrace of globalization and multiculturalism is both anti-democratic and anti-American. They argue that these policies erode services for white, working-class Americans and undermine the nation-state. Indeed, the interests of those pursuing identity politics, in the view of articles on Breitbart (contributors roundly fail to recognize their own arguments as a form of white identity politics), are seen as irreconcilable with those of "real" Americans. Virgil (2016a) writes:

The old Democrats of FDR's time were happy enough with capitalism; they just wanted to extend solidaristic job-protections, and basic social-insurance plans, to all Americans.

By contrast, today's Democrats, filled with Cosmopolitan dreams, want to extend government benefits to the world—and that's not just a budget-buster, it's also a political loser.

In truth, today's Democrats aren't much interested in the well-being of working stiffs. Instead, they are enraptured with new plans to advance identity politics, co-ed bathrooms, and #BlackLivesMatter. All the while, of course, keeping the border open and suppressing energy production and economic activity.

Breitbart, Cultural Communes, and the Problem of Democratic Incorporation

Rousseau famously argued that crafting the identity of a *citizen* is difficult. People are instinctively drawn to small groups, whether they are formed from their local

communities or their near-to-hand social affiliations and identities. Constructing civil solidarity on the basis of an abstraction such as a global world, or even
a nation, is difficult and, ultimately, fragile. Alexander (2006), meanwhile, has
argued that the idea of a "democratic self" is a hard-won achievement, ultimately
premised on people understanding their identities in terms of being a member
of a collective premised on the protection of individual rights, a commitment
to social solidarity and mutual obligation, and civil moral codes that structure
democratic relations.

As Manuel Castells has demonstrated, in a world of global information networks, constructing democratic identities and solidarity is an even more complicated affair. While the global elite has prospered and can now fluidly and
self-reflexively construct their identities, the more common response has been
the flight into cultural communes defined by religion, nation, ethnicity, and
locale. If 2016 has revealed anything, it is the degree to which these defensive
identities have become the refuge of whites across the United States and Europe,
fueled by a growing sense of the loss of their privileged cultural, economic, and
social status in a global world (Hochschild, 2016; Gest, 2016).

Comparatively *older* forms of identity in the United States, and indeed, global
politics, not only have continued relevance, but also, it appears, they are actively
being renewed. As noted above, Castells proposed, two decades ago, that the
construction of identity in the network age could take two forms. The first is the
embrace of hyper-individualized, global forms of identity rooted in expressive
choice, which is only available to elites. Castells goes so far as to refer to "individualism" as a collective identity. The second entails the retreat to the defensive
trenches of nationalism, religion, and ethnic and racial identity. As Castells (2011,
p. 7) argues, in contrast with much of the existing literature:

> It is easy to agree on the fact that, from a sociological perspective, all identi-
> ties are constructed. The real issue is how, from what, by whom, and for
> what. The construction of identities uses building materials from history,
> from geography, from biology, from productive and reproductive institu-
> tions, from collective memory and from personal fantasies, from power
> apparatuses and religious revelations. But individuals, social groups, and
> societies process all these materials, and rearrange their meaning, according
> to social determinations and cultural projects that are rooted in their social
> structure, and in their space/time framework.

What are the consequences of retreat into what can best be conceptualized
as white identity fundamentalism, an identity easily forged from the history of
white supremacy in America and the perceived encroachment of non-whites
on that power? Breitbart provides a window into a future shaped, in no small
part, by a defensive identity defined by conceptions of white group interest.
A significant number of Trump's supporters celebrated his rise precisely because

it symbolically signaled, and would set in motion, the rejection of multicultural democracy in favor of the protection of white interests. Breitbart contributor Virgil (2016b), who published an essay the day after the election entitled "Ten takeaways of the revolution of 2016," argued:

> **Middle America has asserted itself, and these folks have their own ideas.** Throughout the '16 election, the MSM and the rest of the chattering class viewed the American working- and middle class with a combination of contempt and pity. To illustrate, we can look back to July 13, when *The New York Times* headlined a news story, "For Whites Sensing Decline, Donald Trump Unleashes Words of Resistance." We might pause to ask: Would the *Times* use the word "decline" in regard to any group, other than whites? Indeed, as well we all know, the MSM has been joined in its anti-white mockery by big chunks of what's billed, these days, as "comedy. . . ."
>
> Moreover, we can observe that while this smug culture of incomprehension and condescension has been a characteristic of the left, it can also be observed, in milder form, on the right. That is, many Republicans, perhaps even today, just can't quite believe that Trump stands for anything more than reality-TV showmanship. Yet, as anyone who reads Breitbart, for example, knows, serious thinking has been going on about what a populist-nationalist center-right coalition might look like, even if the familiar DC think-tanks haven't been interested.

Breitbart's contributor here entwines white identity with populist-nationalism, celebrating an insurgent Trump candidacy and a new nationalism he rhetorically stood for during the campaign that will benefit white people. Breitbart is the symbolic media, and organizing platform, for a defensive cultural commune that rejects diversity, global institutions, and an expansive, cosmopolitan worldview in favor of white, Christian, and American nationalism. Breitbart also embraces the rejection of establishment Republicanism and older forms of conservatism, especially given its *explicit* (as opposed to *implicit*) racial appeals to white identity and racial framing of the sources of political and social conflict (see Bonilla-Silva, 2010; Hemmer, 2016; McGirr, 2015). At its heart, the defensive cultural commune of the alt-right is a rejection of the pluralism that defines contemporary multicultural democracy.

While on one level the retreat from reflexive global identities is noteworthy against the backdrop of the literature on networked selves, the normative democratic concern lies in the fact that cultural communes, made visible on and constituted through sites such as Breitbart, reject *democratic incorporation*. Democratic politics is possible when individualism is a collective identity, to use Castells's terms. There is no basis for othering or exclusion when everyone is free to construct their own identity; it is a politics premised on a universal individualism.

Cultural communes, however, are premised on exclusion. The history of Western democracies can be understood through the lens of the problem of civic "incorporation," the fight to extend citizenship beyond the boundaries of birth, race, gender, and class—the question of which types of people sharing which identities can and should be incorporated into the civil sphere. Social theorist Jeffrey Alexander (2006, p. 61), for instance, has argued that the historical development of Western democracy came in part through the work of social movements to ground particularistic, excluded identities in terms of democratic universality. There is an almost teleological sense of history in Alexander's account, where the cultural discourses in the founding documents give rise to their later interpretations and ultimately are made manifest in a more inclusive civil sphere. As Alexander (ibid., p. 61) argues:

> Political struggles over the status of lower-class groups, or racial, ethnic, and religious minorities, of women, children, and homosexuals, of those who are constructed as criminals and as mentally, emotionally, and physically handicapped—these conflicts have always involved discursive struggles over whether and how the discourse of liberty can be extended and applied. Insofar as the founding cultural myths and constitutional documents of democratic societies are universalistic, they implicitly stipulated that the discourse can always be further extended, and that it eventually must be.

In the 250 years since the founding of the United States, civil solidarity and formal electoral participation has indeed been extended significantly to include many of these formerly excluded groups. While this liberty does not necessarily mean full economic equality, and the degree to which rights are extended was highly uneven, particularly in the south (Mickey, 2015), universalistic democratic cultural claims have come prior to these broader shifts.

In a world where flexible selves are the predominant mode of constructing identity, incorporation would be less of a pressing issue. In our own time, however, the rise of cultural communes has made the question of democratic inclusion again central to our politics. The particular contours of the "civil" is an ongoing achievement, not a foregone conclusion, and it is not static, it is subject in part to the power of contingent events in history, anxiety about race and status (Hochschild, 2016), and fear about the contours of the body politic (Alexander, 2006). As Castells predicted, the network society can give rise to forms of defensive identity fundamentalism that fuel powerful conservative and reactionary movements. While Castells (2011, p. 63) focused on African-American identity, and saw ethnicity ultimately being *less* powerful than nationalism and religion, it is clear that in the United States *white* cultural communes have extraordinary opportunities to revoke symbolic inclusion and formal rights. As the sociologist Chris Bail (2014) has demonstrated, in our own time the public sphere, dominated by white Christians, has grown more radical in response to terrorism in ways directly counter to the discourse of liberty and equality under the law in calling for the punishing and profiling of Muslim Americans, long before Trump's rise.

The discourses of liberty, equality, and justice at the center of the United States and many Western constitutional democracies are, in the end, historically contingent and an ongoing achievement. They are subject to cultural debates, embedded within fields of power, over what liberty, equality, and justice mean, arguments over how far democratic solidarity should be extended, and elite, institutional, and public evaluations of the values and morals that should govern democratic life. While founding cultural documents, and the communicative and regulatory institutions that give them shape and life, are powerful, defensive movements can draw on their own alternative cultural identities, elaborating their own myths, constituting themselves through media, embedding themselves in powerful institutions, while making fear- and identity-based appeals to the public that enable them to foreclose progressive attempts at democratic equality and expand their defensive cultural communes. And, in so doing, they have the power to weaken democratic identities, norms, values, and institutions. That is the darkest lesson of the cultural commune of the alt-right and Trump's ascendency to America's highest office.

Notes

1 1488 combines two white supremacist symbols: 14 refers to the words "We must secure the existence of our people and a future for white children"; 88 for Heil Hitler (H is the eighth letter of the alphabet).
2 An earlier version of the empirical portion of this chapter appeared in Kreiss (2017).

References

Alexander, J. C. (2006). *The civil sphere*. Oxford: Oxford University Press.
Bail, C. A. (2014). *Terrified: How anti-Muslim fringe organizations became mainstream*. Princeton: Princeton University Press.
Bauman, Z. (2013). *Liquid modernity*. Chichester: John Wiley & Sons.
Benkler, Y., Faris, R., Roberts, H., & Zuckerman, E. (2017). Study: Breitbart-led right-wing media ecosystem altered broader media agenda. *Columbia Journalism Review*, 1(4.1), 7.
Bennett, W. L. & Segerberg, A. (2013). *The logic of connective action: Digital media and the personalization of contentious politics*. Cambridge: Cambridge University Press.
Berry, J. M. & Sobieraj, S. (2013). *The outrage industry: Political opinion media and the new incivility*. Oxford: Oxford University Press.
Block, E. & Negrine, R. (2017). The populist communication style: Toward a critical framework. *International Journal of Communication*, 11(1), 178–197.
Bokhari, A. & Yiannopoulos, M. (2016). An establishment conservative's guide to the alt-right. *Breitbart*, March 29. www.breitbart.com/tech/2016/03/29/an-establishment-conservatives-guide-to-the-alt-right/

Bonilla-Silva, E. (2010). *Racism without racists: Color-blind racism and the persistence of racial inequality in the United States.* Lanham, MD: Rowman & Littlefield.

Calhoun, C. J. (1994). Social theory and the politics of identity. In C. Calhoun (Ed.), *Social theory and the politics of identity* (pp. 9–36). Oxford: Blackwell.

Castells, M. (2011 [1997]). *The power of identity. Vol. 2: The information age—Economy, society, and culture.* Chichester: John Wiley & Sons.

Cramer, K. J. (2016). *The politics of resentment: Rural consciousness in Wisconsin and the rise of Scott Walker.* Chicago: University of Chicago Press.

Dreier, P. & Martin, C. R. (2010). How ACORN was framed: Political controversy and media agenda setting. *Perspectives on Politics*, 8(3), 761–792.

Faris, R., Roberts, H., Etling, B., Bourassa, N., Zuckerman, E., & Benkler, Y. (2017). Partisanship, propaganda, and disinformation: Online media and the 2016 US presidential election. http://nrs.harvard.edu/urn-3:HUL.InstRepos:33759251

Gest, J. (2016). *The new minority: White working class politics in an age of immigration and inequality.* Oxford: Oxford University Press.

Giddens, A. (1991). *Modernity and self-identity: Self and society in the late modern age.* Stanford: Stanford University Press.

Grynbaum, M. M. & Herrman, J. (2016). Breitbart rises from outlier to potent voice in campaign. *New York Times*, August 26.

Haidt, J. (2012). *The righteous mind: Why good people are divided by politics and religion.* New York: Vintage.

Harris-Lacewell, M. V. (2010). *Barbershops, bibles, and BET: Everyday talk and black political thought.* Princeton: Princeton University Press.

Hemmer, N. (2016). *Messengers of the Right: Conservative media and the transformation of American politics.* Philadelphia: University of Pennsylvania Press.

Hochschild, A. R. (2016). *Strangers in their own land: Anger and mourning on the American Right.* New York: New Press.

Hofstadter, R. (1966). The paranoid style. *American politics and other essays.* New York: Vintage.

Kazin, M. (1998). *The populist persuasion: An American history.* Ithaca: Cornell University Press.

Kreiss, D. (2017). Trump, Breitbart, and the rejection of multi-cultural democracy. *Vox*, January 30.

Kreiss, D. & Mason, K. (2017). Here's what white supremacy looks and sounds like now (hint it's not your grandfather's KKK). *Washington Post*, August 17. www.washington post.com/news/monkey-cage/wp/2017/08/17/heres-what-white-supremacy-looks-and-sounds-like-now-its-not-your-grandfathers-kkk/?utm_term=.de0f4c2b29a3

Marwick, A. E. & boyd, d. (2011). I tweet honestly, I tweet passionately: Twitter users, context collapse, and the imagined audience. *New Media & Society*, 13(1), 114–133.

Marwick A. E. & Lewis, R. (2017). Media manipulation and disinformation online. *Report, Data & Society*, May 15.

McGirr, L. (2015). *Suburban warriors: The origins of the new American right.* Princeton: Princeton University Press.

Mickey, R. (2015). *Paths out of Dixie: The democratization of authoritarian enclaves in America's Deep South, 1944–1972.* Princeton: Princeton University Press.

Muller, J. W. (2016). *What is populism?.* Philadelphia: University of Pennsylvania Press.

Nakamura, L. (2013). *Cybertypes: Race, ethnicity, and identity on the Internet.* New York: Routledge.

Panizza, F. (Ed.) (2005). *Populism and the mirror of democracy.* London: Verso.

Papacharissi, Z. (2010). *A private sphere: Democracy in a digital age.* Cambridge: Polity.

Papacharissi, Z. (2014). Conclusion: A networked self. In Z. Papacharissi (Ed.), *A networked self: Identity, community, and culture on social network sites* (pp. 304–318). New York: Routledge.

Pinkerton, J. (2016a). The emerging Trumpian majority. *Breitbart*, August 1. www.breit bart.com/big-government/2016/08/01/the-emerging-trumpian-majority/

Pinkerton, J. (2016b). The worldwide Trumpian majority: Lessons from Brexit, Britain, and the United States. *Breitbart*, August 7. www.breitbart.com/big-government/2016/08/07/worldwide-trumpian-majority-lessons-brexit-britain-united-states/

Ratto, M. & Boler, M. (2014). *DIY citizenship: Critical making and social media.* Cambridge, MA: MIT Press.

Shah, H. & Yamagami, M. (2015). Color-blind racism in television news and commentary: The redemption of Shirley Sherrod. *Howard Journal of Communications*, 26(2), 193–205.

Swoyer, A. (2016). Donald Trump on Brexit: "They took their country back"; "We Will Take Our Country Back." *Breitbart*, June 24. www.breitbart.com/2016-presidential-race/2016/06/24/donald-trump-brexit-took-country-back-will-take-america-back/

Van Dijck, J. (2013). *The culture of connectivity: A critical history of social media.* Oxford: Oxford University Press.

Virgil. (2016a). The ten ideologies of America. *Breitbart*, March 20. www.breitbart.com/big-government/2016/03/20/as-donald-trump-overthrows-the-old-order-a-look-at-the-new-order-the-ten-ideologies-of-america/

Virgil. (2016b). Ten takeaways from the Trump revolution of 2016. *Breitbart*, November 10. www.breitbart.com/big-government/2016/11/10/virgil-ten-takeaways-from-the-trump-revolution-of-2016/

Yiannopoulos, Milo. (2016a). Full text: 10 things Milo hates about Islam. *Breitbart*, September 27. www.breitbart.com/milo/2016/09/27/10-things-milo-hates-islam/

Yiannopoulos, Milo. (2016b). Here's everything i wanted to say about Islam yesterday, but couldn't. *Breitbart*, June 16. www.breitbart.com/milo/2016/06/16/heres-everything-wanted-say-islam-yesterday-couldnt/

3

NEWS AND THE NETWORKED SELF

Performativity, Platforms, and Journalistic Epistemologies

Matt Carlson and Seth C. Lewis

To visit the original Facebook homepage of 2004 is to travel back in time to witness the humble birth of the social media behemoth. Then known as "Thefacebook," the sparse site announced its uses in four bulleted items: "Search for people at your school; Find out who are in your classes; Look at your friends' friends; See a visualization of your social network." These uses get to the voyeuristic side that lies at the heart of the site, but what is notable is what is not there: news. Facebook's original intention was to bring together a fairly homogeneous group—college students at elite universities—to map social space online. But as the site zoomed past 2 billion users, it has inarguably become the world's foremost distributor of news. Yet news dominance was never Facebook's desired goal. It was the users who adopted news as something important and something they wished to share, while news organizations have invested in ways to push their content on the Facebook platform.

This chapter pulls back to offer a bird's-eye view of the constellation of shifting actors, practices, and technologies involved when news moves into the space of social media. At the heart of this chapter is the triad of performativity, platforms, and journalistic epistemology. Performativity speaks to the productive power of the networked self. It encompasses the shift from audiences as passive recipients of news, who, according to classic liberal democratic norms, are expected to transform news into opinion to one in which news users perform through news sharing, commenting, and creation. This newfound power is tempered by constraints that social media platforms place on their users. Platforms are structured spaces that enable and constrain specific action. Both performativity and platforms are viewed through the conceptual lens of journalistic epistemology, defined here broadly as journalism's ways of knowing.

It can be difficult to gain the perspective necessary to critically examine these forces as they shift and change about us, but it remains crucial to step back and gauge what is going on. To do so, this chapter begins by examining what it means for news to be part of the networked self before turning to a discussion of how social media platforms affect news consumption in these spaces. In particular, the politics of algorithms get to this tension between this desire to express ourselves online and the desire of these platforms to shape our content diet in particular ways. We then ask what the consequences are for journalism at an epistemic level when the personal and the political blend.

News and the Networked Self

Human identity is, at heart, a performative one bound up in social conventions, the expectations of others, and the desire to be perceived in particular ways (Goffman, 1959). Identity performance is about negotiating between the self and society, and is carried out through mundane everyday action. The "networked self" marks off the shift to mediated identity performances made possible through social media that encourage personal expression and connection to others as a mode of being (Papacharissi, 2010). Digital media have provided new tools to not only communicate with others, but also to communicate who we are, both as individuals and by virtue of our relations with others. Of course, as the next section will elucidate, these are not neutral spaces for identity performances, but highly constrained ones.

While news is not normally discussed in its relationship to identity, we argue that news engagement also entails a form of identity performance. Engagement here includes practices of news consumption as well as communicating about news. Carey (2009) has most clearly expressed this in communal terms with his ritual view of communication. For Carey, news content should not be examined purely as a means of transmission of specific content, but as a cultural form that provides shared meaning and a way of orienting oneself in the world. In terms of the self, what Carey's argument suggests is that the news produces collective identity as much as it distributes information. Less well developed is how news and identity interact at a local level, but assumptions are embedded in seminal research on the topic. Berelson's (1948) study of a newspaper strike revealed a news audience missing the newspaper as a way of connecting with others. Similarly, Katz and Lazarsfeld's (1955) two-step flow theory was intended to soften claims of strong media effects, but it also demonstrated the degree to which news sharing was part of everyday life. All of this is to suggest that even though news is usually discussed in terms of informational transfer and civic duty among individuals, it clearly is part of identity maintenance.

News and identity performance take on a different character in the context of social media. While news sharing is not a new phenomenon—newspaper articles used to be clipped and sent in the mail, after all—news sharing has become an indelible part of the experience on social media (Kalsnes & Larsson, 2017). The Pew Research Center found that 80% of social media users at least occasionally click on news stories, and nearly half of social media users (49%) share or repost stories. Moreover, sharing of stories on social media occurs across all age groups, with more than half of 30 to 64 year olds sharing news (Mitchell et al., 2016). According to another Pew report, people appear to find news through social media at roughly the same rates that they do by visiting a news website directly (35% and 36%, respectively). When asked to recall the name of the news source that provided the last story they encountered, 10% of respondents wrote in "Facebook" as a specific media outlet (a finding that assumes greater meaning when we consider the "fake news" controversy later in this chapter). Importantly, the study reinforced the cultural embeddedness of digital news, as stories shared by friends and family members elicited the most engagement overall (Mitchell et al., 2017).

Social media thus provide a space for users to interact with news in ways that complicate previous ideas of what it means to consume news (Hermida, 2016). In sharing news, users add their interpretations, which then affect how any story is seen by others (Carlson, 2016). Even more, in sharing news, users may be attempting to shape how *they* are seen by others. Indeed, like virtually all other activities on social media, from posting selfies to polishing profile pages, news sharing is a form of identity manifestation and maintenance—a means of signaling who we are and how we want to be perceived. By virtue of their design, social media sites enable and encourage forms of impression management (Marwick, 2013). Consider, for instance, how changing your Facebook profile photo is almost guaranteed to generate a relatively higher number of impressions in your friends' News Feeds—a form of personal branding that is tied up in the algorithm that promotes it. Because algorithms may surface some posts and not others, and because we are never quite sure who among our friends or followers are active on the network, these social constructions of the self become complicated. The potential audience for them tends to vary from moment to moment, network to network: family and friends, work colleagues and high school classmates, neighbors and strangers—multiple contexts collapsed in a single mediated space, with unclear notions of who exactly is seeing what material posted and why (or why not). The upshot is that social media users are continually performing for audiences that are imagined, never entirely known (Marwick & boyd, 2011).

News sharing is thus one of many ways of organizing the socially mediated self. By choosing what they share—which may vary by content type (e.g. lifestyle vs. business news, listicles vs. long-form narratives), media source (e.g. MSNBC vs. Fox News, *The New Yorker* vs. Breitbart), and tone (e.g. angry vs. optimistic), as well as the frequency of sharing itself—social media users assemble a version of themselves for others. It is a self that is reinforced through news, much like a self reflected in gifs, videos, and memes as well. Purposefully or not, and with varying degrees of personal disclosure about their explicit opinions about the news items they share, social media users thus signal something important about themselves—their political leanings, personal affinities, social concerns, work–life aspirations, and much more.

That social media users share (and share a lot) is clear. *Why* they share is the subject of much ongoing research. The motivations for news sharing, according to a meta-analysis of news sharing on social media, generally fall into three categories: self-serving motives, altruistic motives, and social motives (Kümpel et al., 2015). First, people share news to draw attention, attract followers, and build their status or reputation; second, they share in the hopes of doing good by circulating useful information; and, third, they share to socialize and gain social approval. While the do-gooder side of news sharing is certainly present in many studies, Kümpel and colleagues (2015, p. 8) suggest that "the picture of the self-serving status seeker" is the image that often emerges from studies of news-sharing motivations: "Hyperbolically speaking, news [is] shared by people who want to openly express their own opinions, are prone to social appreciation, and crave for improving their image." Regardless of the motives behind news sharing, and the extent to which they may be self-serving, a construction of the self is entangled in the process of sharing news on social media.

Before turning to the issue of platforms, it should be made clear that while for many news has become part of the networked self, this is not true for everyone. Social media may provide spaces for inadvertent news consumption—even from the early years of the Web many users have reported "bumping into" news online (Pew Research Center, 2014)—but users can also largely abstain from news, choosing instead to surround themselves with other content. This division between news users and non-news users developed in traditional media, particularly with the proliferation of cable television channels catering to different tastes (Prior, 2007). Personalizable digital media both exacerbate this trend toward fragmentation and open up the potential for active disengagement from news. There are "news avoiders" (Ksiazek et al., 2010) as well as others who believe that they do not need to actively seek out news because it will find them when necessary—their peers will keep them informed if something truly important happens. This "news-finds-me perception," while positively associated with exposure to news on social media, appears to have a negative connection with political knowledge over time, leaving such users less and less knowledgeable about public affairs (Gil de Zúñiga et al., 2017). If news discourses become part of online identity performance, it is important to acknowledge the role of disengagement from news as a particular type of identity performance.

Platforms

For news to become a key component of the networked self requires not only the identity work of individuals but the networks where this work takes place.

There are many different sites where the networked self arises, and new sites will undoubtedly emerge in between when this is written and when it is read. Different digital networks or sites have their particular audiences, affordances, and behavioral norms. The rhythms of identity work through posting and interacting on Twitter, for instance, may be quite distinct from those on Instagram, both because of their technical features and affordances (e.g. from the 140-character limit on Twitter to a lack of hyperlinks on Instagram) as well as cultural expectations that develop as users socially construct the spaces. While we wish to make clear that no single site can quite capture the diversity of mediated spaces, this section will focus on Facebook because of its outsized global role as a site for news distribution.

To return to the introduction of this chapter, news—of the public affairs variety—was not part of how Facebook saw itself as it developed. This is evident in Facebook's loose use of the term "news." The center of the Facebook experience is the "News Feed" comprising what the site calls "stories"—labeling that co-opts the vocabulary of news. This is not accidental, but rather a deliberate attempt to borrow the sense of timeliness and importance from the meaning of news while redefining it as a personalized stream that collapses the public–private sphere. This split from traditional understandings of news will be explored in more detail later, but first more explanation of Facebook's approach to content is necessary.

Since it was added to the site in 2006, the Facebook News Feed has evolved over time to become the central focus of the site. A decade later, in 2016, Facebook announced changes to its News Feed algorithm, which it explained in a blog post on June 29 titled "Building a Better News Feed for You." In a section called "News Feed Values," Adam Mosseri, the Facebook vice president in charge of News Feed, laid out the philosophy undergirding the feature:

> Our success is built on getting people the stories that matter to them most. If you could look through thousands of stories every day and choose the 10 that were most important to you, which would they be? The answer should be your News Feed. It is subjective, personal, and unique—and defines the spirit of what we hope to achieve.

Content from friends and family was prioritized, followed by the belief that "Your feed should inform." Facebook did not dismiss news as part of what it does, but it placed it within a larger understanding of news as primarily *what users find relevant*. The blog post articulated it this way:

> We are not in the business of picking which issues the world should read about. We are in the business of connecting people and ideas—and matching people with the stories they find most meaningful.

This connection squares with news and the networked self advanced above. It privileges engagement with content, rather than simply isolated consumption, as the preferred mode of interacting with news.

All of this raises questions about just how Facebook relates to news. As a privately owned public space, Facebook occupies a complicated spot in the larger information ecosystem. It does not produce its own news content but relies on external entities—news organizations as well as regular news users—to supply and circulate journalistic content. Indeed, news organizations have a deeply conflicted relationship with "digital intermediaries" generally and Facebook particularly (Bell & Owen, 2017). On the one hand, news companies see short-term gains in reaching wider audiences where they are on social media platforms—yet, on the other hand, they are waking up to the long-term tradeoffs of becoming dependent on resource-rich digital behemoths and losing control over content distribution (Nielsen & Ganter, 2017). Facebook's enormous size and the degree to which its users engage the site indicate its importance for the creation and circulation of ideas and information within society. But Facebook is not a static place, or really one place at all. It is a platform that houses a variety of content from a variety of sources. It has a set architecture that organizes content, a set of protocols to be followed, and norms about how the site should work.

As a platform, Facebook should be understood as a complex sociotechnical space. This includes its economic imperative to generate revenue by keeping users active and engaged. Facebook converts attention into revenue by selling advertisements, but in a way that is personalized to a user's individual demographics and tastes, in comparison to the impersonal economics of traditional advertising on television or in newspapers. This unique structure drives Facebook's design decisions. The shift in the News Feed algorithm, for example, has its foundation in the site's desire to curate users' content streams as optimally as possible to keep users active—and to keep them coming back, day after day, and for longer periods of scrolling and sharing. Facebook extensively tests and adjusts its features for this purpose.

Facebook, however, is more than a design. The site also presents an idealized version of the social good that it provides in connecting users and creating space for the networked self to develop—a commitment that is also visible in the announcement of the News Feed changes. Facebook thus both constrains and directs users' actions while also constructing a system of ideas about social media as they relate to everyday life.

All of this is to say that, as a platform, Facebook is not a neutral medium but an actor that shapes how people communicate and produces ideas of how people *should* communicate. News sharing, in this sense, is not simply a function of identity performance, carried out among individuals on an almost invisible, nonintrusive platform (see Gillespie, 2010). Rather, the network and its users are mutually constitutive: the networked self as manifest through news construction and circulation emerges out of an interplay of people and the mediated spaces in which they correspond—the social and technical in tandem. Facebook develops its architecture around an idea of who its users are and what they should do, which leads to certain ways of engineering this space. Users also differ in their actions and preferences, pushing the social network in directions that might not have been anticipated. The same dynamics hold true for any other social media site, as they come to have particular uses and communities. To cite but one example: when it was created in 2006, Twitter was intended to be a text-messaging-style mobile platform for having conversations and coordinating with friends; only later, as users adopted it more for information-sharing and retweeting, did Twitter switch its orientation from, we might say, "where are you and what are you doing?" to "what are you thinking about?"

What does this mean for how we understand news and the networked self? We wish to stress the need to examine both news performativity and the platforms where it occurs. Platforms stand between news audiences and journalists. They dictate how the space *can* work, allowing for certain practices while preventing others.

News Performativity and Journalistic Epistemologies

The combination of news performativity and the platforms where this takes place leads to the inevitable question of consequence. The journalistic shifts described above—from the model of passive reception to active engagement and from mass communication channels to the network—affect how journalism works as a form of shared knowledge. In this section, we turn to the topic of journalistic epistemology. Epistemology has a long history in philosophy as the study of knowledge and truth, but our usage here follows Ekström's (2002, p. 260) definition of epistemology as the "rules, routines and institutionalized procedures that operate within a social setting and decide the form of the knowledge produced and the knowledge claims expressed (or implied)." This formulation asks how some idea of news as a form of knowledge assumed to have some correspondence with the reality it chronicles emerges from a combination of practice, context, and discourses of legitimation. It is not about the search for universal truths, but a situated view of how the production of everyday knowledge comes to be legitimated and the means by which it is circulated (see also Lewis & Westlund, 2015b; Matheson, 2004).

Journalistic epistemology can only be understood by examining the total context in which news is produced, distributed, and consumed. In the mass media context, news outlets organized their production around the daily rhythms of the print or broadcast news product. Mass distribution led to a one-way model of consumption such that metrics for traditional media news audiences have always been imperfect and approximate—there were circulation figures and television ratings, for example, but never a granular sense of exactly who was reading/watching and how engaged they were by the content.

In the United States, newspaper competition declined as the objectivity norm took hold (Schudson, 1978). Broadcast media followed the same approach for regulatory and competitive reasons. This environment fostered a constrained news sphere, with a limited number of owners and only few alternative news forms relegated to the margins. And, as journalism education further established a professional approach to news reporting, a certain homogeneity to news production emerged. News was "true" in part because of the reliability of the routines that brought it into being. This institutional arrangement during the twentieth century corresponded with a larger normative outlook about news that coalesced during the turn-of-the-century Progressive Era: a belief that news created a shared information resource consumed by rational actors, thus providing a necessary precondition for democratic self-government. Conveniently, this epistemic formulation—of news as individually incorporated but collectively understood actionable information for democracy—fit the professionalized, objective, one-way model of news. Yet this model has always drawn complaints for its oversights, including its assumptions about the representational fidelity of news (Eason, 1988).

The twin rise of news performativity as a mode of interacting with the news and of social media platforms as key means of human communication raises questions about changing epistemologies of journalism. Much has been written about how digital media radically extend access to mediated channels (Lewis, 2012). For example, when blogs became popular in the early 2000s, they received much attention for allowing readers to become authors. But beyond adding mediated voices, the blogging form was analyzed for the ways in which it affected how information is presented and legitimated (Carlson, 2007; Matheson, 2004; Park, 2009). While blogs vary widely in their forms and practices, they often shared a common approach to the production of knowledge that favors authorial transparency, external linking to provide evidence, open subjectivity of viewpoint, and active engagement with readers. These developments attracted much popular and scholarly attention for how they upended previous structural restrictions for news, ushering in debate about how news was changing and why it mattered.

The types of activities explored in this chapter invite further scrutiny for their epistemic implications—what they mean for news as a form of knowledge. For example, social media facilitate public interaction with news in ways that push us to think about news as a social practice rather than as discrete texts or merely "content." By this we mean that the reception of a news story—how it reaches certain people in a network, how it is interpreted by them, how it may be re-circulated (or not) by those same people, and so on—should not merely be assumed from the text. Instead, any news text is subject to a variety of social and technological actors. Users share or ignore stories in ways that are measured. Algorithms surface or demote stories. Comments get made, stories get liked, and users connect to stories in ways that connect to their identity.

To study journalism as it actually works in such spaces is to study this larger array of sites, actors, and technologies—or what Lewis and Westlund (2015a) refer to as the actors, actants, audiences, and activities that constitute news production and distribution. Understanding news today requires understanding the whole ensemble of humans and machines, people and processes, that shape how news gets fashioned (into words and images) and how news gets negotiated (through subsequent circulations and interactions), altogether contributing to a broader cultural milieu about self and society—including questions of fact and fiction.

From an epistemological standpoint, knowledge is not a static element present in a news text, but something that emerges in the interaction between producers and audiences. It is not enough to look at an individual story; what is needed is a broader perspective that considers the relationship between user activity and the algorithmic processes of social media. In this view, knowledge is something that travels and takes on different shapes as it is traverses social media channels and finds meaning in people's everyday lives. It is sensitive to how knowledge is legitimated and used, not just as a text but as a talisman—a cultural marker as much as a form of information transfer.

To speak of epistemology and news is to invoke a static notion of the news text as an object that is developed and then shared. But the platforms of social media are predicated on an ethos of personalization such that the news for one user is not the same as it is for the next. The basic architecture of Facebook is to provide individualized flows of content that match what it imagines its users want. Doing this at scale requires the intervention of algorithms to make decisions about what users wish to see. On the surface, such decisions may mimic the decisions that journalists make in assembling a news product. But the mass personalization of Facebook indicates a wholly different epistemic prioritization of individual tastes over communal ones. Algorithms make judgments about individual wants that they then cater to, constantly adjusting in real-time as users make selections. This is a far cry from traditional news modes, which the next section makes clear.

Fake News and Real News

The epistemic disparity between traditional mass media models of journalism and social media platforms became apparent in the controversy surrounding "fake news" during the 2016 U.S. presidential election. Fake news here pertains to made-up stories with no basis in fact that pass themselves off as factual. But, as Wardle (2017) makes clear, the term also could include a broad array of content that runs the spectrum from satire and parody (which has no intention to cause harm but may deceive people) to misinformation (the inadvertent sharing of bad information) to deliberately fabricated and manipulated content (which, as disinformation, is intended to deceive). Fake news is, in a word, complicated. Perhaps more pernicious than obviously fake material, as boyd (2017) argues, is the spread of "subtle content" that presents some degree of facticity but is so biased in presentation and framing that it leads people to "make dangerous conclusions that are not explicitly spelled out in the content itself." There are "shades of fakeness" (Gray et al., 2017), which, for technology platforms, makes the automatic detection, deletion, or demotion of such material all the more challenging.

The consternation over fake news is in part a partisan issue: if Donald Trump had lost, the topic likely would have faded into longer ongoing discussions about "clickbait" on digital media. But Trump's election pushed fake news into the spotlight as a potential contributor to his unlikely victory, and the heightened concern has only accelerated since the election. Google has enlisted thousands of content-moderator contractors in a quest to flag fake content, Facebook has sought to retool its algorithm to crack down on tens of thousands of purportedly fake accounts, and governments have launched investigations, hired consultancies, and proposed fines in the millions of euros if social media firms fail to act quickly enough in removing such content—all of which has raised corresponding concerns about "band-aid solutionism" being applied without a true understanding of the social and cultural dynamics driving the phenomenon (Gray et al., 2017). The ultimate question is how and why these stories were able to proliferate despite a total lack of veracity.

A deeper look at fake news starts with recognizing it as a sociotechnical practice. The purveyors of fake news—such as the Macedonian teenagers who famously created the leading "fake news factory" and had an outsized influence on Facebook in the run-up to the U.S. election (Subramanian, 2017)—created texts according to economic or political motives (or both), but the texts themselves relied on social media sharing to become popular enough to have an economic or political impact. These texts may be delinquent on a normative level, but this only became damaging socially and politically with the micro-decisions of thousands of users to share and circulate stories. "The problem," as boyd (2017) put it, "is us"—a deeply cultural dynamic, distorted by a breakdown in the social fabric, played out in clicks, likes, and shares that reinforce tendencies toward polarization. This user distribution is itself complicated as it combines human action with the work of objects—the algorithms that privilege certain stories and further propel their popularity, or the social media bots passing themselves off as human (Howard et al., 2017).

The spread of fake news illustrates how human and non-human components work together to circulate—and therefore amplify—particular narratives. The active human component speaks to the type of news performativity this chapter describes. Online social media users immerse themselves within this environment, crafting their identity through the news they choose to share and comment on. These actions connect them to communities, build allegiances, and set boundaries from others—all part of the networked self. But fake news also points to the importance of attending to the platforms where this identity work takes place. Facebook's Trending Topics algorithm, for example, is a recommendation system that can quickly escalate a story. This may mirror older forms of journalistic awareness as a type of breaking news when something significant occurs, but often it is more organic to the site and reflects the actions of users. For an example of the latter, very soon after Facebook fully automated its Trending Topics feature, the top story became a fake news item about then-Fox News host Megyn Kelly being fired for supporting Hillary Clinton. This was an embarrassing episode for Facebook, and not the only one. It became a symbol of the problems of automation (Carlson, 2018).

Of course, fake news is an example of undesirable outcomes driven by the news audience's power to circulate ideas coupled with the power of platforms to spread them. Other examples demonstrate how this combination can generate positive results. Consider, for instance, that the 2014 police shooting of unarmed black teenager Michael Brown in Ferguson, Missouri, was not immediately national news, and only became so after it spiked in popularity on Twitter. As unrest followed, so did an engagement with larger topics of policing and social justice through social media (Clark, 2016). As with fake news, these communicative flows relied on a combination of human input and platform characteristics that promoted the stories to larger and larger audiences. Optimistically, these forces produce a form of "network framing" (Meraz & Papacharissi, 2013) where multiple users shape news coverage, rather than the other way around. Gatekeeping becomes not just the province of professional journalists, but also something more distributed. This has implications for the types of news knowledge that the public encounters.

Conclusion

As social media continue to grow and embed themselves into more and more domains of social life, different episodes will rise to public consciousness, leading to moments of outcry, as in the case of fake news, or celebration, as in the use of social media to bring nearly invisible acts of wrongdoing to public attention. The lesson of this chapter is that we must favor the complexity of interlocking pieces over privileging any one part. It is tempting to laud social media for creating a new mediated space where users interact with the news in ways that become part of their identity performance. This may be regarded as an engaged form of citizenship that confronts the limits of the traditional news media and the expectations of a one-way information flow. But it also raises epistemic concerns as it creates a cauldron of confirmation bias that leads to the sharing of obviously fake news as real. It is also tempting to privilege the platform above all, reducing users' actions to the dictates of the technology. Such a focus on the algorithm reduces the user to only a thinly realized victim.

We proffer a position that accounts for both the agency of the user engaging in identify performance through news sharing and the power of the structure in shaping what users see and do not see. The user engages with the site out of a desire to speak and to share in the public sphere, and the platform seeks to facilitate this action while also monetizing it. One view without the other is limiting and does not tell the whole story.

We end this chapter by returning to the perspective of news and social media platforms as important on an epistemic level. The production of knowledge is social, and to understand news as vital knowledge about the world around us is to care about its production, circulation, and consumption. The networked self of news is one that is constructive and constrained, one that performs but within a controlled space. The strengths and contradictions of this position will only become more pronounced over time.

References

Bell, E., & Owen, T. (2017). The platform press: How Silicon Valley reengineered journalism. *Tow Center for Digital Journalism.* www.cjr.org/tow_center_reports/platform-press-how-silicon-valley-reengineered-journalism.php

Berelson, B. (1948). What "missing the newspaper" means. In P. Lazarsfeld and F. Stanton (Eds.), *Communication research 1948–1949* (pp. 111–129). New York: Harper.

boyd, d. (2017). Google and Facebook can't just make fake news disappear. *Medium*, March 27. https://backchannel.com/google-and-facebook-cant-just-make-fake-news-disappear-48f4b4e5fbe8

Carey, J. W. (2009). *Communication as culture.* New York: Routledge.

Carlson, M. (2007). Blogs and journalistic authority: The role of blogs in US Election Day 2004 Coverage. *Journalism Studies*, 8(2), 264–279.

Carlson, M. (2016). Embedded links, embedded meanings: Social media commentary and news sharing as mundane media criticism. *Journalism Studies*, 17(7), 915–924.

Carlson, M. (2018). Facebook in the news: Social media, journalism, and public responsibility following the 2016 Trending Topics controversy. *Digital Journalism*, 8(1), 4–20.

Clark, L. S. (2016). Participants on the margins: #BlackLivesMatter and the role that shared artifacts of engagement in the Ferguson protests played among minoritized political newcomers on Snapchat, Facebook, and Twitter. *International Journal of Communication*, 10(26), 235–253.

Eason, D. (1988). On journalistic authority: The Janet Cooke scandal. In J. W. Carey (Ed.), *Media, myths, and narratives: Television and the press* (pp. 205–227). Beverly Hills, CA: Sage.

Ekström, M. (2002). Epistemologies of TV journalism: A theoretical framework. *Journalism*, 3(3), 259–282.

Gil de Zúñiga, H., Weeks, B., & Ardèvol-Abreu, A. (2017). Effects of the news-finds-me perception in communication: Social media use implications for news seeking and learning about politics. *Journal of Computer-Mediated Communication*, 22(3), 105–123.

Gillespie, T. (2010). The politics of "platforms." *New Media & Society*, 12(3), 347–364.

Goffman, E. (1959). *The presentation of self in everyday life.* New York: Anchor Books.

Gray, J., Bounegru, L., & Venturini, T. (2017). What does fake news tell us about life in the digital age? Not what you might expect. *Nieman Lab*, April 6. www.niemanlab. org/2017/04/what-does-fake-news-tell-us-about-life-in-the-digital-age-not-what-you-might-expect/

Hermida, A. (2016). Social media and the news. In T. Witschge, C.W. Anderson, D. Domingo, & A. Hermida (Eds.), *The Sage handbook of digital journalism* (pp. 81–94). Los Angeles: Sage.

Howard, P.N., Bolsover, G., Kollanyi, B., Bradshaw, S., & Neudert, L. (2017). Junk news and bots during the U.S. election: What were Michigan voters sharing over Twitter? Data Memo 2017.1. Oxford: Project on Computational Propaganda. www. politicalbots.org.

Kalsnes, B., & Larsson, A.O. (2017). Understanding news sharing across social media: Detailing distribution on Facebook and Twitter. *Journalism Studies*. doi: 10.1080/1461670X.2017.1297686

Katz, E., & Lazarsfeld, P.F. (1955). *Personal influence*. Glencoe, IL: Free Press.

Ksiazek, T.B., Malthouse, E.C., & Webster, J.G. (2010). News-seekers and avoiders: Exploring patterns of total news consumption across media and the relationship to civic participation. *Journal of Broadcasting & Electronic Media*, 54(4), 551–568.

Kümpel, A.S., Karnowski, V., & Keyling, T. (2015). News sharing in social media: A review of current research on news sharing users, content, and networks. *Social Media + Society*, 1(2), 1–14.

Lewis, S.C. (2012). The tension between professional control and open participation: Journalism and its boundaries. *Information, Communication & Society*, 15(6), 836–866.

Lewis, S.C., & Westlund, O. (2015a). Actors, actants, audiences, and activities in cross-media news work: A matrix and a research agenda. *Digital Journalism*, 3(1), 19–37.

Lewis, S.C., & Westlund, O. (2015b). Big data and journalism: Epistemology, expertise, economics, and ethics. *Digital Journalism*, 3(3), 447–466.

Matheson, D. (2004). Weblogs and the epistemology of the news: Some trends in online journalism. *New Media & Society*, 6(4), 443–468.

Marwick, A.E. (2013). *Status update: Celebrity, publicity, and branding in the social media age*. New Haven: Yale University Press.

Marwick, A.E., & boyd, d. (2011). I tweet honestly, I tweet passionately: Twitter users, context collapse, and the imagined audience. *New Media & Society*, 13(1), 114–133.

Meraz, S., & Papacharissi, Z. (2013). Networked gatekeeping and networked framing on #Egypt. *The International Journal of Press/Politics*, 18(2), 138–166.

Mitchell, A., Gottfried, J., Barthel, M., & Shearer, E. (2016). The modern news consumer. *Pew Research Center*, July 7. www.journalism.org/2016/07/07/the-modern-news-consumer/

Mitchell, A., Gottfried, J., Shearer, E., & Lu, K. (2017). How Americans encounter, recall and act upon digital news. *Pew Research Center*, February 9. www.journalism. org/2017/02/09/how-americans-encounter-recall-and-act-upon-digital-news/

Nielsen, R.K., & Ganter, S.A. (2017). Dealing with digital intermediaries: A case study of the relations between publishers and platforms. *New Media & Society*. doi: 10.1177/146144481770131

Papacharissi, Z. (Ed.). (2010). *A networked self: Identity, community, and culture on social network sites*. New York: Routledge.

Park, D. W. (2009). Blogging with authority: Strategic positioning in political blogs. *International Journal of Communication*, 3, 250–273.

Pew Research Center. (2014). State of the News Media, March 26. http://assets.pewresearch.org/wp-content/uploads/sites/13/2017/05/30142556/state-of-the-news-media-report-2014-final.pdf.

Prior, M. (2007). *Post-broadcast democracy*. New York: Cambridge University Press.

Schudson, M. (1978). *Discovering the news*. New York: Basic Books.

Subramanian, S. (2017). Inside the Macedonian fake-news complex. *Wired*, February 15. www.wired.com/2017/02/veles-macedonia-fake-news/

Wardle, C. (2017, February 16). Fake news. It's complicated. *FirstDraft News*. https://firstdraftnews.com/fake-news-complicated/

4

PUBLICNESS ON PLATFORMS

Tracing the Mutual Articulation of Platform Architectures and User Practices

Thomas Poell, Sudha Rajagopalan,
and Anastasia Kavada

Literature on social media communication during major public events—protests, disasters, elections—is replete with terms to describe the publics formed on these platforms: "networked publics," "calculated publics," "affective publics," "hashtag publics," "issue publics," "ephemeral and transient publics," and "riparian publics" (Berry, 2011; boyd, 2011; Gillespie, 2014; Hestres, 2014; Rambukkana, 2015; Papacharissi, 2015; Postill, 2015). These concepts have been particularly important in highlighting the constantly *changing* character of publicness in online environments. Social media platforms connect thousands and even millions of people, but these connections can also disappear in the blink of an eye when the next wave of trending topics hits the Web. A collective "we" can suddenly emerge, but just as quickly disappear (Juris, 2012; Kavada, 2015; Papacharissi, 2015; Rambukkana, 2015). The different conceptualizations also highlight the *sociotechnical* mediation of publicness. Social media platforms not only enable public exchanges and connections, but also steer through their technologies how these exchanges and connections take shape (Berry, 2011; boyd, 2011; Gillespie, 2014; Galis & Neumayer, 2016; Milan, 2015a; Poell & Van Dijck, 2015). And finally, recent empirical and theoretical work on publics has been important in drawing attention to the *affective* nature of platform-mediated relations of publicness. Affect, emotions, and feelings play a key role in connecting users during public events (Gerbaudo, 2016; Papacharissi, 2015).

This chapter aims to take the exploration of the constitution and continuous transformation of online publics a step further by examining and theorizing publicness as a *communicative process that follows specific trajectories*. While the different conceptualizations of online publics have been highly productive in identifying the characteristics of these publics, they also stimulate researchers to produce "snapshots" of moments of publicness rather than account for the continuous changes that characterize platform-mediated publicness. Moreover, by concentrating on the identification of particular publics, researchers tend to downplay the variation between social media platforms in how they steer public exchanges. Thus, rather than focusing on publics as the outcome of a process of communication, we try to untangle publicness as a communicative process. This process is always grounded and context-specific: the particular sociotechnical configuration, as well as the historical and political context in which publicness is articulated, shapes how it unfolds (Kavada & Poell, 2017). By shifting the analytical focus from the identification of particular publics to the exploration of processes of publicness, we hope to produce more accurate empirical descriptions of such processes, as well as gain a deeper understanding of the political (and democratic) implications of specific episodes of (contentious) publicness.

Conceiving of publicness as a process that follows a specific "trajectory," means that we need to be attentive to how relations of publicness are spatially, temporally, and materially instantiated. In this chapter, we will do so by concentrating on the role of specific social media platforms in two episodes of public contention. The one concerns the Twitter communication in the year following the New Delhi gang rape of December 2012, which sparked mass protests. This case study builds on the analysis of a set of over 1 million tweets, as well as interviews with feminist activists and journalists (Poell & Rajagopalan, 2015).[1] The second case study focuses on the Egyptian Kullena Khaled Said (We are all Khaled Said) Facebook Page, which became a vital stage for the expression of grievances about the Mubarak regime in the months leading up to the uprising of early 2011. For this case study, we have collected all available data—14,072 posts, 6.8 million comments, and 32 million likes—exchanged through the entire lifetime of the page from June 2010 to July 2013. The analysis specifically focuses on the period from June 2010 to mid-February 2011, when the Mubarak regime fell (Poell et al., 2016; Rieder et al., 2015).[2] The two case studies should be seen as "slices" from larger trajectories of publicness, which incorporated many more actors, locations, media, issues, exchanges, and so on than can be discussed in this chapter.

By putting the interactions on two social media platforms under the microscope, we can gain a more precise sense of how platform-based relations of publicness transform over time and vary across platforms. Operationalizing this inquiry, we will, in the next section, reflect on how *platform architectures* mediate relations of publicness. What role do particular platform technologies play in the construction of publicness? Building on work in platform and software studies, we understand the formation of social relations and the instantiation of publicness through social media as the mutual articulation of technological architectures and user practices (boyd, 2011; Van Dijck, 2013; Gillespie, 2014; Langlois et al., 2009; Poell, 2014). Platform architectures consist of interfaces and algorithms that format, organize, and process the flow of user data. These architectures steer how users interact with each other, but, vice versa, users also shape the meaning and impact of platform technologies by using and interpreting them in specific ways. Networked sociality cannot be reduced to one or the other. Hence, the second section of the chapter focuses on *user practices*, examining how users have adopted particular platform affordances in the two contentious episodes. Finally, as recent scholarship has made clear, platform-mediated publicness also centrally involves the mobilization of affect and emotions. To gain insight into how *affective ties* that bind publics together are assembled and reassembled, we will analyze how users, in the course of contentious episodes, project, invoke, and experience collectivity in streams of contentious social media communication.

Platform Architectures

Social media platforms are characterized by specific "architectures of participation" that shape the relations of publicness constituted through them. Such architectures involve specific rules of engagement and communication, regulating who communicates with whom, as well as how such communication unfolds. The rules or codes that underlie social media platforms are inscribed in the terms of service and community policies that regulate interaction on these platforms (Van Dijck, 2013; Noveck, 2005). And, they are encoded in the platforms' technical design: in the interfaces between users and platforms and in the algorithms through which user activity is processed. Platform architectures are not static, but constantly evolving—they differ across platforms, depending on the goals, cultures, and business models of the specific corporations that develop and manage them. As we noted before, while these architectures do not determine social practices, they do shape how this practice unfolds.

In light of these considerations, we can observe key differences between the two platforms at the center of our case studies: Facebook Pages and Twitter. Starting with Pages, similar to broadcasting's one-to-many design, Facebook Pages provide its administrators with a public stage to distribute messages to large numbers of people. Given the architecture of Facebook Pages, admin posts are displayed on the page timeline and directly visible to users. By contrast, user comments, except for the last few, can only be accessed through further clicking. On large pages such as Kullena Khaled Said on which users post many comments in a short time, user comments are like a continuous stream or a rapidly increasing number with the admin post as the frame. The administrators, in this respect, very much set the agenda for interaction on the page. This hierarchical structure of communication corresponds with how Facebook envisions Pages, as marketing tools to "give your brand, business or cause a voice on Facebook and connect with the people who matter to you" (Facebook, 2017). Strikingly, developing key platform features, such as Pages and Groups, Facebook effectively pushes users who want to communicate with large numbers of people to Pages by setting limits on other functionalities. As Coretti and Pica (2015, p. 958) note in their analysis of the Italian Popolo Viola, the movement, around 2010, quickly ran into the 5000 user limit set on Groups. Consequently, it migrated to Pages, which did not allow for the same forms of interaction as Groups. These authors also note that the evolving architecture of Pages over time became more hierarchical, providing admins with advanced instruments to steer the interaction on their page (ibid., p. 963). In this regard, architectural changes affect how key elements of social interaction, including leadership relations, collective identities, and formations of publicness take shape.

Connecting with users in the framework of Facebook Pages also means being able to gain insight through a range of metrics into how users engage with the content posted on the page. Through the freely available Facebook Insights, page owners are provided with detailed metrics concerning the number of page likes, unique users engaging with the page, and the demographics of these users, as well as when page followers are online each day of the week, and what type of post—for example, "status update," "photo," or "video"—generated the highest reach and engagement (Lee, 2013). In the Kullena Khaled Said case, it gave the admins detailed insight into the interest of users and especially their willingness to pursue particular protest activities. These insights, as will be discussed, very much guided the interaction between admins and users. The real-time and detailed metrification of user activity is an essential element of how publicness evolves on Pages.

In comparison to Pages, the dynamic of exchange on Twitter is evidently much more distributed. While hashtags are employed to organize streams of communication on particular issues, these do not provide a prefixed structure, like a Facebook page, but instead preferred hashtags frequently change and multiple hashtags are used in parallel. Furthermore, the relationship between users, like in the case of friend networks on Facebook, is in principle more horizontal than on Pages.

This also affects how metrics about user activity are made available. Although Twitter users have access to metrics regarding the engagement with their Tweets, given the networked nature of Twitter communication it does not provide the kind of overview afforded to Pages administrators. Having said this, it is, simultaneously, important to note that there are large differences between Twitter users in number of followers. Whereas most users come close to the average number of about 200 followers, there are some users that have tens of thousands or even millions of followers. These power users are in a somewhat similar position to the admins of major Facebook pages, broadcasting their messages to large numbers of users. These observations are particularly interesting in the light of frequent claims about online publicness as revolving around participation by the crowd and around two-way communication (Bennett and Segerberg, 2012; Bruns, 2008; Shirky, 2008).

Given the specific affordances of the examined networked technologies, it appears particularly vital that researchers are careful when trying to generalize their observations concerning specific platforms to make claims about online publicness more generally. From this perspective, it is also noteworthy that research on online contention has heavily focused on Twitter, for which user data is more readily available than for Facebook, let alone for Snapchat, Whatsapp, and Telegram. Over the past years, various studies have been published on activist Facebook Pages, but the arguably more important terrain of Facebook friend networks remains largely unexplored (Coretti and Pica, 2015; Gerbaudo, 2016; Hendriks et al., 2016; Poell et al., 2016; Swann & Husted, 2017). Thus the particular dynamic of specific modes of online publicness also remains largely unexplored.

Contentious User Practices

Of course, as we have argued, exploring different modes of online publicness entails analyzing not only the affordances of particular platforms, but also the contentious practices that shape the meaning and impact of specific technologies. Looking at user practices, it is first important to note that in both Egypt and India the use of social media in the years around 2011 was distinctly an urban middle-class phenomenon. In Egypt in 2011, there were about 5 million Facebook users in a population of 92 million. Many of these users were located in Cairo (Lim 2012, p. 235). In India in 2012, there were about 93 million Facebook and 33 million Twitter users in a total population of 1.3 billion (Patel, 2014). In this regard, whatever connections of publicness were established and expressed through social media in the examined episodes of contention, these only actively involved the middle-class section of the population in both countries. With this major caveat in mind, we will now focus on how contentious practices were articulated through the specific social media platforms.

In the Kullena Khaled Said case, the interaction between admins and users, as structured by page architecture, is especially interesting. The analysis of this interaction suggests that the social exchanges on the page were mostly triggered and guided by what can be labeled as "connective leadership" (Poell et al., 2016). As the page received 250,000 likes during its first three months and rapidly developed into a stage where users shared grievances about the Mubarak regime, the page provided an important framework for protest communication and mobilization (Lesch, 2011; Lim, 2012).

The page admins carefully developed this framework by explicitly cultivating the page as "participatory." The admins constantly invited user contributions, which informed further initiatives and activities developed through the page. A prime and successful example of this was a call to users to photograph themselves holding up the "Kullena Khaled Said" (We are all Khaled Said) sign, a tactic which was, a year later, replicated on a much larger scale during the Occupy protests with the "We are the 99%" slogan (Gerbaudo, 2015; Milan, 2015b). This expression of collectivity, while involving the active participation of users, was not simply a bottom-up dynamic, but one that was at least partly engineered by the admins, an observation confirmed by parallel research by Gerbaudo (2016) on the administrators of the Kullena Khaled Said page and of the Spanish Real Democracy Now page, which played a key role in the May 2011 protest. He observes how the admins incited enthusiasm among users by posting hopeful, emotional messages.

The impression of intricate engineering of collectivity by connective leaders is further reinforced, when we consider how Ghonim and colleagues solicited user feedback and consulted page metrics to develop campaigns that resonated with the majority of page users. For one, they regularly held polls to determine what further activities the users were interested in developing through the page. And, they systematically read user comments to be able to adequately respond to feedback. It is also through such feedback that calls for street protests were formulated and circulated through the page, including the call for mass protest on January 25, 2011. Hence, a carefully curated form of contentious publicness comes into view, constructed through the interaction between specific platform technologies and activist strategies. This managed public is enabled by the hierarchical structure of Facebook Pages and accomplished through the careful marketing tactics of the page admins (Kavada, 2015; Gerbaudo, 2016; Poell et al., 2016).

Yet, although Facebook Pages afford admins extensive control over user interaction, in practice this control and the relations of publicness constructed through these tactics are highly unstable. The connective mode of leadership exercised by the admins effectively commands little, if any, loyalty from the assembled users because these leaders do not and cannot publicly identify themselves as leaders. And given the completely open character of Facebook communication, their activities can also be easily undermined by political opponents. This became very clear on the Khaled Said page when supporters of the Mubarak regime hijacked the communication on the page from the moment the mass protests started on January 25, 2011. With newly created Facebook accounts, these supporters began spreading false rumours and accusing the administrators of being foreign agents, secretly working for Israel.

While the relations on the Kullena Khaled Said page can be conceptualized as a particular type of networked or affective public, this does not help to trace the fundamentally evolving character of relations of platform-mediated publicness. Exploring how such relations evolve, we observe moments of collectivity but also their sudden collapse. Before we turn to this discussion, we will demonstrate, by looking in more detail at the Indian case study, how other networked technologies and other user practices can produce very different sociotechnical relations.

Whereas the Kullena Khaled Said page constituted, at least initially, a framework for the construction of collectivity, the Twitter communication following the New Delhi gang rape and the mass protests revolved much more around publicity and global networks. The Facebook page was composed as a particular space for public contention, while the Twitter communication was completely open. This should not simply be seen as the consequence of different techno-logical architectures. There are prominent instances of contentious Twitter com-munication in which users intensely communicate with each other through particular hashtags that establish a frame or space for the articulation of collectiv-ity. For example, during the Tunisian uprising #sidibouzid functioned as such, as did #Egypt during the early stages of the Egyptian uprising (Papacharissi & de Fatima Oliveira, 2012; Poell & Darmoni, 2012).

In our Indian case study, we observed a different dynamic. The analysis of our Twitter data shows that various hashtags were employed, but no issue-specific hashtag stood out. Instead of tagging their messages through issue-specific hashtags, such as #Damini and #Nirbhaya, users tweeting on the gang rape case chose to use general hashtags, such as #India and #Delhi. Even when we focused the analysis on the Twitter accounts of prominent women's organizations and feminist activists and bloggers, we did not find intensive use of issue-specific hashtags (Poell & Rajagopalan, 2015). This image was also put forward by the feminist activists and journalists we interviewed, who emphasized that they espe-cially used Twitter to network and disseminate information.

Of course, these kinds of connections can be considered as a public: one that brings together a heterogeneous set of geographically distributed actors. Yet, this was by no means a stable public, but rather one that was continuously transform-ing. Especially following the mass protests incited by the gang rape incident, a lot of international women's organizations and feminist activists began to make statements on Twitter about the problem of gender violence in India and in other parts of the world. Over the period of our investigation, we could observe a rapid expansion in relations of publicness mediated through Twitter, but also a rapid decrease, when the public interest in the gang rape incident receded.

Acutely aware of the ephemeral character of Twitter attention, most of our interviewees considered the platform as only the first step in developing more durable relations. In developing such relations, Twitter was particularly important in a country as vast as India, in which women's organizations and activists based in different parts of the country may otherwise not have found each other. For example, Binalakshmi Nepram, the founder of the Manipur Women Gun Survivors Network, stressed that 90% of her Twitter followers were located in other parts of India.[3] Moreover, as Rita Banerji, founder of the women's organization 50 Million Missing, makes clear, the platform not only allows Indian feminists to overcome geographical distances, but also allows them to address a variety of societal actors, ranging from other activists, jour-nalists, and NGOs to academics, public servants, politicians, governments, and international organizations.[4]

As this list of actors already indicates, this is very much an elite network. Many of these actors can be understood as connective leaders. Some of the activists and journalists had large numbers of followers and were connected to prominent activist organizations and news media. Just like Ghonim and his fellow page admins, they employed networked technologies to invite, connect, steer, and stimulate activism. Yet, the type of contentious publicness they engineered was distinctly different than in the Egyptian case. Although we can identify prominent Twitter users that acted as connective leaders, the relationship with their follows was much more horizontal than in the Kullena Khaled Said case. For our Indian interviewees, publicness on Twitter took the shape of a heterogeneous set of relations, while for Ghonim the Facebook page especially functioned as a broadcasting platform to a mass of users. As such the page constituted a framework for engineering collectivity, whereas the Indian Twitter communication produced a more open-ended network.

So far, this exploration provides two key insights for the study of platform-mediated publicness. First, while the sociotechnical relations observed on Twitter and Facebook can be understood as networked publics, these are fundamentally unstable publics, which are constantly evolving. This dynamic should not be seen simply as the consequence of changing user practices, but also as driven by the techno-commercial strategies of platforms. To sustain a high level of online engagement, social media platforms are geared toward identifying and promoting trending topics rather than generating sustained interest in contentious issues that hold publics together (Barassi, 2015; Poell & Van Dijck, 2015). Second, beyond such general observations, the investigation demonstrates that publicness takes shape differently on each platform. These differences result from the interaction between particular platform architectures and specific user practices.[5]

Evolving Affective Relations

It is through the interaction between platform technologies and user practices that *imagined collectives* emerge. These collectives need to be consider as "imagined" for the same reason as Benedict Anderson (1983) considered nations as imagined communities: most users in mass processes of contentious social media communication will never know or meet each other. Nevertheless, collectivity is constantly projected onto these processes. Participants may develop affiliative ties, an abstract sense of "we" deriving from their shared affiliation to the same cause (Bimber et al., 2012). However, they may also create interpersonal bonds of solidarity if they engage in direct interpersonal communication with each other (ibid.). While in both case studies we observed such instances of collectivity, there are distinct differences in how collectivity was articulated and how it evolved.

The clearest expression of a collective "We" could be observed on the Kullena Khaled Said Facebook page. This was triggered by streams of emotional user messages, as well as by the architecture of Facebook Pages. Given how Pages directs user attention toward the admin posts, it constitutes an ideal space for the articulation of collectivity by the admins. Strikingly, user metrics played a vital role in this process. These metrics have a strong affective quality, they incite administrators and users to develop further activity and they confirm that many users are involved (Gerlitz & Helmond, 2013; Kavada, 2012). The admins of the Kullena Khaled Said page constantly cited rapidly growing user numbers to mobilize and to unite. In one of the first posts, on June 10, 2010, they maintained "we've reached 300 people in two minutes, we wanna reach a hundred thousand . . . we have to unite so as to make a firm stand against those who lord it over us." And, six months later, when the call for protests on January 25, 2011 circulated on the page, the admins wrote "The Jan25 invitation reached 500,000 Facebook users . . . 27,000 have RSVPed . . . [. . .] Let's do this, Egyptians."

Using metrics as validation, the admins rhetorically constructed the page as the stage for unity against oppression. This was a constantly evolving process. Initially, in the summer of 2010, the admins and users connected with each other over their shared horror and anger over the murder of Khaled Said. They organized so-called silent stands in Alexandria and changed their profile picture to the image of Said, giving substance to their collective identity "We are all Khaled Said" (Ghonim, 2012). Over the following months, as more users joined the page and expressed their grievances, the scope of oppositional publicness expanded to develop into a national collective: the united Egyptian people against corruption, torture, terrorism, nepotism, and radicalism. This vision was especially clearly pronounced in early January 2011, when the bombing of a Coptic church in Alexandria threatened to divide the page users. The admins posted "We have to meet despite our differences . . . despite misunderstands and blurred visions that sometimes come to our minds . . . We have to stand next to each other . . . and say we are Egyptians . . . We are one." Many page users met this call with enthusiasm. As one user argued, "if they want the Copts, we in Egypt are all Copts, and if they want the Muslims, we in Egypt are all Muslims."

Yet, when the mass protests against the Mubarak regime started on January 25, 2011, this sense of national unity immediately fell apart. The admins and users disagreed whether and how to revolt against the regime. Some of the users strongly supported the call for an uprising, providing strategic advice on how to limit the chances of being arrested, disable armored vehicles, and draw international media attention. Others feared the response of the security forces, arguing that protests would lead to a blood bath. And when the protests turned into a genuine uprising at the beginning of February, the page users began to disagree on whether or not the Mubarak regime would have to resign.

The page, however, especially lost its role as a key platform for staging a united public front because regime supporters began to subvert the exchanges on the page. After the protests had started, it was clear from the analysis of the most engaged-with comments that the regime indeed systematically targeted the page. These counterpropaganda efforts were part of a larger campaign to immobilize online opposition. From January 27 to February 2, the regime famously shut down the Internet in the entire country. While this measure proved to be ineffective in stopping the protests, it did bring the activity on the page to an almost complete halt. Consequently, the focal point of oppositional publicness shifted from Kullena Khaled Said and the Internet more generally to the streets, especially to the occupied Tahrir Square. The role of the page changed from staging public opposition and collectivity to publicizing images and reports of on-the-ground protests.

Strikingly, the analysis of the communication on other social media platforms during the mass protests does show strong expressions of collectivity. In their study on the Twitter exchanges through the #egypt hashtag in the period from January 25 to February 25, 2011, Papacharissi and de Fatima Oliveira (2012, p. 275) found that the "Tweets documenting events and expressing opinion reflected overwhelming expressions of solidarity." The authors observed constant calls to "fellow brothers and sisters" to join the cause and to "unite" against the Mubarak regime (ibid.). These observations reveal the complexity and variation of platform-mediated publicness. Thus, examining online expressions of collectivity, it is vital to be aware that these can substantially vary across platforms and even across hashtags.

We can observe how platform-mediated publicness evolves along particular trajectories. At any point along the trajectory followed by Kullena Khaled Said, we can label the connections and exchanges on the page as a networked public. The real challenge is to trace the *changes* in the form and dynamic of these connections and exchanges. As a result of these changes, the role of the Facebook page in Egyptian public discourse and politics substantially transformed over time. To understand what publicness entails in a social media stream, we need to account for these changes and transformations.

Turning from Egypt to India, from Facebook to Twitter, and from protests against an authoritarian regime to protest against gender violence, we encounter a trajectory of platform-mediated publicness that started with mass protests and strong online expressions of collectivity. Our analysis focuses on the year that followed these protests. In this year, feminist activists and women's organizations tried to build on the momentum of the protests to develop sustainable networks and communities to combat systemic gender violence and patriarchy.

Before we turn to these efforts, it is important to briefly discuss the power moment of collectivity that took shape during the mass protests immediately following the gang rape incident. As various studies have documented, the mass protests were driven by collective frustration with the justice system and the police to hold rapists culpable and to provide basic security and protection. In this turbulent period, the communication on Twitter and other social media platforms was characterized by pervasive social outrage (Ahmed et al., 2017; Belair-Gagnon et al., 2014; Chaudhuri & Fitzgerald, 2015). The online communication was vital in translating individual anger into collective action. As Ahmed and colleagues (2017, p. 460) maintain "the online Nirbhaya movement was able to channel individual expressions of anger into collective action as an offline protest." This process was guided by activists who formulated a common cause for the protests: "Justice for Women" (ibid.).

In the year following the protests, such a collective identity was no longer as clearly present. Rather than revolving around the articulation of collectivity, the Twitter communication was predominantly focused on generating public attention for new cases of gender violence and to mobilize support for the persecution of perpetrators. Particularly striking was also that many of the emotionally charged exchanges on Twitter were very much tied to the mass media, with Indian and international celebrities figuring prominently. Many of the interviewed feminist activists and journalists experienced this close connection with the mass media as rather problematic. Journalist Anindita Sengupta emphasized that most Twitter users appeared primarily interested in the "crime of the day" and questions of suitable punishment and retribution.[6] Like in many mass media, there was relatively little attention in the most retweeted messages for the larger enduring problem of systemic gender violence and patriarchy.

Reflecting the mass-media-driven dynamic, the Twitter communication was only occasionally organized through issue-specific hashtags, such as Suryanelli and Tejpal, which referred to other rape cases that were in the news. Following the mainstream news cycle, these hashtags trended for a short period to subsequently disappear again. Crucially, our interviewees did not see themselves as part of a particular public on Twitter either, but rather as individual members of (global) interpersonal networks, who briefly connect through particular hashtags. As individuals they were primarily positioned in following and follower networks, allowing them to promote their cause. On Twitter, they focused on growing these networks, targeting influential actors within them, and promoting strategically important information.

Community-building efforts primarily took place beyond Twitter. The interviews indicate that a great investment was made to build ties beyond the "moment." The interviewees realized the need to channel the publicity, public anger, and protest triggered by the gang rape incident into a larger societal movement against all kinds of everyday forms of gender violence and patriarchy. Twitter was frequently the starting point to pursue this aim, but not the end point. A prominent example, in this regard is "Justice for Women," which started as a Twitter hashtag. Its founder, Sakshi Kumar, began to use the hashtag #justiceforwomen in the summer of 2012 after a young woman from north-east India was assaulted by a group of twenty to twenty-five men. The hashtag was meant to raise awareness and to function as an open call to ask people what could be done against gender violence. As the assault case triggered a lot of media attention and public anger, the hashtag quickly began to trend in India and, subsequently, worldwide. And in December 2012, "Justice for Women" became the central slogan of the mass protests.

Encouraged by all the publicity, Kumar developed the idea to set up a network to organize self-defense workshops for women in cities across India. This was an effort that quite quickly extended beyond Twitter and other social media. Kumar emphasizes that while social media were employed to publicize the workshops and to find volunteer martial artists, hardly anyone showed up through Twitter. People were primarily mobilized through other means, banners, word of mouth, and networks of friends. It was ultimately through these on-the-ground connections and the workshops themselves that a more sustainable community and sense of collectivity grew.[7] The need to look beyond social media platforms to build more enduring collectives was expressed by many of our interviewees. This involved on-the-ground activities, but also other types of mediated exchanges. For example, Natasha Badhwar, columnist and filmmaker who co-curates Genderlog, a crowd-sourced group website on gender violence in India, emphasized the importance of writing long-form reflexive pieces in print media or on blogs rather than immediately responding on Twitter. It is through such "slow" forms of civic journalism that attention can be generated for more fundamental problems.[8] In other words, to gain insight into the dynamic of episodes of public contention, it is crucial to also trace how relations of publicness take shape beyond social media platforms.

Conclusion

Exploring our two case studies, we have come to a few crucial insights that can help future research. Given the highly dynamic, constantly evolving character of platform-mediated publicness, we suggest *shifting the analytical focus from the identification of publics to tracing processes of publicness*. Doing so, we can observe how through the interaction between user practices and platform technologies, relations of publicness substantially change shape over time. Moreover, as technologies, users' practices, and the composition of user populations substantially differ from platform to platform, publicness also takes shape differently on each platform. Since this is by no means a uniform process, tracing larger trajectories of publicness can be particularly challenging. It entails analyzing how particular platforms and specific pages or hashtags become vehicles of public expression and connection. Subsequently, we need to examine how such specific sites of publicness become tied to other spaces, both online and offline, and how in the process new actors become involved and new issues are raised (Kavada & Poell, 2017).

As we have observed, platform-mediated publicness has an important affective dimension: notions of collectivity are continuously projected onto streams of social media communication. Yet, even though such imagined collectives are vital for bringing people together and setting off collective action, they are never self-evident or stable. In fact, our analysis suggests that collectivity tends to disappear as quickly from social media platforms as it appears. The relations between platform-mediated and offline processes of publicness are especially interesting in this regard. Sometimes platform-based moments of collectivity are translated to offline collective action and vice versa. This is, however, never guaranteed. It is especially difficult to translate fleeting online expressions of collectivity to more sustainable communities. Our Indian case study showed the hard work that goes into building enduring connections. Whatever the examined episode of public contention, the analytic challenge is to untangle such translations, tracing how connections and expressions of publicness take shape across particular technologies and locations.

Notes

1 After the New Delhi gang rape incident of December 2012 and the large protests that followed, a dataset was collected of approximately 15 million tweets containing the words "rape" or "gangrape," sent by more than 5 million unique users over the period of a year, from January 16, 2013 until January 16, 2014. These tweets have been scraped and analyzed with the Twitter Capture and Analysis Toolset of the Digital Methods Initiative (Borra and Rieder, 2014). Subsequently, from this dataset, the ten keywords most frequently included in tweets pertaining to the Delhi gang rape case have been selected: "India," "Delhi," "Nirbhaya," "Damini," "Delhigangrape." "Delhirape," "MumbaiGangRape," "Asaram," "Suryanelli," and "Tejpal." Querying the full dataset on the basis of the ten keywords generated a subset of 1,008,460 tweets, specifically focused on the Delhi gang rape case and related issues. These tweets were sent by 311,611 unique users. To contextualize the analysis of the Twitter data and to gain further insight in the social relations constructed in relation to the Twitter communication, we conducted, between February and April 2014, fifteen semi-structured interviews via Skype with eight Indian feminist activists and seven journalists and bloggers involved in the Twitter communication on the Delhi gang rape.
2 All available data exchanged through the entire lifetime of the Kullena Khaled Said page, from June 2010 to July 2013, was extracted via a customized version of the Netvizz application (Rieder, 2013). Given that the most intense communication on the page took place between January 1 and February 15, 2011, three days after Mubarak stepped down, we have focused the analysis on this period. In these one and a half months, 1629 admin posts and 1,465,696 user comments were made on the page. Examining this material, we have translated and analyzed the most engaged with messages: the posts that received most comments and likes, and the comments that received most likes. Furthermore, to gain insight in the larger political, sociocultural configuration in which this communication took place, we have consulted the many studies on social media and the Egyptian uprising.
3 Binalakshmi Nepram, Skype interview by Sudha Rajagopalan, April 2, 2014.
4 Rita Banerji, Skype interview by Sudha Rajagopalan, March 13, 2014.
5 These observations do come with an asterisk. Exploring the Facebook page, we could only examine the interaction on the page itself. We could not observe what happened in user news feeds. Hence, we know little about the interactions between individual users triggered by Kullena Khaled Said posts and comments. In the case of Twitter, we did get insight into individual interactions around particular issues. This affects how we understand the nature of the relations between users. Of course, this is, to an important extent, also true for the Facebook and Twitter users themselves. Platform architectures shape how users perceive and imagine their relationship to a larger collective.

6 Anindita Sengupta, Skype interview by Sudha Rajagopalan, April 4, 2014.
7 Sakshi Kumar, Skype interview by Sudha Rajagopalan, March 11, 2014.
8 Natasha Badhwar, Skype interview by Sudha Rajagopalan, March 21, 2014.

References

Ahmed, S., Jaidka, K., & Cho, J. (2017). Tweeting India's Nirbhaya protest: A study of emotional dynamics in an online social movement. *Social Movement Studies*, 16(4), 447–465.

Anderson, B. (1983). *Imagined communities: Reflections on the origin and spread of nationalism.* London: Verso.

Barassi, V. (2015). Social media, immediacy and the time for democracy: Critical reflections on social media as "temporalising practices." In L. Dencik and O. Leistert (Eds.), *Critical approaches to social media protest: Contentions and debates* (pp. 73–88). Lanham, MD: Rowan and Littlefield.

Belair-Gagnon, V., Mishra, S., & Agur, C. (2014). Reconstructing the Indian public sphere: Newswork and social media in the Delhi gang rape case. *Journalism*, 15, 1059–1075.

Bennett, W. L. & Segerberg, A. (2012). The logic of connective action: Digital media and the personalization of contentious politics. *Information, Communication & Society*, 15(5), 739–768.

Berry, D. (2011). *The philosophy of software: Code and mediation in the digital age.* Berlin: Springer.

Bimber, B., Flanagin, A., & Stohl, C. (2012). *Collective action in organizations: Interaction and engagement in an era of technological change.* Cambridge and New York: Cambridge University Press.

Borra, E. & Rieder, B. (2014). Programmed method: Developing a toolset for capturing and analyzing tweets. *Aslib Journal of Information Management*, 66(3), 262–278.

boyd, d. (2011). Social network sites as networked publics: Affordances, dynamics, and implications. In Z. Papacharissi (Ed.), *A networked self: Identity, community, and culture on social network sites* (pp. 39–58). New York and London: Routledge.

Bruns, A. (2008). *Blogs, Wikipedia, Second Life, and beyond: From production to produsage.* New York: Peter Lang.

Chaudhuri, S. & Fitzgerald, S. (2015). Rape protests in India and the birth of a new repertoire. *Social Movement Studies*, 14, 622–628.

Coretti, L. & Pica, D. (2015). The rise and fall of collective identity in networked movements: Communication protocols, Facebook, and the anti-Berlusconi protest. *Information, Communication & Society*, 18(8), 951–967.

Facebook. (2017). Create a page. www.facebook.com/pages/create

Galis, V. & Neumayer, C. (2016). Laying claim to social media by activists: A cyber-material détournement. *Social Media + Society*, 2(3), e2056305116664360–e2056305116664360.

Gerbaudo, P. (2015). Protest avatars as memetic signifiers: Political profile pictures and the construction of collective identity on social media in the 2011 protest wave. *Information, Communication & Society*, 18(8), 916–929.

Gerbaudo, P. (2016). Constructing public space| rousing the Facebook crowd: Digital enthusiasm and emotional contagion in the 2011 protests in Egypt and Spain. *International Journal of Communication*, 10, 20.

Gerlitz, C. & Helmond, A. (2013). The like economy: Social buttons and the data-intensive web. *New Media & Society*, 15(8), 1348–1365.

Ghonim, W. (2012). *Revolution 2.0: The power of the people is greater than the people in power: A memoir.* New York: Houghton Mifflin Harcourt.

Gillespie, T. (2014). The relevance of algorithms. In T. Gillespie, P.J. Boczkowski, & K.A. Foot (Eds.), *Media technologies: Essays on communication, materiality, and society* (pp. 167–193). Cambridge: MIT Press.

Hendriks, C.M., Duus, S., & Ercan, S.A. (2016). Performing politics on social media: The dramaturgy of an environmental controversy on Facebook. *Environmental Politics,* 25(6), 1102–1125.

Hestres, L.E. (2014). Preaching to the choir: Internet-mediated advocacy, issue public mobilization, and climate change. *New Media & Society,* 16(2), 323–339.

Juris, J.S. (2012). Reflections on # Occupy Everywhere: Social media, public space, and emerging logics of aggregation. *American Ethnologist,* 39(2), 259–279.

Kavada, A. (2012). Engagement, bonding, and identity across multiple platforms: Avaaz on Facebook, YouTube, and MySpace. *MedieKultur: Journal of Media and Communication Research,* 28(52), 21.

Kavada, A. (2015). Creating the collective: Social media, the Occupy Movement and its constitution as a collective actor. *Information, Communication & Society,* 18(8), 872–886.

Kavada, A. & Poell, T. (2017). Trajectories of public contestation: Tracing the temporal, spatial, and material articulations of popular protest through digital media. Paper presented at the *Digital Media and the Spatial Transformation of Public Contention workshop of ECPR Joint Sessions Workshops,* Nottingham, UK, April 26–29.

Langlois, G., Elmer, G., McKelvey, F., & Devereaux, Z. (2009). Networked publics: The double articulation of code and politics on Facebook. *Canadian Journal of Communication,* 34(3), 415.

Lee, J. (2013) An introduction to Facebook's new page insights. *Search Engine Watch,* October 14. http://searchenginewatch.com/article/2300218/An-Introduction-toFace books-New-Page-Insights

Lesch, A.M. (2011). Egypt's spring: Causes of the revolution. *Middle East Policy,* 18(3), 35–48.

Lim, M. (2012). Clicks, cabs, and coffee houses: Social media and oppositional movements in Egypt, 2004–2011. *Journal of Communication,* 62(2), 231–248.

Milan, S. (2015a). When algorithms shape collective action: Social media and the dynamics of cloud protesting. *Social Media + Society,* 1(2). doi: 10.117/2056305115622481

Milan, S. (2015b). From social movements to cloud protesting: The evolution of collective identity. *Information, Communication & Society,* 18(8), 887–900.

Noveck, B.S. (2005). A democracy of groups. *First Monday,* 10(11). www.uic.edu/htbin/cgiwrap/bin/ojs/index.php/fm/article/view/1289/1209

Papacharissi, Z. (2015). *Affective publics: Sentiment, technology, and politics.* Oxford: Oxford University Press.

Papacharissi, Z. & de Fatima Oliveira, M. (2012). Affective news and networked publics: The rhythms of news storytelling on # Egypt. *Journal of Communication,* 62(2), 266–282.

Patel, Atish. (2014). "India's social media election battle." *BBC News India,* March 31. www.bbc.com/news/world-asia-india-26762391.

Poell, T. (2014). Social media and the transformation of activist communication: Exploring the social media ecology of the 2010 Toronto G20 protests. *Information, Communication & Society,* 17(6), 716–731.

Poell, T. & Darmoni, K. (2012). Twitter as a multilingual space: The articulation of the Tunisian revolution through # sidibouzid. *NECSUS. European Journal of Media Studies,* 1(1), 14–34.

Poell, T. & Rajagopalan, S. (2015). Connecting activists and journalists: Twitter communication in the aftermath of the 2012 Delhi rape. *Journalism Studies*, 16(5), 719–733.

Poell, T. & Van Dijck, J. (2015). Social media and activist communication. In C. Atton (Ed.), *The Routledge companion to alternative and community media* (pp. 527–537). London: Routledge.

Poell, T., Abdulla, R., Rieder, B., Woltering, R., & Zack, L. (2016). Protest leadership in the age of social media. *Information, Communication & Society*, 19(7), 994–1014.

Postill, J. (2015). Public anthropology in times of media hybridity and global upheaval. In S. Pink and S. Abram (Eds.), *Media, anthropology, and public engagement* (pp. 164–181). New York: Berghahn.

Rambukkana, N. (2015). *Hashtag publics: The power and politics of discursive networks*. New York: Peter Lang.

Rieder, B. (2013, May). Studying Facebook via data extraction: The Netvizz application. *Proceedings of the 5th annual ACM web science conference* (pp. 346–355). New York: ACM.

Rieder, B., Abdulla, R., Poell, T., Woltering, R., & Zack, L. (2015). Data critique and analytical opportunities for very large Facebook Pages: Lessons learned from exploring "We are all Khaled Said." *Big Data & Society*, 2(2). doi: 10.1177/2053951715614980

Shirky, C. (2008). *Here comes everybody: The power of organizing without organizations*. London: Penguin.

Swann, T. & Husted, E. (2017). Undermining anarchy: Facebook's influence on anarchist principles of organization in Occupy Wall Street. *The Information Society*, 33(4), 192–204.

Van Dijck, J. (2013). *The culture of connectivity: A critical history of social media*. Oxford: Oxford University Press.

5

THE BOT PROXY

Designing Automated Self Expression

Samuel Woolley, Samantha Shorey, and Philip Howard

Harry, a developer who specializes in the production of social media bots, was one of the first people to give our research team an explanation of the complex relationship between the bot and its builder. Referencing the work of Ian Bogost (2012) he stated, "bots are independent objects that do the work of the philosopher." This is a concept that requires some unpacking. First, Harry wanted to make it clear that bots are separate from their creators. They are autonomously functioning. Second, he elaborated on the position of the philosopher-builder as someone who builds functions into these digital objects and then relinquishes the majority of control over their activities in the world. Yes, bots do the work of the person that constructs and releases them, but they also have their own identity, they interact with the Internet in ways removed from that builder.

Like Harry, we see the role of the social bot as something that should be complicated rather than simplified. Bots are more than tools, but they are not sentient or independently emotive. They reflect the thoughts and emotions of the builder, while also reacting to the networked computational systems in which they operate. After many discussions with people who build and launch highly automated accounts on social media platforms, we have come to see bots as extensions of their creators. A bot stands in, and often does the will of the person who built it. However, a bot can also challenge the authority of its maker. It functions and interacts with its environment, independently and automatically. The builder is not the bot and the bot is not the builder. Rather, the bot is a separately functioning representative of its creator; the bot is its creator's proxy.

The Computational Propaganda Project

For the past four years we have been interviewing bot makers. This work has been done in conjunction with two connected projects at the University of Washington and the University of Oxford, concerned with the study of what we have termed "computational propaganda" (Woolley & Howard, 2016). Our goal has been to develop understandings of social automation online. We are specifically concerned with communication-oriented problems surrounding the use of "social bots"—automated software programs on social media built to look and act like real people. In some ways, this work has been a theoretical endeavor aimed at understanding the particular capacities of social bots as social actors. Bots can be used as simple tools on social media platforms, to automate pre-programmed messages on Twitter or to moderate posts on Reddit. They can also be drivers of sociality in unique ways. They can be constructed to learn communication skills from other users, an unpredictable venture in and of itself, or be deployed and left to interact with their environment with little oversight.

The empirical goal of our research project has been to understand these unique automated tools by talking to the people who build them. We have traveled to several countries and interacted with makers building and deploying bots over social media for all sorts of reasons: to curate news, to manipulate political conversations, to create art, to comment on social problems, and more. These interactions, and the projects in question, have revealed a special relationship between bots and the people who build them. Bots act as a proxy for their makers; they help them to creatively interact with digital systems.

At the outset we had a tendency to personify the social bot. Social media users talk about creations like @OliviaTaters or XiaoIce as if they were thinking automatons: human-like artificial intelligence akin to C3PO or eccentric robot helpers more like R2D2 (Lloyd, 2016). Creators often give their bots human names and creative personalities, they speak about them like friends or pets. Social bots, however, are still built to do tasks specified by developers and even advanced machine-learning bots, such as Microsoft's @Tay, reveal the imperfections and biases of their builders (Neff & Nagy, 2016). Most bots on social media are semi-automated tools that allow the person who launches them to interact with platforms in both an obscured infrastructural and shared interactive capacity. In other words, social bots communicate with servers, applications, and databases on the backend of websites, but they also interact with human users on the frontend of those same sites.

We argue that social bots help users to reveal, exploit and change aspects of digital systems that otherwise go unquestioned. These changes occur through interactions directed from human to computer, but also those initiated from computer to human. However, it is too simplistic to say that automation on sites like Twitter or Facebook is purely functional. Bots are more than lines of code. The reality of social bots' capability exists somewhere in between the poles of bots as wholly autonomous entities or bots as programs or tools. Our interviewees have shown a consistent desire to place themselves as separate but related to, or invested in, the bots they build. They challenge the rigid separation between humans and technologies, makers and mediums.

Thinking of bots as proxies for their creators allows us to treat bots as surrogates, but also to see their function as entities that enact change on a system while they themselves are also changed. As bots interact with complex social systems, they do things beyond the expectations of their builders, they achieve the unexpected.

I'm Not a Bot

In the course of our interviews with bot builders, and in our work revealing the manipulative political uses of bots during elections and security crises, we have regularly discussed the complicated user–bot relationship. During two events in 2016, the "Brexit" referendum in the U.K. and the presidential election in the United States, our team worked to identify automated Twitter accounts working to amplify partisan points of view in attempts to manufacture trends and project consensus. However, we received pushback from the programmers behind accounts we had described as bots.

One programmer, a developer from the United States, wrote an email to our project in which he stressed that *he* was not a bot, but a person who used software to automate his presence on Twitter. This particular user had, in his relatively brief tenure on the platform, produced hundreds of thousands of messages. Most were heavily in favor of a particular political perspective or, at times, heavily against oppositional views. The account tweeted nearly every second, with a high degree of topical specificity, both markers of automated activity. It was, however, diverse in the way it interacted with content and other users: it was able to both like and retweet existing posts and also to generate original messages.

It would be true to say that this user was harnessing a bot in order to bolster his online presence. By definition, a bot is a piece of automated software used to do automated tasks that a human would otherwise have to do. But our interaction with him complicates a mutually exclusive division between him and the software automating his profile. He saw his profile as being reflective of his views. For him the software was mostly functional, it allowed him to have some kind of online presence at all hours. The software, however, is not the person. In this case it was the software, and not this user, that was actually generating tweets and interacting with sites. But, the bot did not exist by itself. It was made as an extension of its creator. While people shape the content and trajectory of automation used to streamline interaction on and over social media, they are also separate from that technology and vice versa.

The Bot as a Proxy

Anecdotes like this reveal the usefulness of thinking of bots as proxies. The word "proxy" describes organizations, activities, and people who "act as a substitute for another" (Proxy, 2016). We use this definition when referring to a social bot as a proxy for a human user. The bot is endowed with agency or power, and can exercise that agency on behalf of the builder. Because a person must construct the code that allows the bot to function, they can have a degree of faith—and culpability—in what the bot does or will do. However, the expectations of creators are challenged on social media platforms where the bot interacts with other people or programs. Here a diverse range of inputs and outputs can affect the actions of a bot. In short, is it hard to predict exactly how any social program will function under different stresses. Tay was an example of this. The case of a bot built by developer Jeff van der Gloot (Weaver, 2015), wherein the bot said it wanted to kill people, stands as another. Here, a proxy behaved in a way that its creator did not intend. The bot went beyond the tasks its builder believed he had programmed.

A social bot is, therefore, an automated software program built to stand in for, represent, or extend a human user. We argue that these digital automatons allow users the unique ability to interact with both systems and social spheres in ways that otherwise they could not. Socially, bots allow users the ability to act exhaustively. While a user has to sleep, a bot does not. They allow users to multiply their presence online, as one person can control many bots. They allow users to speed up their actions online, to computationally enhance the ability to complete tasks. They allow users the ability to veil their actions, providing a degree of separation and anonymity between the user, the message sender, and their target, the message receiver. They allow and facilitate communication; they mediate conversations and can be seen as a new medium in their own right (Woolley & Guilbeault, 2017).

Bots are also infrastructural elements of social media systems built on top of existing platforms. The work of deploying a bot over Twitter or Facebook does not require direct collaboration or involvement of platform designers or engineers in order to change or allow for original features that users want to make possible. For example, users can build and deploy bots to translate text from one language into another. This accessibility can be harnessed in very practical ways. Several interviewees argued that they were most generally using bots to add additional functionality on systems already in use. Still others argued that this ability allowed for genuine creativity. Bots have been used to generate art based upon user's profiles and preferences (Katie Rose Pipkin's @mothgenerator), to critique news media (Darius Kazemi's @twoheadlines), even to argue with other users (Sarah Nyberg's @arguetron). All varieties of bots offer new possibilities for interaction on, and with, social networking sites.

In this chapter, we explore bots as a form of networked self-expression. When a person types and sends a tweet, it is clear that they are motivated by a desire to convey a thought or feeling. But, when the text is produced through combination and sent automatically by a computer script, these motivations become less clear. This means that it is exceedingly important to look beyond the content of automated messages to the bot designers, themselves. While it is possible to interpret the desired effects of a bot based on its messages, talking to bot makers helps us understand their design goals—elements that have a meaningful impact on the form and features of bots. Through forty qualitative interviews with bot makers, we discovered that bots both enable and extend the communicative reach of their builders. Our interviewees made it clear that social bots function well beyond the purview of simple automated messaging, that they have a unique capacity for complex interaction. Because some bots are built to learn from their ecosystem, they often display startling characteristics borne from factors outside of their original code. They are not human, but they are invested with power that can be directed diversely and unpredictably.

Automation and Social Life

There is persistent concern within both media studies and science and technology studies regarding the relationship of algorithms and, often proprietary, software to various aspects of social life. Today, algorithms and other computational tools play an important political role in arenas such as news consumption, issue awareness, and cultural understanding (Gillespie, 2012; Sandvig et al., 2014). Research on bots, in particular, has largely focused on their potential for political effects. Building upon prior work in the computer sciences (Ferrara et al., 2016; Metaxas & Mustafaraj, 2012; Wagner et al., 2012), communication and media-oriented work has shown that political actors around the globe make social media bots in efforts to both facilitate and control communication (Woolley, 2016). Bots have been used by political campaigns and candidates in attempts to manipulate public opinion by thwarting activist attempts to organize or to create the illusion of popularity. This work suggests that modern social bots are increasingly sophisticated and that pernicious use of them threatens social spheres on and offline. Moreover, it suggests these tools in the hands of powerful political actors are now being widely used in attempts to manipulate public opinion.

Alternatively, building and using bots has also been discussed as a kind of agnostic commercialism. Bot builders act as "hired guns," selling bots on sites like Fiverr, with little concern for how they are used and by whom. Using bots to spread advertisements or attack online adversaries has a long history and has existed over email and other chat mediums before it spread to platforms like Twitter and Facebook (Holz, 2005). Newer forms gather information on other users or push a particular argument, agenda, or hashtag (Hwang et al., 2012). Experiments on the efficacy of such bots reveals that they can infiltrate networks on sites like Facebook with a large degree of success and that they are successful in bypassing extant security systems meant to protect from just such attacks

(Boshmaf et al., 2011). Those who build and deploy such programs have told us in no uncertain terms that their work is mercenary, apolitical in their view and driven by a desire to make money online.

Less scholarly attention has been paid to the sense-making of bot builders: how bot makers give meaning to their work, frame their activities within technological systems, and evaluate the effectiveness of their creations. Yet, the creative practices of makers—and the social practices of individuals writ large—are constitutive of the practices of large-scale institutions and organizations (Neff, 2012). The unique ways that bots are harnessed by non-commercial makers are often taken up by companies and normalized by powerful political actors. Scholars such as Castells (1996) and Howard (2011) have called for media research that studies media infrastructure, media content, and the "individuals who produce and consume content over media" (Howard, 2011, p. 2).

In this chapter, we interview bot makers to better understand the processes and relationships that determine the shape of automated technologies. From this perspective, bots can be analyzed as part of the "expressive equipment" available to social network users (Papacharissi, 2011, p. 307). Bots, like other forms of text and images, are tools for the strategic sharing of information. They enable users to make statements about current political issues, illuminate crucial details in mountains of information, and reveal biases in computational systems. Rather than doing so using personally crafted messages, they can rely on automated processes (known as "algorithms") that draw on existing data (known as a "corpus") to produce messages. Bots are a constituent part of the networked publics in which social media users operate; they "reorganize how information flows and how people interact with information and each other" (boyd, 2011, p. 3). The application programming interface (API) of platforms like Twitter is the bridge that affords publics this exchange. It is through the API that users build and launch software applications, including social bots. These creations play important ecological roles in both the backend and the frontend of social media sites.

Bots have the power to "extend and modify" the functionality of online platforms (Geiger, 2014). Moreover, bots can extend and modify the capabilities of humans who use those systems. We agree with Tsvetkova and colleagues' assertion (2017) that the curatorial roles given to bots on sites like Wikipedia allow "even relatively 'dumb' bots to give rise to complex interactions" (p. 1). However, in this context bots are not "predictable automatons that do not have the capacity for emotions, meaning-making, creativity, and sociality" (p. 1). While we do not, by any means, argue that bots have emotions or the ability to make meaning, we do argue that they have a capacity for effecting sociality in ways beyond those envisioned by their creators. This effect is not a conscious decision on the part of the bot. Rather, it is a motion set in action via the bot through a diverse ecological social system that prioritizes not only the intent of the developer but also that of a broad, and networked, public comprising people, software, and machines. As Guilbeault (2016) argues, social media platforms and a diverse range of inputs and outputs "propel bots into agency" (p. 5004).

Wise (1998) argues that software programs like bots serve programmers as "intelligent agents" or "digital butlers," that they are the digital embodiment of their creator. Our research suggests, however, that bots as proxies exist somewhere between conceptions of bots as pure extensions of their builders and arguments that see bots as only rigid tools. There is a strong current of humanity encoded into the social bot; indeed, many successfully and duplicitously mimic human users. Though, within humanistic definitions of feeling, the bot is not truly sentient. Sentience is best defined as the ability to "perceive or feel things" (Oxford Living Dictionaries, 2017). While the bot can parse information and use this data to react to its environment, the builder constructs the bot to respond to data according to her wishes. The bot, however, can respond in surprising ways when unforeseen intake results in similarly unexpected output. The bot is neither its builder nor only its builder's tool, but something in between.

Steyerl (2014) discusses the politics of using media and technology systems in a proxy capacity, and is the first to refer to bots as an example of this representation. This work theorizes that bots are an example of "post representation," like a mask or persona that functions as a generic placeholder. Our own evidence and analysis pushes perspectives of representation further, with more specificity placed upon the meaningful relationship between the bot and maker.

Networked Field Work

There is a short, but rich, history of using ethnographic methods, including interviews, to study technology-oriented communities. The proliferation of digital qualitative methods has grown out of the work done by the social scientists and humanistic scholars throughout academic history. Scholars have struggled with both the proper terminology for studying culture online, vacillating between methods that are digital, virtual, net-based, "netnographic," and data-centric, but also with how to represent culture online (Howard, 2002; Bowler, 2010). Those interested in internet methods early on were particularly concerned with the separation between the "real" world offline and the artificial one online. This separation itself has since been criticized as artificial, especially in light of the ever-increasing "wired" nature of society.

Markham and Baym (2009) strike down the notion of online/offline separation by arguing that sectioning off certain aspects of social life as real or digital is a colloquial endeavor, one that has no place in empirical research. They argue, moreover, that "qualitative research requires a tolerance for chaos, ambiguity and inductive thinking" (p. ix). By being open to the potential for multiple, and concurrent, meanings—to subjectivity—qualitative researchers are able to work toward contextual understandings of new phenomena as well as new ways of thinking about existing phenomena. This perspective is crucial when theorizing about the social capabilities of technology.

Schools of thought from actor network theory to activity theory seek to answer the complex questions associated with the ability of technology to affect change. Social bots are an obvious object of analysis within the category of technology with a social function. Our concept of the bot as a proxy allows the simple polarization of the technical and the social to be complicated. Our conversations with bot builders made it impossible to simply classify bots as the technical outcomes of social creators. Bot builders regularly negotiated their relationships to the bots they built. Their expressions of reflexive identification and moments of comparison between themselves and these automated social programs illuminated the proxy nature of bots.

Interviews, and other ethnographic methods, allow STS researchers to get to the heart of intentionality. They ask technology makers why they built what they did, how they built it, and what they believe it does. This strain of research is in contrast to user-based studies, which seek user reactions and interpretations of media. This is not to say that the two cannot be complementary. Here, however, we are concerned with the relationship between builders and their bots, so we have conducted over forty interviews with the bot-building community. In this chapter we focus mostly on builders who make Twitter bots, but this research has implications for other social platforms where bots are being used: Facebook, Reddit, Instagram, Snapchat, Kik, Periscope, Firechat, Wechat, Telegram, Slack, Weibo, and many others.

Our interviewees come from a diverse range of professional, demographic, and cultural backgrounds. Some of them work as professional software developers; others are digital artists, educators, lawyers, journalists, political consultants, entrepreneurs, or writers. Many have day jobs with no connection to bot development or the digital sphere but engage in bot building as a hobby or activist practice. We spoke to men, women, and those who self-identified as non-binary. Some were in their late teens or early twenties, others were in their thirties, forties, or fifties. Politically, interviewees spanned the range from conservative to liberal. Some have worked for political campaigns, others consider themselves anarchists. One thing brings this otherwise heterogeneous group together, they all build bots. The ideas in this chapter, therefore, come from technology makers.

Our interview process involved establishing contact with potential interview subjects, disclosing the nature of the study, and asking for consent. Second, we conducted the interview, taking notes and recording as appropriate. Finally, we prepared a thematic memo for each interview. We audio recorded all interviews, unless asked not to by interviewees. We completed an interviewee information statement for every interview. This sheet included demographic information and also general questions about the person's level of coding experience and professional background. We gave all informants pseudonyms. This was a considered choice made in the beginning stages of our project and continues for two main reasons: first, to protect informants' identity, especially when confidential or politically sensitive information is being shared; and second, to allow for open conversation, so that thoughts and feelings can be shared without hesitation. In order to protect our data, we followed ethics guidelines established by both the University of Washington and the University of Oxford, but also those of funders including the U.S. National Science Foundation and European Research Council.

Bot Success

Bot makers defined the success of their bots in two ways: intention and attention. Does the bot do what it is designed to do? And does the bot have followers, does it have viewers and does it garner engagement? For some bot makers, the intention of their bots was practical. Bots extend people's abilities to rally volunteers, gather signatures for political petitions, or translate across language barriers on social networks. For others, the intention was more artistic. Bots are tools for commentary, creating imagery, and making rhetorical points.

In terms of attention, bots extend people's ability to reach audiences, circulate content, and bait political adversaries into arguments. The capacity of bots to increase attention is complementary to the intentions of designers; making their practical goals more achievable and the audience for their expressive goals larger. Bots automate familiar forms of interpersonal interaction, such as tweets and @-replies. Importantly, bots are also uniquely equipped to interact with trending algorithms to heighten awareness and visibility around a particular topic.

Intention and attention are not disparate goals. They do not divide bot makers into two groups motivated by two different aims. Rather, almost all the bot makers we talked to referenced *both* intention and attention as the primary criteria for evaluating the success of their creations. Bots are made with both expressive motivations and functional outcomes in mind. These coexisting, though sometimes competing, aims have to be balanced by makers in the process of designing bots.

Intention

Intentionality gives power to designers. Here, success is based on what a bot achieves, relative to what its creator wanted it to do. Bot makers often spoke of bots as a "tool" and compared them to "paintbrushes" or "instruments." This overarching focus on the intention of designers may appear to imply a view of technology as neutral or impartial, as a conduit for the visions of the humans who build them. However, bot makers often spoke directly about the powerful ideologies that are present in computers and computer-based tools. For these bot makers, intention is seen as a *corrective* to systems that are either inherently biased or easily take on the bias of the communities they interact with. Bot makers who neglect ethical directives were seen as careless and irresponsible.

Rather than mitigating culpability—as one might say with "the best of intentions"—intention is essential for building ethical systems. Quinn, a bot-making artist, stated this directly: "Bot making itself is political. Sometimes quite explicitly, but in general too." Bot makers have to consider what they want their bots to express, "to take special care to ensure that they aren't going express things that we don't mean for them to express, like they don't use oppressive language for instance." Bot making, as a form of technology design, means encoding the values of the designer into what is being built. In writing the scripts with care and intention, they are attempting to ensure that the bots they build reflect their own values as a human.

Modeling

Hannah is poet and teacher, who uses bots as part of her creative practice. She has been making bots since 2007, when the earliest adopters of Twitter were considering what the nature of computers—automation, randomness, combination, repetition—could contribute to the arts. Hannah's work is wildly popular, with tens of thousands of twitter followers, and inspired many of the people making bots today.

At the most basic level, bots are rule-based. Like any algorithm, bots on Twitter require instructions: conditionals, if this/then that. But, bots that function on Twitter also operate on a platform where information is experienced synchronously. "Bots are a response to the fact that Twitter is real time." She explains, "any effect that you want, has to keep happening. It has to happen over and over." Automation is ideal for repetitive tasks. Once the initial commands are written, reproducing an action takes no additional energy. If you can determine the formula, the basic structure of a statement or pattern of an interaction, it can be automated.

Repetition, as an artistic feature, has a revelatory capacity. Take for example the knock-knock joke, the most unoriginal of all joke formats. Knock-knock jokes work through using a formula: the first two interactions (knock-knock / who's there?) are always the same. The third introduces the punch line. The fourth is just the third + the word "who." And the fifth, the punch line, plays on the third. If you have never experienced a knock-knock joke before, each aspect of the script might seem novel. It is only through repetition—through hearing it over and over—that the underlying system becomes clear.

For Hannah, formula and repetition are central to the communicative capacity of bots. In that tweets generated by people have the power to express the writer's perspective, tweets generated by bots have the power to express the perspective of computers: "I'm trying to expose the guts of these techniques, so it becomes more clear how they work internally." One of the best ways to do this is to show the procedure, the rules of the system, and how the outputs come about.

As Hannah explains it, writing the code for bots requires that the maker define a system. This process of definition requires that makers determine the rules of a message, then make a model of it through code. Beyond highlighting these patterns, modeling also concretizes knowledge that may otherwise remain tacit. This tacit knowledge may be the logic of computer systems or the logics of particular human actions, but in creating bot proxies one can express these logics visibly and legibly to those who may view them.

Concretizing

Charlene is an investigative journalist who uses bots to help with reporting. Her area of expertise, campaign finance, requires sifting through massive databases and monitoring congressional filings. Stories come from finding expenditures which are often deliberately buried in piles of unremarkable information. Bots are an excellent tool for this kind of "boring" and repetitive work, which just requires observing and relaying simple facts. But, automating aspects of the journalistic process requires that bot makers write the informal knowledge of seasoned journalists into formal, rule-based code.

Formal knowledge, in this case, is the rules of campaign finance. For example, every political campaign must file with the Federal Elections Commission on an orderly schedule. But this formal knowledge is also accompanied by the informal knowledge that, in any big filing, there will always be small bits of money that are being used for alternative purposes. These cynical-seeming maxims "aren't written down anywhere" but can be used to inform the bot-making process. "That's the core," she says "taking what you know to be true and writing it as rules in a system."

Building bots makes these tendencies and patterns explicit. The mechanisms become legible to interested parties who can read the code. And, the outcomes of those mechanisms produce information that is relevant and understandable to lay audiences. Charlene sees bots and humans "working together" in the field of journalism—both helping journalists to do their jobs and performing basic journalistic tasks, like sharing information. For other politically driven makers we spoke to, bots served similar purposes. Rather than a person sifting through dense logs in search of pertinent information, bots can watch information as it is produced. They act as monitors or alarms, using the intuition of journalists to overcome the data density that (perhaps deliberately) obstructs understanding.

Exploiting

Aaron is a computer programmer who builds bots as a form of activism. He began building bots in a period of unemployment, which exposed him to the "horrible bureaucracy" of modern unemployment security departments. People receiving unemployment benefits must be actively searching for a job. Rather than assessing qualitatively, the government measures this criterion by counting the number of jobs a recipient has applied to. The applications are often online, highly impersonal, and repetitive. They require sifting through large amounts of information in job postings and classifieds. As Hannah and Charlene observe, both these qualities make job applications an ideal task for automated tools. But, more than that, Aaron fundamentally disagrees with the idea that benefits are based on "the filling out of forms" and human experience is not taken into account at any step of the process. So, he wrote a bot to do job applications for him.

While it is easy to frame this activity as a clever work-around, Aaron ascribes significant meaning to the script he created. Automating job applications is exploiting a system through the mechanisms of the system itself. The government essentially automates the process of assessing job seekers through the counting of applications. Yet, unemployment is rife with experiences that do not fit into a quantitative framework. It is a "computational metaphor placed on top of people, and they're expected to go along with it. I'm fond of disrupting that." The expressive power of bots is not purely in the content of social media messaging, in the political declarations made over and over again in tweets and postings. They can perform acts of resistance.

The stories of Hannah, Charlene, and Aaron illuminate the ways in which bot making, as a creative practice, allows people to question the quiet functioning of everyday life. Bots achieve instrumental goals: performing repetitive tasks and surfacing relevant content. But, the meaning of bots goes beyond their practicality. They bring to light the computational, political, and societal patterns that govern our everyday activities. They are constructed with a spirit of candor; driven by honest expression. As proxies they mitigate the complexity of algorithms, the magnitude of data, and the triviality of bureaucracy.

Attention

One participant put it simply: "Following is the lifeblood of bots." Bots, as communication technologies, need an audience. This is most true for bots that have a frontend communication focus, a mandate to interact with other users—including humans and other bots—on platforms such as Twitter, Facebook, or Reddit. Without followers, or at the very least, viewers, bots can generate hundreds of messages easily but with limited frontend effects. It nearly impossible to change a person's ideas on a social issue, for instance, without that person interacting with the ideas—or, online, even seeing the posts—you are sharing. The importance of followers for user-to-user communication, regardless of whether the user is a bot or person, is due, in large part, to the nature of interaction on Twitter. While moments and hashtags draw from public content produced across the platform, most users experience Twitter through their personalized feed (Java et al., 2009).

Bots can, however, be used to push particular hashtags in a quantitatively driven attempt to get topics to trend on the platform's sidebar. This type of bot communication is distinguished from user to user, or frontend, communication in that it is between the bot (or botnet) and the platform's "trending" or "newsfeed" algorithm, or backend. In this type of information exchange bots are constructed in attempts to affect these algorithms in order to prioritize hashtags that users see. The trending algorithm on Facebook, for instance, now operates quantitatively without human oversight (Thielman, 2016). It computes trends based around how many times content is shared and various other pieces of predetermined input and output. As recently as a year ago, human moderators had a role in filtering content on Facebook. This has changed, due to allegations that these news "curators" were politically biased. Now the algorithm arbitrates what content shows up in users' newsfeeds, but the algorithm only has the illusion of objectivity. Not only can the algorithm be gamed—by bots amplifying information in order to manufacture false trends, for instance—it is also laden with human judgment. People construct algorithms and encode them with particular values.

Really, most algorithms built to prioritize information based upon social behavior online can be manipulated. The twitter feed chronologically displays content from followed users, and retweets and @-replies from those users. If bots can garner human followers, their content will show up in human users' feeds. If they tweet enough, even without human followers (many bots rely on armies of bot followers to meet expectations of having followers), they can count on causing hashtags to trend or on their tweets to show up as a "most popular" when they fall into a particular search category. In both of these circumstances, bot-driven information can be consumed and repurposed by other users. Being retweeted by human users gives the information legitimacy, reaching their networks through a trusted relationship. If bots are built to learn from their surroundings, they can be programmed to draw interaction from their followers. However, most social bots are not, at present, built to use machine learning.

The bots that have the most success in gaining human attention via the tactics mentioned above are quite simple. They often either 1) communicate over popular channels, or on/around popular topics, and/or 2) shout—metaphorically speaking—in order to be heard. Hans, a bot builder who has experimented with launching bots on Twitter in attempts to affect people's perception of social issues, explained the former strategy by stating that he builds the bot with an implicit and explicit goal. Explicitly, the bot will tweet using hashtags and content related to a relatively benign issue—football, for instance. Once the bot gets an audience, however, it begins injecting conversations with content related to a particular belief or concept. It garners a following by engaging in chat about sports and once it has built rapport it begins sharing articles on, say, the science behind global warming. This is the implicit goal of this type of bot. The second type of bot makes use of sheer numbers to get a point across. It shouts, or amplifies information, in order to get the algorithm and/or people to notice content. Three mechanisms allow bots to attract attention: listening, evoking, and shouting.

Listening

The bots created by Hans (the bot maker mentioned above) often observe interaction on social media. These bots "listen" to the hum of a platform, constantly searching Twitter for relevant conversations. Using hashtags, listener bots find and participate in specific topics and engage with specific users. For instance, to engage with supporters of Donald Trump one might build a bot that listens for conversations connected to #MAGA or #Draintheswap. These bots garner attention through tweeting using the same hashtags as human users—making their statements visible to anyone following discussions on that topic. Or, the bot tweets at hashtag-users directly, engaging them in conversation. After a response, a human user may take over. The listener bot effectively automates the laborious process of finding interlocutors. This tactic is especially useful if the builder is working to further the cause of a particular ideology, policy or politician. Like the journalistic bots described by Charlene, these bots can leverage databases of information while also monitoring newly created information online. They then share that information to make a clear political statement or draw attention to an action or issue acting as a proxy relationship for their builder. Other listener bots can monitor sites and databases for manipulation or wrongdoing, then share that information with the public. Wikiedits bots, for instance, are created to track politicians' edits to Wikipedia pages (Ford et al., 2016).

Alternately, listener bots can work through distraction. Roadblock bots, a type of listener, are built to generate noise. They monitor feeds for a particular topic and then attempt to push users away from it through generating a wealth of nonsensical or off-topic posts. The volume of tweets makes it difficult for users to find the pertinent information needed to organize online—or, they are distracted by misinformation or attacks. Such bots have been used to demobilize activists trying to organize and communicate on Twitter but they can also be used to drive traffic from one cause, product, or idea to another (Woolley, 2016). These bots can do more than drown out activists or drive people to ideas. They can also be used to direct targeted noise in an attempt to harass other users.

Evoking

Pan is an educator and software developer, who builds and launches bots that tweet historical data in order to draw parallels to contemporary events. An example of a bot that Pan would build would be one that accesses and publicly tweets databased information about the fallout of nuclear arms use in Japan during WWII to critique ongoing proliferation of nuclear arms by both democracies and countries like North Korea. Pan's bots evoke the past to critique the present.

They are stand-alone informational bots that exist with a consistency akin to public art. Once Pan launches a bot she allows it to continue tweeting on its own from a corpus or database. The bot either gains followers or does not, it either spurs conversation or it does not.

Many art bots function in an evoking capacity. They produce statements or images that, far from being political, are built to create a subjective reaction from other users. Pan has built several popular bots that mash together strings of words to create bot poetry or that send out images related to a particular subject over Twitter. Her bots evoke emotions by consistently tweeting images related to, for instance, Americana.

These bots can also be purposefully strange or provocative, a variety that one interviewee called "dancing bear-ware." This type of bot is built to draw attention by saying odd, quasi-human, phrases related to a particular topic—say, affirmative action—in order to get people to engage. Like a dancing bear, they engage in unexpectedly human behavior in order to get other users to communicate with them. Such bots can, and have, then been used to argue with people about politics or distract those who engage in racist behavior (such as @argutron).

Shouting

Shouting bots work to garner attention by messaging in high numbers to get algorithms and/or people to view a particular message. While the actions of listening and evoking bots are topic-centered, shouting bots work mostly through volume. They say something so often—so loudly—it becomes difficult to ignore. Listening and evoking bots are also more targeted than shouters: baiting people into engagement or statically sharing an idea in order to evoke an emotion.

Shouting bots can be built to talk at someone until they listen. They can speak directly to a user through @-ing them or tagging them in images. This means content shows up in mentions, and is potentially displayed to others in their network. The number of people involved in this tactic used to be limited by the twitter character limits, but as this chapter was being written @-replies have been exempted from character counts leading to a potentially infinite number of @s.

An example of this type of bot was given to us by a respondent, who said they had tracked a bot-driven smear campaign. In this instance a builder or group of builders deployed hundreds of bots to tweet rumors about another user. These tweets were feasibly visible to anyone who looked at the embattled user's profile. Though distressful, the respondent felt that the attack was ultimately not very successful in mimicking a crowd of real human attackers because the bots were newly created and had no followers, and thus no audience. "In order for bots to be effective (in spreading a message)" said the respondent, "you have to be able to verify your message is reaching people." This bot did, however, cause emotional distress to the person who was targeted—regardless of whether it was seen by other people. It also caused them to delete their Twitter account. In this sense, the bot was in part successful in its—decidedly abusive—task of silencing those being attacked. Bots like this can also circumvent the need for reaching users directly by tweeting many times so that the trending algorithm picks up their hashtag or ideas as part of a popular movement. The information the bot maker wants to get to users still reaches them but through an additional layer of obfuscation.

Bots and Networked Self Expression

Whether bots work through means of intention, attention, or—as is often the case—a combination of these two mechanisms, they act as proxies for their creators. They allow their builders to construct additional layers of infrastructure upon a social platform, typically using an API. These layers of infrastructure function beyond the purview of the original platform developers. While bots on social media sites can function as tools for users hoping to alter or stretch their network footprint, they also exist as proxies for those who create them. They are imbued with intentions of their creator, deputized in order to undertake particular communicative actions. As proxies, however, they are separate entities.

Bots are built to do simple and direct functions, but even in these instances they interact with users and systems in ways that are complex and meaningful. Practical goals are accompanied by expressive outcomes—motivated by bot builder's perspectives on the mediated world in which they live. Beyond amplifying political declarations, bots engage and exploit the nature of social systems. Through writing automated scripts, bot makers write (and re-write) the computational logics, journalistic practices, and public deliberations that organize political participation.

Thinking of bots as proxies means to consider them more than a mask for a user, but less than a fully independent sentient entity. Bots do not think and feel. They can, however, have effects upon the social spheres in which they operate. This effect is driven not only by the bot's builder, but also by the networked system—all the users, other bots, protocols—with which the bot interacts. Intention and attention make bots more than a tool or set of commands; it makes them exceed their automation.

Acknowledgments

For their help and feedback, we would like to acknowledge all of the bot makers and trackers who spoke to us in the course of this work. We would also like to thank the other members of the Computational Propaganda Research Project team at the University of Oxford. We are also grateful to the faculty at the Department of Communication at the University of Washington, the Oxford Internet Institute at the University of Oxford, and the research team at Google Jigsaw. Please direct any correspondence to Box 353740, Communication

Department, University of Washington, Seattle, WA 98105. Parts of the research for this project were supported by the National Science Foundation, the European Research Council, and Google Jigsaw. Any opinions, findings, and conclusions or recommendations expressed in this material are those of the authors and do not necessarily reflect the views of the University of Washington, University of Oxford, the National Science Foundation, the European Research Council, or Google Jigsaw.

References

Bogost, I. (2012). *Alien phenomenology*. Minneapolis, MN: University of Minnesota Press.

Boshmaf, Y., Muslukhov, I., Beznosov, K., & Ripeanu, M. (2011). The socialbot network: When bots socialize for fame and money. *Proceedings of the 27th Annual Computer Security Applications Conference* (pp. 93–102). New York: ACM. doi: 10.1145/2076732. 2076746

Bowler, G. M. (2010). Netnography: A method specifically designed to study cultures and communities online. *Qualitative Report*, 15(5), 1270–1275.

boyd, d. (2011). Social network sites as networked publics: Affordances, dynamics, and implications. In Z. Papacharissi (Ed.), *A networked self: Identity, community and culture on social network sites* (pp. 39–58). New York: Routledge.

Castells, M. (1996). *The rise of the network society*. Malden, MA: Blackwell.

Ferrara, E., Varol, O., Davis, C., Menczer, F., & Flammini, A. (2016). The rise of social bots. *Communications of the ACM*, 59(7), 96–104. doi: 10.1145/2818717

Ford, H., Dubois, E., & Puschmann, C. (2016). Keeping Ottawa honest—one tweet at a time? Politicians, journalists, wikipedians, and their twitter bots. *International Journal of Communication*, 10, 4891–4914.

Geiger, R. S. (2014). Bots, bespoke, code and the materiality of software platforms. *Information, Communication & Society*, 17(3), 342–356. doi: 10.1080/1369118X.2013.873069

Gillespie, T. (2012). Can an algorithm be wrong? *Limn*, 1(2). http://escholarship.org/uc/item/0jk9k4hj

Guilbeault, D. (2016). Growing bot security: An ecological view of bot agency. *International Journal of Communication*, 10, 19, 5003–5021.

Holz, T. (2005). A short visit to the bot zoo [malicious bots software]. *Security & Privacy, IEEE*, 3(3), 76–79. doi: 10.1109/MSP.2005.58

Howard, P. N. (2002) Network ethnography and the hypermedia organization: New media, new organizations, new methods. *New Media & Society* 4(4), 550–574. doi: 10.1177/146144402321466813

Howard, P. N. (2011). *Castells and the media*. Cambridge: Polity Press.

Hwang, T., Pearce, I., & Nanis, M. (2012). Socialbots: Voices from the fronts. *Interactions*, 19(2), 38–45. doi: 10.1145/2090150.2090161

Java, A., Song, X., Finin, T., & Tseng, B. (2009). Why we twitter: An analysis of a microblogging community. *Lecture Notes in Computer Science*, 5439, 118–138. doi: 10.1007/978-3-642-00528-2_7

Lloyd, A. (2016). Our friends, the bots? *Data & Society: Points*, February 25. https://points. datasociety.net/our-friends-the-bots-34eb3276ab6d

Markham, A. N. & Baym, N. K. (2009). *Internet inquiry: Conversations about method*. Los Angeles: Sage.

Metaxas, P. T. & Mustafaraj, E. (2012). Social media and the elections. *Science*, 338(6106), 472–473. doi: 10.1126/science.1230456

Neff, G. (2012). *Venture labor: Work and the burden of risk in innovative industries.* Cambridge, MA: MIT Press.

Neff, G. & Nagy, P. (2016). Talking to bots: Symbiotic agency and the case of tay. *International Journal of Communication*, 10, 17.

Oxford Living Dictionaries (2017). "Sentient." Oxford: Oxford University Press.

Papacharissi, Z. (2011). *A networked self: Identity, community and culture on social network sites.* New York: Routledge.

Proxy. (2016). *Merriam-Webster.* www.merriam-webster.com/dictionary/proxy

Sandvig, C., Hamilton, K., Karahalios, K., & Langhort, C. (2014). Auditing algorithms: Research methods for detecting discrimination on internet platforms. In *Data and discrimination: Converting critical concerns into production inquiry.* Paper presented at preconference for the International Communication Association, Seattle, WA.

Steyerl, H. (2014). Proxy politics: Signal and noise. *e-flux*, December. www.e-flux.com/journal/60/61045/proxy-politics-signal-and-noise/

Thielman, S. (2016). Facebook fired trending team and algorithm without humans goes crazy. *The Guardian*, August. www.theguardian.com/technology/2016/aug/29/facebook-fires-trending-topics-team-algorithm

Tsvetkova, M., García-Gavilanes, R., Floridi, L., & Yasseri, T. (2017). Even good bots fight: The case of Wikipedia. *PLOS ONE*, 12(2), e0171774. doi: 10.1371/journal.pone.0171774

Wagner, C., Mitter, S., Körner, C., & Strohmaier, M. (2012). When social bots attack: Modeling susceptibility of users in online social networks. *CEUR Workshop Proceedings on Making Sense of Microposts*, vol. 838 (pp. 41–48). CEUR-WS.

Weaver, J. F. (2015). Who's responsible when a twitter bot sends a threatening tweet? *Slate*, February 25. www.slate.com/blogs/future_tense/2015/02/25/who_is_responsible_for_death_threats_from_a_twitter_bot.html

Wise, J. M. (1998). Intelligent agency. *Cultural Studies*, 12(3), 410–428. doi: 10.1080/095023898335483

Woolley, S. (2016). Automating power: Social bot interference in global politics. *First Monday*, 21(4). doi: 10.5210/fm.v21i4.6161

Woolley, S. & Guilbeault, D. (2017). Bots aren't just service tools—they're a whole new form of media. *Quartz*, April 10. https://qz.com/954255/bots-are-the-newest-form-of-new-media/

Woolley, S. C. & Howard, P. N. (2016). Introduction: Political communication, computational propaganda, and autonomous agents. *International Journal of Communication*, 10, 9.

6

THE EMOTIONAL ARCHITECTURE OF SOCIAL MEDIA

Karin Wahl-Jorgensen

This chapter traces the political consequences of the emotional architecture of social media. It is part of a larger project of taking seriously the place of emotion in mediated contexts (Wahl-Jorgensen, forthcoming), and views social media as a key site in this respect. As with the architecture of other public spaces, design decisions around the affordances of social media are sometimes *intended* to structure forms of expression, whereas in other cases, the consequences of decisions are coincidental and unexpected by-products. Increasingly, a great deal of thought goes into tailoring emotional architectures toward more positive and pro-social forms of expression—in part as a result of the greater potential to monetize positivity and commodify users' emotional labor. On this basis, the chapter suggests that there is a dynamic and ongoing negotiation of the emotional affordances of social media, which is vital to our formation of networked identities. It considers the case of Facebook's reaction emoji, which exemplifies the ways in which the emotional architecture of social media contributes to the shaping of public debate.

The idea animating this chapter is that the design of public spaces—and the forms of emotional interaction enabled within them—has a concrete impact on the conditions for public debate. Architects, urban planners, and philosophers are among those who have argued that the design of space shapes the public life of communities in the way in which, for example, the presence of playgrounds and green urban spaces allows for children to play outside and adults to meet and interact, while the monumental buildings and sweeping avenues of Fascist states signal the authority of absolute power. The social dynamics of public space enable particular social, political, and cultural formations and agency while discouraging others (Harvey, 2000). For example, Kevin DeLuca and colleagues (2012) have written about the "architecture of oppression." Analyzing the experience of the

Occupy movement, DeLuca and his colleagues suggested that as public spaces have been increasingly privatized and subjected to legal frameworks limiting their use, this has had a detrimental impact on rights of assembly. David Brain (1997) is one of several scholars calling for engagement with processes of architectural production on the basis of their consequences for public life, arguing that "the discipline of design has also played a key role in constructing the symbolic vocabularies and representational practices which shape the experience and interpretation of meaning in the built environment" (p. 240).

In the same way, information architecture, or the architecture of information systems, including virtual environments, has wide-ranging consequences (whether intentional or not) for the types of public interaction and participation possible (e.g. Raboy, 1997). Often, this is referred to as an "information infrastructure."[1] Other metaphors for the interactions between the structuring of space and place and emotional responses call to mind the natural environment. They emphasize complex interactions between the architectures, social visions, and sometimes haphazard decisions that shape the spaces we inhabit. Here, I prefer the term "architecture" because of the connotations of the deliberate design of public space with the intent of encouraging certain kinds of interaction and discouraging others.

All spaces for mediated public participation have particular emotional architectures. For example, the letters to the editor section, one of the most long-lived participatory formats within conventional media, has been characterized by an emphasis on relatively formal contributions written in the language of rationality (e.g. Wahl-Jorgensen, 2007). Newspapers have sought to construct letters sections as a civic and civil public space in which participants are radically accountable for their statements due to the very publicness of their contributions. Contributions which do not conform to norms of civility, rationality, and other key deliberative ideals are excluded from publication by the gatekeepers who make constant decisions which are, among other things, designed to sanitize and improve the neighborhood of public discourse (Wahl-Jorgensen, 2007).

This chapter views emotional architecture as a key factor in shaping engagement with and participation through social media, looking more closely at Facebook. While social media vary in their functionality and focus (Kaplan & Haenlein, 2010), they emphasize an "injunction to share" material, views, and information—personal, social, and political—with others in the network (Hermida, 2014; Van Dijck, 2013). In the United States, upwards of 80% of the population use social media (Statista, 2017b), while in the UK, 59% of the population do so (Think Digital First, 2017). Globally, social media sites account for the majority of time spent online, with a penetration of 37% in 2017 (Kemp, 2017). In this chapter, much of the attention focuses on the emotional architecture of Facebook as the social media site, which is most prominent as a news source, and also the one which has most successfully monetized its activities through the careful architectural policing of emotional expression. As of February

2017, Facebook has close to 2 billion users on a global basis (Fiegerman, 2017), with 214 million users in the United States alone (Statista, 2017a). Close to half of people in the United States use Facebook to access news, and for the vast majority of these audiences, the social media platform is their most important news source (Lichterman, 2016). Industry analysts believe that the site is only increasing its emphasis on news (Read, 2016). What this means is that Facebook now needs to be taken seriously as a major news organization which is shaping our shared conversations—as well as the knowledge we bring to these conversations. The architecture underpinning these conversations—whether visible, through emoji reactions and other affordances, or invisible, through algorithmic curation—is shaped by an explicit concern for managing the emotions of users in a positive and pro-social direction.

I am not alone in taking an interest in how the architecture of social media shapes public debate and interaction. Goodwin and colleagues (2016) have argued that Facebook's architecture promotes particular forms of sharing behavior online, compelling young people to enact a "precarious popularity" through the sharing of images of social alcohol consumption. For Goodwin and colleagues "this expanded imperative to share is a governing dimension of Facebook's overall architecture" (ibid., p. 9). Similarly, Papacharissi (2009) has researched what she referred to as the virtual geographies of social media, specifying an interest in "the underlying structure or architecture of these sites, on the premise that it may set the tone for particular types of interaction" (p. 199). To her, the architecture of social media "is defined as composite result of structure, design and organization" (ibid., p. 205). It does not overdetermine behavior online, but rather creates particular parameters for interaction, which can then be modified, challenged, or resisted by users. As Papacharissi (ibid.) cautions:

> [O]nline social networks simultaneously suggest genres of behavior through their architectural elements and submit the same architectural elements to the behavioral idioms of their users, who customize them to connect better their offline and online interactions. So, while the architecture of social networking sites is suggestive, it does not have to be inherently limiting, depending of course on the culture and orientation of the online social network.
>
> *(p. 203)*

This observation provides a useful reminder of the interaction between human agency and the technological architecture. That is, the range of expression is not overdetermined by the affordances of the emotional architecture, but particular forms might be structurally encouraged. Here, it is worth acknowledging that social media architectures are not narrowly *emotional* but also have a series of other, often closely related, consequences, including political, economic, and social ones. Decisions about whether to enable advertising on a site, whether to allow comments, and whether such comments may be anonymous all contribute to shaping the types of interaction encouraged in the virtual environment.

The increasing ubiquity of social media, the ease of participation, and the varying degrees of publicness and political action associated with them raise important questions about the changing nature of public participation in the networked age. In today's "media life" (Deuze, 2012) where we do not merely *consume* media, but also increasingly live our lives *through* the media—and social media in particular—the complexity of emotional management regimes online increasingly mirrors those prevailing in the offline world. However, social media are far more ontologically complicated than conventional media. Social media challenge conventional divides between the private and the public, the individual and the collective, and the personal and political.

Social media are heavily predicated on deliberate identity construction and self-branding (e.g. Marwick, 2013; Seargent & Tagg, 2014; Thumim, 2012). In the era of the networked self, it is also the case that "to be authentic to yourself, one must first be authentic to others" (Banet-Weiser, 2012, p. 80). The presentation of a desirable self is a key preoccupation of social media participants (e.g. Kaplan & Haenlein, 2010). This self-presentation takes place through what Donath and boyd (2004) described as "public displays of connection," which "serve as important identity signals that help people navigate the networked social world, in that an extended network may serve to validate identity information presented in profiles" (p. 219). This, in turn, means that emotional architectures of social media—ranging from our emotional reactions to news from our private and public life, to our performative alignment with particular causes—are central in facilitating the identity construction of networked selves.

Unlike "old" or "conventional" media, social media are frequently discussed in terms of emotion—both positively and negatively. The dominant narrative surrounding conventional media has emphasized rationality and objectivity, and emotionality has been denigrated as a "bad" object—a corrupting and deviant influence (e.g. Wahl-Jorgensen, 2013). By contrast, social media represent an emerging set of venues in which the elicitation of emotional expression and reaction are explicitly discussed and encouraged by information architects and others involved in crafting their discursive parameters. And these architectural decisions have a profound impact on the potential for political discussion and action.

The Emotional Life of the Virtual World

In the early days of the internet, there was substantial optimism about, and emotional investment in, the potential of the virtual world to bring about democratized forms of public participation. A generation of "cyberoptimists" proclaimed the possibilities of new "virtual communities" to generate "electronic agora" enabling new and liberating forms of participation (e.g. Rheingold, 1993). Early enthusiasts celebrated the creation of a *community* of like-minded individuals—connecting on issues ranging from parenting, health, politics, and gaming through a fairly basic information architecture enabling the formation of groups exchanging text-based information. This celebration was couched in deliberately emotional terms, contrasting their own strong attachment to the coldness and inhumanity usually associated with computers. As Howard Rheingold (1993) wrote in the early days of the Internet:

> The idea of a community accessible only via my computer screen sounded cold to me at first, but I learned quickly that people can feel passionately about e-mail and computer conferences. I've become one of them. I care about these people I met through my computer, and I care deeply about the future of the medium that enables us to assemble. I'm not alone in this emotional attachment to an apparently bloodless technological ritual.
>
> *(p. 2)*

Rheingold's position captures the emotional tenor associated with the excitement over the democratizing potential of networked modes of participation and forms of community available online, invoking "passion" and "care"—deeply embodied emotions that contrast with the understanding of interactions with "cold" and "bloodless" machines. It also represented an early articulation of what many now take for granted: that the machines, cold, bloodless, inorganic, and dispassionate though they may be, are tools for connecting us with distant others in the virtual world for whom we can care as deeply and intimately as those in our immediate physical surroundings.

However, as empirical research began to demonstrate the limitations of the online environment, scholars became more pessimistic about the liberating and empowering potential of the virtual world. An alternative set of arguments emerged, rejecting early cyperoptimist perspectives. The critiques suggested that new media technologies, rather than inevitably bringing about democratic and social utopia, might instead be subject to the same problems that characterize "real-world" encounters, and that these problems might, in fact, be exacerbated by the emotional architecture of the online world.

The anonymous and disembodied nature of interactions online—enabled by the minimally restrictive and "open" architecture of early forums for public participation—appeared to allow participants to dispense with behavioral norms of civility and respect and to engage in incivil behavior through verbal aggression, hostility, and attacks. Observers were particularly interested in investigating anti-social behaviors associated with the expression of negative affect. Drawing on the term "flaming," or "the hostile expression of strong emotions and feelings," scholarly and popular discussions expressed concern about the discursive environments generated by the emotional disinhibition and lack of social control of the online world (e.g. Lea et al., 1992). Early internet scholars thus observed that participants, unmoored from the strictures of social convention, were swearing, name-calling, attacking, and just being plain rude to others whose views they found offensive (Lea et al., 1992).

If anything, these preoccupations have only accelerated with the emergence of social media, particularly in the light of high-profile examples of online hate speech, such as the #gamergate incident which entailed the harassment of women working in the video game industry (Shepherd et al., 2015). This has further intensified in the increasingly polarized political climate following on from the rise of Donald Trump in the United States, and closely related forms of populism in other countries around the world (Karpf, 2017).

Flaming and trolling have been broadly viewed as destructive and anti-social affective behaviors—and are often punished with exclusion and social sanction by virtual communities. They are seen as detrimental to the communities in which they occur, because they constitute deliberate attempts at disrupting communicative norms which ensure pro-social behavior (e.g. Bishop, 2014; Gurdu, 2013).

The preoccupation with bad emotional behavior online is not merely reflected in scholarly debates, but also reverberates in contemporary popular discourse. If anything, the narrative of the online world as a "bad neighborhood" of public participation—an irrational environment dominated by negative affect—is well entrenched. Underpinning popular and media interest is the assumption that such behavior is on the rise. The past few decades have seen growing attention to problems of cyberbullying, especially amongst young people (e.g. Snakenborg et al., 2011). In the U.K., for example, the Crown Prosecution Services issued new legal advice in 2016 on the prosecution of cyberbully cases, including the proliferating use of fake profiles for harassment (Osborne, 2016), and by 2017, police had stepped in to intervene in nearly 6,300 cyberbullying cases in one year, following more than 19,000 reports (Cole, 2017). In the United States, research suggests that more than a quarter of middle and high school students experienced cyberbullying between 2007 and 2016, with figures rising to over a third since 2014 (http://cyberbullying. org/statistics). Melania Trump made cyberbullying her key cause as First Lady during the presidential campaign, even if there has subsequently been little evidence of her plans coming to fruition (Puente, 2017). Concerns about the closely related practice of hate speech online have increased, with new legislative frameworks emerging across the world (Banks, 2010).

The Commodification of Emotional Labor: Encouraging Positive and Pro-Social Expression

As a result of such concerns about the detrimental consequences of anti-social affective expression online, issues around the expression of emotion have been central to the generation of social media architectures. At stake here is the attempt at understanding how the complex motivations and behaviors of individuals map onto the discursive opportunities and restraints constructed in networked environments. Walzer (1986) coined the term "open-minded" public spaces to describe areas designed for multiple and sometimes unforeseen purposes, and in which users "are prepared to tolerate the broad utility of the space" (Fernback, 1994, p. 38). He contrasted these to single-minded public spaces, designed for distinctive purposes and therefore less likely to encourage diverse uses (Walzer, 1986). Early environments for online interaction were characterized by open-mindedness, and came with both dangers and opportunities for particular affectively charged interactions. As Fernback (1994) observed:

> Cyberspace has this "open-minded" quality; users of all stripes flock here, with only the rules of social propriety and "netiquette" to guide them, and engage with one another. Flaming and virtual harassment in cyberspace, like the Spanish Inquisition's *auto-da-fé* ceremony of public torture, illustrate the dark character of CMC's public arena, but this darkness is often the price exacted for the tolerance required to realize and maintain truly open-minded public space.
>
> *(p. 38)*

The vocabulary of open-mindedness versus single-mindedness is problematic in several respects. It gives agency to technologies of space by granting them a mind of their own, and generates a dichotomous opposition between open-mindedness and single-mindedness. Further, in Fernback's (1994) reading, it implies a necessary trade-off between enabling the expression of negative affect and creating the conditions for open discussion and tolerance. At the same time, the distinction is helpful in calling attention to the architecture of virtual worlds, and the ways in which it shapes behavior in public spaces.

Here, I will suggest that even as popular discourses have focused on the expression and elicitation of *negative* emotion online, decisions around the emotional architecture of social media are made to ensure the preponderance of *positive* and *pro-social* emotions, and that this development has palpable consequences for the types of public debate made possible. In an environment where there is increasing pressure for users to express positive emotions, the space for conflict, contestation, and argument are structurally limited.

Historian of emotion William Reddy (2001) suggested that our expression of emotion may be "overlearned" insofar as we, through processes of socialization, learn to channel our emotional reactions into socially acceptable forms. Sociologist Arlie Hochschild (1983), in her study of airlines stewardesses, developed the concept of "emotional labor" to describe the ongoing work that we engage in to maintain relationships. Emotional labor entails the "handling of other people's feelings and our own" (Hochschild, 1983; see also Baym, 2015[2]). Social media both enable and require emotional labor just like the face-to-face interactions they mimic. But unlike the emotional labor of the stewardesses that Hochschild

(1983) studied, social media users are encouraged to engage in unremunerated forms of emotional labor (see also Van Dijck, 2013). The idea that media audiences participate in various forms of unremunerated labor is not a new one. Ever since Dallas Smythe (1981) first discussed the notion of the "audience commodity," scholars have been aware of the fact that audiences/users are actively engaged in the production of value.

Lazzarato (1996) has discussed what he refers to as "immaterial labor"—activities which contribute to producing the cultural content of particular commodities. These forms of labor are not necessarily recognized as work—instead they constitute activities "involved in defining and fixing cultural and artistic standards, fashions, tastes, consumer norms and, more strategically, public opinion" (ibid., p. 137). Drawing on Lazzarato's work, Michael Hardt describes this as "affective" immaterial labor which involves the production and manipulation of affects and requires "human contact and proximity" (Hardt, 1999, p. 93, cited in Andrejevic, 2011a, p. 282). Hardt and Lazzarato thus call attention to the ways in which emotional labor plays a central role in adding value to cultural artifacts. What is distinctive about the emotional labor carried out by social media users is not just its contribution to performative self-branding in public, but also the ways in which it is harnessed by social media organizations for financial gain. Particular forms of emotional expression are structurally encouraged, while others are discouraged. This occasions careful architectural management by those seeking to shape and profit from it. As this chapter will now discuss, in the case of Facebook, the emphasis of the architectural management is on the expression and elicitation of positive and pro-social emotion toward the cultivation of an emotional economy that benefits the social media organization.

The Commercialization of Emotional Labor on Facebook

The emotional architecture of Facebook is a direct result of the site's commercial orientation. As Heyman and Pierson (2015) have noted, through a variety of features, on Facebook, "the private space is subsumed under the commercial space and [. . .] the colonization reconfigures the public space" (p. 1). This "colonization" has several concrete consequences. Mark Andrejevic (e.g. 2011a, 2011b) has pointed to the relative flexibility of Facebook—the way it "can constantly change its capabilities and affordances, and frequently does." It does this to facilitate greater activity by its users, only to exploit that activity by "capturing a broader spectrum of information about user activity" (2011a, p. 280). This allows the site to market products to users more effectively, as well as to sell information about audiences to corporate clients (ibid.). Andrejevic points out that offering a plethora of interactive opportunities and structures, whilst empowering users to engage in gratifying forms of virtual socializing, also represents a somewhat sinister development. This is because this strategy is premised on compiling, aggregating, and classifying information shared by users to sell it on to companies.

It engenders a form of commodified "instrumentalized hyper-sociality" (ibid.) whereby mediated social interaction is exploited for commercial means.

Along those lines, Facebook—like other social media sites—channels social interaction in particular directions designed to maximize user engagement and therefore profits. There is growing pressure to move away from the "open-minded" architecture of early virtual public spaces, and toward a more "single-minded" model. In her examination of the architectures of social media, Papacharissi (2009) argued that Facebook:

> [E]merged as the architectural equivalent of a glass house, with a publicly open structure, which may be manipulated (relatively, at this point) from within to create more or less private spaces. Looseness of behavioral norms obliges users to construct their own, but the network provides tools with which individuals may construct and leave behavioral cues for each other.
>
> *(p. 215)*

The affordances of Facebook may facilitate varied forms of participation, but the site also structurally encourages particular forms of engagement organized around the mobilization of positive and pro-social forms of engagement. For Tim Berners-Lee (2010), Facebook is a "walled garden" whose principles go against the universality and openness so central to the normative premises underpinning the World Wide Web. As Gerlitz and Helmond (2013) put it, "Facebook's very definition of the social web falls together with an increasingly structured, preformatted and traceable web. Being social online means being traced and contributing to value creation for multiple actors including Facebook and external webmasters" (p. 1359). The history of Facebook's reactions emoji highlights the deliberate ways in which the platform has sought to direct its users toward positive and pro-social forms of expression.

Emotional Architectures and Public Debate: The History of Facebook Reaction Emoji

I am here focusing on Facebook reactions emoji as an example of a particularly influential emotional architecture which has significant structuring consequences for public debate online. As Stark and Crawford (2015) have noted, emoji should be seen as "conduits for affective labor in the social networks of informational capitalism" (p. 1). Their incorporation into devices and platforms exemplifies "techniques of computational control" (ibid., p. 2). As such, their use is restrained by the commercial orientation of "informational capital":

> Emoji offer us more than just a cute way of "humanizing" the platforms we inhabit: they also remind us of how informational capital continually

> seeks to instrumentalize, analyze, monetize, and standardize affect. Representations of feeling in general, and happiness in particular, are often painted across the exterior of money-making ventures. Emoji are an exuberant form of social expression but they are also just another means to lure consumers to a platform, to extract data from them more efficiently, and to express a normative, consumerist, and predominantly cheery world-view.
>
> *(Ibid., p. 8)*

The distinctive history of Facebook's reactions emoji shows how the site's emotional architecture generates a commodified affect control structure which calls for universalized expressions of emotion which can, at the same time, be easily aggregated (e.g. Pariser, 2011). Facebook's first step toward structuring reactions toward positive and pro-social forms of emotion took place when the Like button was introduced in 2009. The button was rolled out on Facebook in February 2009, and across the Internet from 2010 (Gerlitz & Helmond, 2013). With the introduction of the button, it became possible to "Like" "status updates, photos, links or comments. Initially only available within the platform, the Like came with a counter showing the total number of likes as well as the names of friends who clicked it" (ibid., p. 1352). It was presented "as a shortcut to commenting in order to replace short affective statements like 'Awesome' and 'Congrats!' (ibid.). Indeed, Facebook's Like button feature was, for a month during the design process, known as the "Awesome" button until the design team decided on "Like" as a more universal expression of positive affect (Pariser, 2011, p. 149). The Like button was rolled out across the Web in 2010.

Following on from its introduction, the button had a major impact on the online business environment, occasioning widespread discussion of how to make money from the "Like Economy" (e.g. Carter, 2013), which also involves the labor of users as both social activity and one which produces value for the company (Gerlitz and Helmond, 2013).

The universalizable positivity of the Like button was celebrated among social media marketers. For example, Ayelet Noff (2011), the CEO of social media PR company Blonde 2.0, argued that "Facebook is a social community and in order to survive there needs to be positivity in the air. Negative energy can only lead to negative content which in turn would harm such a network." When media architectures and content are first and foremost designed to facilitate consumption, there is a strong pressure for light-hearted and positive content, which creates a "buying mood" (Baker, 1995).

The Like button reflects the dominance of what Pariser (2011) referred to as a "friendly world syndrome." Pariser suggested that "the stories that get the most attention on Facebook are the stories that get the most Likes, and the stories that get the most Likes are, well, more likable" (ibid., p. 149). These observations highlight how the emotional architecture of Facebook has concrete consequences for the tone of public discourse by generating an environment where light-hearted, positive content is emphasized over weightier "bad news" stories which might involve important social, political, and personal issues. Other scholars studying the phenomenon across social media have suggested that there is a prevalent "positivity bias" (e.g. Reinecke & Trepte, 2014) which means that social media users are overwhelmingly likely to share posts expressing positive emotion as they seek to construct desirable networked selves (Utz, 2015). The picture of the online world of public interaction drawn by these observations is a very different place from the hostile, uncivil neighborhood discerned in earlier analyses of online public participation. It suggests that if audiences increasingly use Facebook as a news source, they will view the world through glasses tinted by emotional positivity.

The dominance of the Like button—and the positivity it encouraged—generated significant critical debate. In 2012, a campaign on Facebook to add a Dislike button garnered three million people signatures. The idea of a dislike button was rejected by Facebook "on the grounds that it would sow too much negativity" (Frier, 2016), reflecting the company's concern with maintaining a positive discursive neighborhood. Nonetheless, the company continued to grapple with the problem of ensuring that its architecture facilitates the measurement and expression of user emotions as accurately as possible, while directing these emotions toward greater positivity. Since 2009, Facebook has hosted "Compassion Research Days" where programmers have considered how best to tinker with the site's features to facilitate the expression of compassion. At the 2013 meeting, programmers proposed introducing a "sympathize" button (Meyer, 2013). *Atlantic* technology editor Robinson Meyer (2013) speculated that, "Facebook may be reluctant to add too many buttons that signify specific emotions. Give users options—Like, or *sympathize?*—and they may feel like neither gets at their feelings."

Despite such concerns, Facebook made it a priority to build into its architecture a more nuanced palette of human emotions. By September 2015, Facebook announced the decision to roll out "a technical way to express regret or sympathy in a situation" (Meyer, 2015). As *Slate*'s Will Oremus (2015) observed:

> [I]t makes sense for Facebook to consider some alternatives, because understanding when users are expressing things like sympathy, outrage, or laughter rather than approval will help Facebook fine-tune its newsfeed algorithms. More nuanced responses means more data for Facebook to mine and monetize—and if you dislike that, then you're on the wrong social network.

This observation points to the fact that Facebook has been a key driver of the emergence of an "emotional economy," where emotional engagement serves as a commercial currency, and its accurate elicitation and measurement translates into commercial gain. As *Forbes*'s Amit Chowdhry (2016) noted:

> If Facebook offers an ideal mix of content for its users, then it would be able to ensure that users spend more time on the social network. And users that spend more time on the social network will see more ads, thus generating additional revenue.

Facebook's decision to roll out additional reactions was based on the aim of giving

> users more authentic ways to quickly and easily respond to posts, whether they are sad, serious, funny or happy. Before emoji "Reactions," users were often put in the awkward position of resorting to "liking" a post about a death or one that expressed frustration or disappointment, without distinction from how one would "like" an engagement photo.
>
> *(Chaykowski, 2016)*

Extensive research went into the design of the reactions emoji. Facebook worked with linguistics scholars to analyze the sentiments expressed most frequently by users in their comments in stickers, emoji, and one-word reactions, seeking to distill this range of reactions into a manageable set of universalizable emoji (Stinson, 2016):

> People used the hearts-in-the-eyes emoji more than any other. They were also prone to expressing humor, sadness, and shock through visual means. The team took a subset of reactions that cut across the emotional spectrum and removed redundancies like sympathy and sadness, and joy and love. Then they tested them with users . . . Reactions needed to fulfill two main criteria: universality and expressivity.

The reactions emoji were rolled out in February 2016 and included, in addition to the existing "Like" button, Love, Haha, Wow, Sad, and Angry, as shown in Figure 6.1.

The reactions emoji share a pro-social orientation: although they do enable negative emotions ("Sad" and "Angry"), they function first and foremost to

| Like | Love | Haha | Wow | Sad | Angry |

FIGURE 6.1 Facebook reactions emoji

facilitate the easy expression of sympathy for the poster in response to "Bad news" disclosures—whether personal or political. Further, they were introduced into a particular expressive environment whose architecture was premised on positive and pro-social emotional expression. And the algorithmic curation of user timelines ensures that the posts with the most likes continue to figure most prominently. This facilitates the persistence of the "Friendly World Syndrome," while enabling a more nuanced regulation of the diversity content based on emotional reactions.

Facebook is not the only social media organization to erect emotional architectures for commercial gain, but the prominent example of its reactions emoji highlights the fact that the "positivity bias" of social media has been carefully engineered. It operates alongside the algorithmic curation of content to profoundly shape the horizons for public debate and networked identity construction.

The evolution of reactions emoji is the most prominent example of the ways in which Facebook has sought to direct the emotions of its users. Other high-profile—and perhaps more controversial—examples include the large-scale "emotional contagion" experiment that Facebook carried out in 2014 on almost 700,000 users without their knowledge or consent. In this experiment, they demonstrated an emotional contagion effect by manipulating user newsfeeds:

> When positive expressions were reduced, people produced fewer positive posts and more negative posts; when negative expressions were reduced, the opposite pattern occurred. These results indicate that emotions expressed by others on Facebook influence our own emotions, constituting experimental evidence for massive-scale contagion via social networks.
>
> *(Kramer et al., 2014, 8788)*

More recently, Facebook has been granted a patent to use smartphone cameras and webcams to monitor user feelings and use it to deliver content and advertising tailored to their moods (Billington, 2017). These examples illustrate how Facebook's architectural practices—as well as future plans—foreground emotion as the driver of user engagement. But it also shows us that the social media organization, as one of the most influential news platforms in the world, has little hesitation in the manipulation of users—in terms of the news they are exposed to, and the emotions they experience as a result—for the purpose of commercial gain. Along those lines, our networked selves also constitute emotional selves. And these networked emotional selves, it seems, are shaped by the platform architecture to afford only a limited range of emotion.

Conclusion

If Facebook is now the world's most important news medium, the ontology that underpins the architecture of the platform matters hugely to the public sphere.

The centrality of emotion in shaping the architecture of Facebook shows a paradigm shift in thinking about public debate as it takes place through social media. Whereas emotion has long been vilified as an enemy of rationality in the public sphere, it is now at the forefront of the concerns of the architects designing the social media platforms through which so many of us get our news.

The history of the Facebook emoji reactions highlights the commodification and marketization of public emotion, or what we might characterize as the emotional economy of our mediatized world. In particular, the privileging of pro-social positive emotion has coincided with the colonization of the public sphere by corporate interests. These corporations are more interested in targeting and tailoring content to interested consumers than in creating the conditions for a diverse public debate which has inevitable affective components that come in both positive and negative forms. If our news consumption increasingly takes place in environments predicated on the architectural management and algorithmic manipulation of our emotions, it is more important than ever to take emotion seriously as an object of study, and to understand its central place in public life.

Notes

1 In comparison to "architecture," the notion of "infrastructure" is far more strongly connected to ideas of transportation and efficiency.
2 For Baym (2015), relational labor is distinctive from emotional labor, as stipulated by Hochschild (1983), because it is ongoing and tied to economic contexts. However, these features could be seen as central to Hochschild's original conception of emotional labor.

References

Andrejevic, M. (2011a). Surveillance and alienation in the online economy. *Surveillance & Society*, 8(3), 278–287.
Andrejevic, M. (2011b). The work that affective economics does. *Cultural Studies*, 25(4–5), 604–620.
Baker, C. E. (1995). *Advertising and a democratic press*. Princeton: Princeton University Press.
Banet-Weiser, S. (2012). *Authentic: The politics of ambivalence in a brand culture*. New York: New York University Press.
Banks, J. (2010). Regulating hate speech online. *International Review of Law, Computers & Technology*, 24(3), 233–239.
Baym, N. (2015). Connect with your audience! The relational labor of connection. *The Communication Review*, 18, 14–22.
Berners-Lee, T. (2010). Long live the web: A call for continued open standards and neutrality. *Scientific American*. www.scientificamerican.com/article.cfm?id=long-live-the-web
Billington, J. (2017). Facebook wants to secretly watch you through your smartphone camera. *Ibtimes*. www.ibtimes.co.uk/facebook-wants-secretly-watch-you-through-your-smartphone-camera-1625061?utm_source=social&utm_medium=facebook&utm_

campaign=%2Ffacebook-wants-secretly-watch-you-through-your-smartphone-cam
era-1625061

Bishop, J. (2014). Representations of "trolls" in mass media communication: A review of
media-texts and moral panics relating to "internet trolling." *International Journal of Web
Based Communities*, 10(1), 7–24.

Brain, D. (1997). From public housing to private communities: The discipline of design
and the materialization of the public/private distinction in the built environment. In
J. Weintraub and K. Kumar (Eds.), *Public and private in thought and practice* (pp. 237–267).
Chicago and London: University of Chicago Press.

Carter, B. (2013). *The like economy: How businesses make money with Facebook.* Indianapolis,
IN: Que Publishing.

Chaykowski, K. (2016). Facebook no longer just has a "like" button, thanks to global
launch of emoji "reactions." *Forbes*, February 24. www.forbes.com/sites/kathleen
chaykowski/2016/02/24/facebook-no-longer-just-has-a-like-button-thanks-to-
global-launch-of-emoji-reactions/#44635689692d

Chowdhry, A. (2016). Facebook emoji "reactions": Are there ulterior motives? *Forbes*,
February 29. www.forbes.com/sites/amitchowdhry/2016/02/29/facebook-reactions/
#5c920fe31a62

Cole, H. (2017). Throw the book at them. *The Sun*, May 7. www.thesun.co.uk/
news/3502815/police-called-to-step-in-into-nearly-6300-cyber-bulling-incidents-
on-facebook-last-year-prompting-fresh-fears-social-media-giants-not-doing-enough-
to-tackle-abuse/

DeLuca, K.M., Lawson, S., & Sun, Y. (2012). Occupy Wall Street on the public screens
of social media: The many framings of the birth of a protest movement. *Communication,
Culture & Critique*, 5(4), 483–509.

Deuze, M. (2012). *Media life.* Cambridge: Polity.

Donath, J. & boyd, d. (2004). Public displays of connection. *BT Technology Journal*, 22(4),
71–82.

Fernback, J. (1994). The individual within the collective: Virtual ideology and the realization of collective principles. In Jones, S. (Ed.), *Virtual culture: Identity and communication
in cybersociety* (pp. 36–54). Newbury Park, CA: Sage.

Fiegerman, S. (2017). Facebook is closing in on 2 billion users. *CNN*, February 1. http://
money.cnn.com/2017/02/01/technology/facebook-earnings/index.html

Frier, S. (2016). Inside Facebook's decision to blow up the like button. *Bloomberg, Business-
week*, January 27. www.bloomberg.com/features/2016-facebook-reactions-chris-cox/

Gerlitz, C. & Helmond, A. (2013). The like economy: Social buttons and the data-
intensive web. *New Media & Society*, 15(8), 1348–1365.

Goodwin, I., Griffin, C., Lyons, A., McCreanor, T., & Moewaka Barnes, H. (2016). Precarious popularity: Facebook drinking photos, the attention economy, and the regime
of the branded self. *Social Media + Society*, 2(1). doi: 10.1177/2056305116628889

Gurdu, C. (2013). Codes of ethics in discussion forums. In J. Bishop (Ed.), *Examining the
concepts, issues and implications of internet trolling.* Hershey, PA: IGI Global.

Hardt, M. (1999). Affective labor. *boundary 2*, 26(2), 89–100.

Harvey, D. (2000). *Spaces of hope.* Berkeley: University of California Press.

Hermida, A. (2014). *Tell everyone: Why we share and why it matters.* Toronto: Doubleday
Canada.

Heyman, R. & Pierson, J. (2015). Social media, delinguistification and colonization of
lifeworld: Changing faces of Facebook. *Social Media + Society*, 1(2). doi: 10.1177/2056
305115621933

Hochshild, A.R. (1983). *The managed heart: Commercialization of human feeling.* Berkeley, CA: University of California Press.

Kaplan, A.M. & Haenlein, M. (2010). Users of the world, unite! The challenges and opportunities of Social Media. *Business Horizons* 53(1), 59–68.

Karpf, D. (2017). Digital politics after Trump. *Annals of the International Communication Association*, 41(2), 198–207.

Kemp, S. (2017). Digital in 2017: Global overview. *We are social*, January 24. https://wearesocial.com/uk/special-reports/digital-in-2017-global-overview.

Kramer, A.D., Guillory, J.E., & Hancock, J.T. (2014). Experimental evidence of massive-scale emotional contagion through social networks. *Proceedings of the National Academy of Sciences*, 111(24), 8788–8790.

Lazzarato, M. (1996). Immaterial labour. http://strickdistro.org/wp-content/uploads/2011/09/Week-1_Immaterial-Labour_Lazzarato.pdf

Lea, M., O'Shea, T., Fung, P., & Spears, R. (1992). *"Flaming" in computer-mediated communication: Observations, explanations, implications.* London: Harvester Wheatsheaf.

Lichterman, J. (2016). Nearly half of U.S. adults get news on Facebook, Pew Says. *Nieman Lab*, May 26, www.niemanlab.org/2016/05/pew-report-44-percent-of-u-s-adults-get-news-on-facebook/

Marwick, A.E. (2013). *Status update: Celebrity, publicity, and branding in the social media age.* New Haven: Yale University Press.

Meyer, R. (2013). Facebook considers adding a "sympathize" button. *The Atlantic*, December 13. www.theatlantic.com/technology/archive/2013/12/facebook-considers-adding-a-sympathize-button/282126/

Meyer, R. (2015). Facebook says it's introducing a "dislike" button. *The Atlantic*, September 15. www.theatlantic.com/technology/archive/2015/09/facebook-says-its-introducing-a-dislike-button/405514/

Noff, A. (2011) Happy birthday to Facebook's Like button. *Socialmedia.biz*, April 22. www.socialmedia.biz/2011/04/22/facebooks-like-button/

Oremus, W. (2015). Is Facebook finally building a "dislike" button? Not exactly. *Slate*, Sept 15. www.slate.com/blogs/future_tense/2015/09/15/facebook_dislike_button_not_exactly_mark_zuckerberg_confirms_new_buttons.html

Osborne, C. (2016). UK to prosecute online trolls, cyberbullies and fake account creators. *ZDNET*, March 3. www.zdnet.com/article/uk-to-prosecute-online-trolls-cyberbullies-and-fake-account-creators/

Papacharissi, Z. (2009). The virtual geographies of social networks: A comparative analysis of Facebook, LinkedIn and ASmallWorld. *New Media & Society*, 11(1–2), 199–220.

Pariser, E. (2011). *The filter bubble: What the Internet is hiding from you.* London: Penguin.

Puente, M. (2017). What's up with Melania Trump's cyber bullying campaign? It's "a work in progress." *USA Today*, May 9. www.usatoday.com/story/life/people/2017/05/09/whats-happening-melania-trumps-cyberbullying-campaign-not-much-yet/101212182/

Raboy, M. (1997). Cultural sovereignty, public participation, and democratization of the public sphere: The Canadian debate on the new information infrastructure. In B. Kahin & E.J. Wilson (Eds.), *National information infrastructure vision and policy design* (pp. 190–216). Cambridge MA and London: MIT Press.

Read, A. (2016). Where social media is headed in 2017: The biggest trends to watch for. *BufferSocial.* https://blog.bufferapp.com/state-of-social-media

Reddy, W. (2001). *The navigation of feelings: A framework for the history of emotions.* Cambridge: Cambridge University Press.

Reinecke, L. & Trepte, S. (2014). Authenticity and well-being on social network sites: A two-wave longitudinal study on the effects of online authenticity and the positivity bias in SNS communication. *Computers in Human Behavior*, 30, 95–102.

Rheingold, H. (1993). *The virtual community: Homesteading on the electronic frontier*. Cambridge, MA: Addison Wesley.

Seargeant, P. & Tagg, C. (Eds.). (2014). *The language of social media: Identity and community on the Internet*. Berlin: Springer.

Shepherd, T., Harvey, A., Jordan, T., Sray, S., & Miltner, K. (2015). Histories of hating. *Social Media + Society*, 1(2). doi: 10.1177/2056305115603997

Smythe, D. W. (1981). The audience commodity and its work. In D. W. Smythe (Ed.), *Dependency road. Communications, capitalism, consciousness, and Canada* (pp. 22–51). Norwood, NJ: Ablex.

Snakenborg, J., Van Acker, R., & Gable, R. A. (2011). Cyberbullying: Prevention and intervention to protect our children and youth. *Preventing School Failure: Alternative Education for Children and Youth*, 55(2), 88–95.

Stark, L. & Crawford, K. (2015). The conservatism of emoji: Work, affect, and communication. *Social Media + Society*, 1(2). doi: 10.1177/2056305115604853

Statista. (2017a). Number of Facebook users in the United States as of January 2017, by age group (in millions). www.statista.com/statistics/398136/us-facebook-user-age-groups/

Statista. (2017b). Percentage of U.S. population who currently use any social media from 2008 to 2017. www.statista.com/statistics/273476/percentage-of-us-population-with-a-social-network-profile/

Stinson, E. (2016). Facebook reactions, the totally redesigned Like button, is here. *Wired*, February 24. www.wired.com/2016/02/facebook-reactions-totally-redesigned-like-button/

Think Digital First. (2017). The demographics of social media users in 2017. www.think digitalfirst.com/2016/01/04/the-demographics-of-social-media-users-in-2016/

Thumim, N. (2012). *Self-representation and digital culture*. London: Palgrave Macmillan.

Utz, S. (2015). The function of self-disclosure on social network sites: Not only intimate, but also positive and entertaining self-disclosures increase the feeling of connection. *Computers in Human Behavior*, 45, 1–10.

Van Dijck, J. (2013). *The culture of connectivity: A critical history of social media*. Oxford: Oxford University Press.

Wahl-Jorgensen, K. (2007). *Journalists and the public*. Creskill, NJ: Hampton Press.

Wahl-Jorgensen, K. (2013). Future directions for political communication scholarship: Considering emotion in mediated public participation. In K. A. Gates (Ed.) *Media Studies Futures* (pp. 455–478). New York: Blackwell.

Wahl-Jorgensen, K. (forthcoming). *Emotions, media and politics*. Cambridge: Polity Press.

Walzer, M. (1986). Pleasures and costs of urbanity. *Dissent*, Fall, 470–475.

7

"THE MORE I LOOK LIKE JUSTIN BIEBER IN THE PICTURES, THE BETTER"

Queer Women's Self-Representation on Instagram

Stefanie Duguay

> I've had somebody recently ask me if I was a boy or a girl, so I had to clarify and let him know, yes, I'm a lesbian female and I dress as a male. But like, it's just me. You know what I mean? Like, I live *me* so I don't think it's different but I guess I have to explain to people who don't know. So when I hashtag "lesbian," it's basically, I'm just letting them know what I like and my lifestyle.
>
> *@kelzz32*

Kelzz explained her reasons for including #lesbian among the multiple hashtags she added to her Instagram photos. Her excitement about recently gaining followers and getting her videos noticed was tangible throughout our Skype call. Living in the western United States, she works most days at a warehouse but spends the rest of her time practicing hip-hop and urban dancing. She planned to go on tour with her dance partner soon, hoping that the attention she received for her dance videos on Instagram would attract audiences sizable enough to pay for their trip. Her identification as lesbian was evident from her hashtags and also implied in her fashion style and flirty messages directed at female audiences. Rather than maintaining this aspect of her identity separate from her career aspirations, it was fully integrated throughout her self-representation on Instagram.

In this chapter, I share the experiences of eight queer female[1] Instagrammers to demonstrate how sexual identity features in their networked self-representations on this platform. I view self-representations on Instagram—photos, videos, and the interactions surrounding them—as the building blocks for networked stories of the self that individuals shape and curate through platform affordances. Working with Alice Marwick's (2015) observation that gaining attention on

Instagram requires a combination of microcelebrity practices and stylized references to celebrity and popular culture, I identify how these women incorporate sexual identity into their integration of these self-representational approaches. Microcelebrity has long comprised a set of practices that users of participatory digital media adopt in order to forge connections with audiences (Senft, 2008). In her early work, Theresa Senft (2008) pioneered this concept, identifying that microcelebrity involves reflectivity, reflecting a desired image to oneself and others, reflexivity in the form of ongoing dialogue with audiences, and refraction in the way that various audiences perceive self-representations differently. Marwick (2016) points out that microcelebrity approaches shift across social media platforms, adapting to their technological affordances and social contexts. I integrate these notions to examine how queer women's reflectivity, reflexivity, and management of refraction with regard to sexual identity can forge the strategically intimate connections required for microcelebrity while also referencing the styles and popular cultures that garner notoriety on Instagram. This notoriety, often measured by follower counts, is what Marwick (2015) terms "Instafame." Recognizing these approaches to self-representation on Instagram highlights platform affordances, constraints, and challenges that queer women face in posting images and making connections that convey a desired networked self. It also demonstrates everyday users' creativity and agency in producing self-representations in the service of their personal and economic aspirations.

Queer Women's Mediated Representation

Instagram first caught my attention because it struck me as presenting different opportunities for queer women's representation from those perpetuated through broadcast media. Prior to the 1990s, LGBTQ people were largely absent from screen media, with one-off episodes introducing gay characters for dramatic effect but denying them focal plot lines or on screen relationships (Walters, 2001). This lack of visibility was intensified for queer women, whom Terry Castle (1993) describes as being subject to a "ghost effect." Their invisibility stems from women's sexuality being conceivable only in relation to men's sexuality due to gender discourses that deny women sexual agency (Jagose, 2002). Therefore, it is no surprise that the increase in queer women's representation throughout the 1990s was termed "lesbian chic," as television, film, and magazines depicted queer women as normatively feminine to retain male audiences (Ciasullo, 2001). This trend has continued into the 2000s, with the rise of "heteroflexible" (Diamond, 2005) characters and celebrities who perform hyperfemininity and interact with each other sexually for men's attention, such as Madonna and Britney Spears kissing at the 2003 MTV Video Music Awards. While queer women's alternative media, such as zines and feminist music (Allen, 1997; Collins, 1999; Sport, 2007), have included a range of gender representations and targeted queer audiences, several decades of broadcast media have portrayed narrow representations of queer women in relation to men's sexual desires.

While today's representation of queer women in television, film, and streaming online media is more diverse, it still tends toward heteronormativity and other normative categories of identity to attract mainstream audiences. Smith and Tyler (2017) assert that contemporary media depictions of lesbians that appear to be groundbreaking actually reinforce post-feminist values. They analyze an episode in *Coronation Street*, a show with typically older audiences, which purports to push boundaries by including a lesbian wedding. However, the characters' feminine, white wedding dresses and traditional marriage ceremony reinforce the patriarchal gender roles and heteronormativity that post-feminism elides. This scene reflects a general tendency toward "gaystreaming" (Ng, 2013) in which shows cast white, upper middle-class LGBTQ characters who appeal to multiple audiences through their exhibition of lavish, luxury lifestyles. Julia Himberg (2014) identifies this trend in television shows with lesbian characters and critiques it as ignoring "the realities of most sexual minorities, particularly sexual minorities of colour, of lower socioeconomic status, and those in rural and conservative parts of the country" (p. 300). While there are exceptions, such as *The Wire*'s multiple African American and non-gender conforming lesbian characters (Dhaenens & Van Bauwel, 2012), gaystreaming remains prevalent across popular broadcast media. Even LGBTQ YouTubers support their careers as "social media entrepreneurs" (Cunningham et al., 2016) by valorizing gender norms and idealized lifestyles. For example, popular YouTuber Ingrid Nilsen's make-up tutorials appeal to heterosexual audiences and corporate sponsors alike. Since many of the most visible representations of queer women today still frequently involve white, feminine, and upper middle-class individuals, I became interested in how queer women's self-representations on Instagram deviated from, reproduced, or remixed these in various ways.

Microcelebrity and Instafame

Microcelebrity involves ways of relating to audiences that developed with earlier forms of participatory technology and have shifted with the introduction of new platforms. Senft (2008) first described microcelebrity in her study of camgirls, women using webcams in the late 1990s to share about their lives. She explained that while conventional celebrity is generally tied to capital (fame supported by large amounts of money), which separates celebrities from "average" people, microcelebrity involves forging a connection with the audience, regardless of capital and without guarantee of profit. As Senft observed camgirls' everyday lives, she noted three themes of microcelebrity in their activity, which included: reflectivity, as mediated self-representations served "as mirrors for those who choose to display themselves to the world"; reflexivity as "the way our dialectical exchanges place us in a continual feedback loop with others"; and refraction, occurring "when one person's definition of public is another's definition of private or professional" (p. 34). These themes of microcelebrity practice show how individuals share reflections of themselves that forge connections with audiences and, in turn, must be managed in how they are received.

As microcelebrity practices have become integrated into everyday users' approaches to self-representation on social media, scholars have built upon this concept. Later observing the proliferation of microcelebrity practices, Senft (2013) further defines microcelebrity as the contemporary imperative for individuals to form a coherent, branded self through social media. Alison Hearn (2008) notes that social media enable individuals to build inventories of branded selves, which serve as commodities for public consumption. Through social media's affordances, individuals engage in the labor of producing "a public persona that might be of practical or relational use" (ibid., p. 213) within unstable neoliberal economies. Brooke Duffy (2016) pinpoints this labor as central in many women's use of social media for creative entrepreneurship. She conceptualizes it as "aspirational labour" constituting "creative activities that hold the promise of social and economic capital" (ibid., p. 443). Aspirational laborers brand themselves through intimate displays of authenticity, forging affective relationships, and demonstrating brand devotion in ways that reinforce gendered histories of using women's bodies to sell commodities. Through these recent studies and critiques, it is clear that contemporary microcelebrity involves the labor of self-branding within economic and gendered systems of inequality.

Instagram provides a particular set of technological affordances and social context for microcelebrity and self-branding practices. In my previous work, a close reading of the app's interface and company materials revealed an emphasis on visual aesthetics, as Instagram's features and discursive materials encourage users to transform their photos into "works of art" (Duguay, 2016). Noting this focus on visuals resonates with Marwick's (2015) observations about Instafame as a platform-specific variety of microcelebrity. With Instagram's emphasis on images and the dominance of selfie-taking, she argues that direct relationships with audiences take a backseat to visual self-presentation. Instafamous users attract audiences by reproducing "conventional status hierarchies of luxury, celebrity, and popularity that depend on the ability to emulate the visual iconography of mainstream celebrity culture" (ibid., p. 139). In her analysis of highly followed accounts, she found that microcelebrity on Instagram rests on the ability to produce stylized visuals, displays of conspicuous consumption, and references to celebrity culture. Crystal Abidin's (2016) study of "Influencers" in Singapore also supports notions of an Instagram-specific variety of microcelebrity. Influencers gain attention and subsequent commercial profits through their use of high-end digital cameras to produce sleek selfies, showcasing luxury commodities and lifestyles. As these studies demonstrate cases of Instafame enacted by highly popular users, this raised questions for me regarding how queer women might negotiate Instafame in their everyday Instagram use.

Investigating Representations on Instagram

Aiming to understand queer women's representations on Instagram and the platform's influence on these representations, I engaged with multiple methods that built upon each other. Mentioned earlier, I conducted a close reading of Instagram using the walkthrough method (Light et al., 2016) to examine the app's affordances and the way the company framed its purpose for users. With this foundational knowledge about the app, I used textual analysis (McKee, 2003) to examine more than 400 photos with hashtags related to queer women (e.g. #lezzigram, #lesbehonest, #girlswholikegirls). The majority of content was split between pornographic/solicitous images selling sexual services (e.g. pornography subscriptions) and individuals' representations of themselves and their everyday lives, often in the form of selfies. Focusing on individual users' self-representations, I sifted through hundreds of images of everyday women who were smiling at the camera, flexing in front of the mirror, on holidays with their partners, or posting in other poses and locations. I knew I needed to speak with them to understand what they considered when creating their self-representations: what were they trying to depict and for what outcomes? What did it mean to them to include queer hashtags or other indicators of their sexual identity?

I gathered interview participants by sending direct messages through Instagram to women whose self-representations appeared in my content sample. Six responded and two more approached me after I posted about my study on Facebook and Twitter. I held Skype or telephone interviews with eight women in total, who ranged in age from 24 to 46, lived in Australia, Canada, Thailand, and the United States, came from a range of ethnic backgrounds, and worked in many different sectors. All participants identified as women, with one additionally identifying as genderqueer, one as gender non-conforming, and another as transfemale. Seven participants identified as lesbian and one identified as gay. Some participants asked me to include their Instagram username to give credit to their photos and publicize their accounts; I have included these upon first mentioning a participant and have otherwise used pseudonyms for those who did not wish to be identifiable.

This chapter focuses on my interview data because it most clearly captures a variety of queer women's approaches to self-representation on Instagram. Throughout my analysis, it became clear that participants' self-representations involved at least some forms of microcelebrity practice as aspirational labor toward economic and/or personal aims. Kelzz dreamed of making it big with her dancing and leaving her warehouse job. Alex (@a1exthehuman) created a second account (@dapperdykes) to promote her clothing line for gender non-conforming people. Emi showcased her tattoo business while her girlfriend Queenie (@Queenie_von_curves) promoted her modeling and burlesque shows. Kamala hoped to draw bookings for her motivational-speaking seminars and Julie spread the word about her children's yoga and recreational programs. Those without economic motivations still sought to build a particular reputation: Thea portrayed herself as a well-read college student and Mïta (@mitagibson) advocated for trans rights as a vocal trans activist. Indicators of sexual identity were prominent throughout their aspirational labor and were communicated through enduring microcelebrity practices and Instafamous tactics. Senft's (2008) themes of microcelebrity as involving reflectivity, reflexivity, and the negotiation of refraction were evident as individuals shared intimately about their sexual identity to forge relationships with audiences. These women's labor of producing stylized images, displaying commodities related to sexual identity, and referencing popular, recognizable forms of "lesbian" or queer identity were also interwoven throughout microcelebrity themes. The following sections investigate this integration of microcelebrity and Instafamous strategies more closely as queer women enacted them in their networked self-representations.

Reflective Identity Building

Participants included intimate portrayals of sexual identity to forge relationships with audiences while engaging in popular platform practices and referencing queer culture to construct a reflection of their perceived "self" personally and for broader audiences. They largely achieved this by using hashtags, displaying relationships, and posting strategically tailored selfies. In the opening quote, Kelzz described hashtags like #lesbian as an indicator of "what I like and my lifestyle." This highlights how such hashtags enable her to personally claim a particular sexual identity while also referencing a collectively constructed lesbian "lifestyle" outside of the norm. Alex also seamlessly strung together these aspects of personal and broader reference, "If I feel like I look really gay, I probably will use #gay just, again, it's a big part of my identity." She discusses #gay as essential to her identity while also noting that she often "looks gay," as a reference to overarching notions of gay fashion and styles. Therefore, sexual identity hashtags serve as a personal declaration while also connecting individuals with the volumes of other Instagram users who also incorporate these hashtags in their self-representational practices. Several participants used broad and specific sexual identity terms for these dual purposes. Mïta used #translesbian to reflect her identity and also because "#lesbian is such a big cloud . . . that's when you have to get into the multiple hashtags . . . to kind of filter people, like, to funnel people that are similar to you." Resembling how Instafamous users reference luxury lifestyles (Marwick, 2015), sexual identity hashtags reference LGBTQ lifestyles made imaginable through media representation, stereotypes, and commercialization. Instead of sticking with particular identity labels, participants often used multiple sexual identity hashtags, such as #lesbiansofinstagram with #dykesofinstagram, to reflect their membership in such lifestyles in order to gain LGBTQ followers and queer-friendly audiences.

For participants in relationships, references to their partners reflected personal aspects of identity while also often tying into broader cultural references. Julie aimed to be out on Instagram but was still concerned about homophobic parents boycotting her children's programs. She occasionally posted subtle couple selfies to portray her sexual identity:

> I think it's very hard for me to actually communicate my identity as a lesbian in a selfie without being with my partner because of—in terms of the way people sort of stereotype LGBT people, I don't think I necessarily fulfill any of the stereotypes.

Since her appearance did not signal her sexual identity according to collective notions of queerness and she did not want to turn off audiences through overt sexual identity hashtags, Julie worked small displays of affection toward her partner into her photos. However, since queer women in relationships are often disregarded as platonic "gal pals" (McBean, 2016), other participants displayed their relationships alongside more salient references to sexual identity and LGBTQ popular culture. Emi described the unique "couple hashtag" she created with Queenie, #rainbowdashandsoarin4ever: "My girlfriend has rainbow hair and so she gets called Rainbow Dash a lot and then my, uh, drag persona that I have is, looks a lot like the other pony, Soarin. So we've decided those are our names." The hashtag references *My Little Pony*, a show that has been appropriated by LGBTQ online fandom communities that reimagine the characters as queer.[2] The couple combines this personal hashtag with popular platform practices. Queenie remarked to Emi, "I #moonday-ed your butt" and showed me a couple selfie she posted as part of the platform trend of sharing a butt-related photo on Mondays. The photo displays the women in matching rainbow underwear showing off tattoos representing their *My Little Pony* personas. Couples' self-representations are personal portrayals of sexual identity and intimate relationships. They can also appeal to broader audiences by reproducing platform trends, mimicking celebrity practices of posting couple selfies (e.g. Bayley, 2017), and referencing popular culture.

Participants who were not posing with partners in selfies relied on styles associated with lesbian stereotypes or queer fashion in their self-representations. Thea described one of her selfies as "actually a very staged photo" and noted that wearing a backwards hat was a key component of the photo because it was

> a lesbian thing. Actually, like I wear a lot of backwards hats to sort of make a statement to people who—because I don't—because I think I look straight, so it sort of lets people know . . . so yeah, other lesbians are going to know, generally.

With her otherwise feminine appearance, Thea adopted the backwards hat as a more masculine fashion item to signal her lesbian identity. The hat owes its potency as an indicator of sexual identity to its association with lesbian identity in popular media, such as celebrity YouTuber Hannah Hart's iconic snapback hat,[3] and its association with lesbian culture alongside other stereotypical fashion items, such as the plaid shirt or karabiner key ring (Cauterucci, 2016).

Participants' emphasis on fashion in selfies was associated with their desire to mimic celebrity styles that reflected their sexual identity and affiliated them with glamorous lifestyles. As I discussed with Alex about her numerous stylized selfies, portraying creative angles of her flat-brimmed hat, short haircut, and tattoos, she joked, "The more I look like Justin Bieber in the pictures, the better." Lesbian culture has appropriated Bieber's feminine masculinity as an indicator of queerness expressed through drag performances, fashion items, and the iconic Bieber-style haircut (Brickman, 2016).[4] Since Bieber's fashion attempts to assert his masculinity, which is routinely called into question by his boyish mannerisms and emotional songs, replicating his gender representation gives an ironic nod to this fluidity. It also portrays a soft masculine presentation, characteristic of the "boi" gender identity label (in contrast to hard masculine "butch" gender presentation), popular among some lesbian celebrities, such as Ruby Rose (Hoff, 2015). By incorporating celebrity styles into her self-representations, Alex not only depicts her gender and sexual identity but also situates herself in relation to attention-grabbing, celebrity lifestyles.

By producing personal, stylized, and culturally recognizable self-representations, participants felt a sense of self-validation and that they were presenting audiences with a particular image of LGBTQ people. Alex's use of Instagram allowed her to "see what a lot of other people are doing" and she noted that, "It's kind of helped me find myself in a lot of ways." Similarly, Kelzz experienced a shift after she started sharing her photos publicly, "It kind of broke the shell I was hiding in—in a way, and it opened me up to be even more okay about who I am." For Mita, who added #LGBTfamily to several photos of herself with her wife and baby son, she viewed her self-representations as challenging normative discourses. She aimed

to portray just gender broadness and just LGBT awareness, you know, there's not just a man and a woman who can have a family. There can be two women that can have a family; there can be two women that can have kids—genetic kids—you know what I mean?

These women's microcelebrity practices share similarities with those of trans YouTube vloggers, whose videos chronicling their transitions reflect their gender identity back to them while also making visible trans identities that challenge normative gender discourses (Raun, 2014). However, whereas trans YouTubers tended to focus on their personal stories, these queer women's self-representations drew on Instagram-specific elements in their microcelebrity techniques. Through platform features, stylized staging of selfies and couple photos, and references to popular culture, women shared intimately about their sexual identity while also asserting their association with shared and glamorized lifestyles in ways that increased their potential to attract audiences.

Reflexive Self-Promotion

Aligning with Senft's (2008) observation that microcelebrity involves reflexive dialectical exchanges, participants' use of hashtags and other platform features also connected them with others for the purpose of accumulating audiences as fan bases, which provide attention and feedback. To further attract audiences, individuals engaged in a process of observing popular or celebrity Instagrammers, replicating their techniques, and adjusting their posts based on user response (e.g. gains in followers, increases in likes). Several women carefully chose aesthetically pleasing backgrounds and angles for images, such as Kelzz's repurposing of a parking lot in her neighborhood into a sleek dance video backdrop. Kamala often shot thematic photo series: "Maybe ten, twenty, thirty in the one location . . . just to know, what did you see from the same location?" She felt that showcasing interesting locations around Thailand could spark dialogue with her followers. Mita eschewed Instagram's filters for manually adjusting photo saturation and hue while Emi and Julie used third party apps to add borders and create collages. Several participants also created personal hashtags, such as #tattoosbyemi and #kingkelzz32, serving to further transform the self into a recognizable and memorable brand. These reflexive upskilling and self-promotional practices, involving individuals' iterative tailoring of techniques to suit their aspirations, provided the means for attaining the stylized aesthetics that Marwick (2015) notes as essential to Instafame.

With polished self-representations, participants built their audiences through networking techniques, drawing attention to their personal brands. Several participants regularly used the @mention feature, which tags another user in a photo or caption, to "shout out" other accounts in attempts to invoke their attention and attract their followers by showing affiliation with them. When Queenie posted meals made with ingredients from a nearby "vegan butcher shop," she shouted out their account, gaining attention from other vegans on Instagram as well as the shop, which eventually offered her a job. In turn, many participants aimed to have celebrities or Instafamous accounts shout out or regram[5] their photos to grab the attention of the celebrities' followers. This practice resembles collaborative videos where popular YouTubers feature each other or up-and-coming users to share audiences (Morris & Anderson, 2015). Kelzz's recent increase in followers was attributable to a celebrity regramming one of her dance videos. Similarly, Alex's @dapperdykes account owed many of its fans to a popular trans user who shouted it out to his followers early in its creation. Alex experienced an even greater influx as this practice collided with celebrity culture when a Ruby Rose fan account shouted out @dapperdykes in a photo, "There was a picture of Ruby Rose holding a pair of my boxers that came out, and I sold a few hundred pairs that week." Through these networking practices and Instagram's affordances for building large, interconnected audiences, even everyday users are able to accrue sizeable fan bases.

As these women anticipated and responded to audiences by adjusting their techniques, demonstrating affiliations, and sharing self-representations, their audiences also provided feedback. Since Queenie participated in body-positive campaigns, such as #rockthecrop, a trending hashtag encouraging women of any size to wear any clothes they want (including crop top shirts), she received many positive messages from her followers. They also frequently recognized and complimented her in person:

> We went to a roller derby event Saturday night and one of the roller girls came up to me and said, "Oh my God, Queenie Von Curves, I stalk you on Instagram." . . . I feel like, especially locally, I have a really great exposure to people through Instagram.

This instance demonstrates the permeation of Queenie's digital microcelebrity into physical spaces, as her fan base provides feedback on the app and in person, indicating that her content resonates with her followers.

Other participants engaged in sustained back-and-forth dialogue with followers who reached out to them. Mïta received daily messages from trans people or their partners, asking about her transition and requesting advice. She responded to each message because, "I was once one of those people that was struggling with how to do this, you know, so I get back to everybody that is looking for help." She also compiled an album of Instagram photos, featuring her family and showcasing her life post-transition, posting it to Reddit to support and inspire trans users on that platform. This cross-platform sharing extended her dialogue to new audiences while also drawing them to her self-representations on Instagram. Marwick (2015) notes that with Instagram's minimal space for and emphasis on text comments, Instafame diverges from models of microcelebrity that rely on reaching out to audiences directly and textually through comments and written acknowledgments. However, participants' behind-the-scenes private messages with followers and photo-inspired dialogue on other platforms demonstrate the endurance of these forms of direct interaction, which are less outwardly visible and harder to trace than on-platform, public-facing conversations. These other approaches to microcelebrity combine with Instafamous practices relying on visuals and affiliations, such as through the use of @mentions and cultural references in images. Altogether, these examples demonstrate multiple levels of dialectical reflexivity in participants' self-representational practices.

Managing refracted selves

Senft (2008) mentions "refraction" as the way some audiences perceive the personal aspects of self-representations as suitable for public viewing and others perceive them as content that *should be* private. For me, this theme also conjures the scientific concept of refraction: as light hits a target, it can be refracted, or deflected, to other surfaces in the process. While social media users produce their images for an imagined audience (Marwick & boyd, 2011), these representations can be inadvertently refracted to, or received by, other unanticipated audiences. On Instagram, queer women negotiated the refraction of self-representations that communicated their sexual identity to unintended audiences, which included: known acquaintances, who were likely to be offended or react negatively; unknown and pseudonymous audiences, who responded in crass, harmful, and violent ways; and Instagram's moderators, who imposed platform values derived from dominant discourses. Participants managed these refractions by separating audiences, ignoring harassers, and self-censoring their images.

Since all participants had public accounts, they were aware that anyone could view their self-representations and intended for them to be viewed widely. Emi put this bluntly, "Well, what's the point of doing it if—how do you get all this attention for things if only the people I select see it? Kind of defeats the purpose." Most of the women knew family, friends, or colleagues who would view their images negatively and while some spoke of these acquaintances as homophobic, others discussed them as being more "traditional" or "sensitive" and viewing sexual identity as a private matter. However, few participants were concerned about these audiences seeing their Instagram images because they mainly congregated on Facebook. Mïta explained:

> There are pictures on Instagram that are a little bit more risqué . . . like, there's more boob-age or whatever, and having my grandparents or uncles and aunts on [Facebook]—it's like, if they want to see it, they can go on my Instagram, you know what I mean?

Rather than posting her photos on Facebook, where they could pop up in her extended family's News Feeds, she maintained them on Instagram knowing they would require extra effort on her family's part to access. Participants were careful to maintain this divide, such as by Thea disabling Instagram's feature for automatically cross-posting to Facebook so her friends would not be drawn to her account if they saw an Instagram-style photo in their News Feeds. These practices reflect microcelebrity techniques for differentially targeting audiences, which have become widespread in everyday users' social media practices (Marwick & boyd, 2011; Senft, 2013).

Several women received harassing and sexual messages and comments from users who were previously unknown to them. Mïta recalled only two messages from users discriminating against trans people but she was accustomed to a regular barrage of sexual messages and "dick pics." While she attempted to counter this by capitalizing the words "LESBIAN" and "MARRIED" in her profile biography, the messages persisted. Since Queenie often posts photos promoting her burlesque dancing, she perceived dealing with sexual messages and comments as "just part of what I have to deal with in the industry I'm in." However, she noticed an increase in angry and violent comments after she started posting photos with Emi:

> I think for some of the straight, male followers that I had, who would comment or like the photos that I had that were scantily clad or things like that, I think knowing I was a lesbian was a turn-off for them because they couldn't imagine things, to be honest.

While these messages reflect the volumes of harassment and gender-based violence that women encounter regularly on digital media platforms (Citron, 2009; Jane, 2014), sexually entitled messages targeting queer women gain fuel from broadcast media representations that perpetuate heterosexualized lesbian fantasies for male audiences (Diamond, 2005; Jackson & Gilbertson, 2009). When Queenie disrupted this fantasy by including couple selfies with Emi, whose masculine appearance does not fit heteronormative perceptions of attractiveness, her followers became upset. Harassers' use of pseudonyms and throwaway accounts, along with Instagram's limited features for monitoring user activity, leaves women with little recourse. Similar to Marwick's (2015) finding that Instafamous accounts largely ignored critical or hate-filled comments, many participants blocked commenters, ignored messages, and ceased to engage with these users any further.

Some participants also managed refractions of sexual identity that came to the platform's attention. To promote her underwear line, Alex posted a photo to @dapperdykes that featured a feminine-presenting woman embracing a more masculine-presenting woman. Both women were in their underwear and their breasts were obscured or covered. Although the photo did not violate Instagram's Terms of Service by portraying full nudity, the image was flagged as inappropriate. Alex pointed out that other underwear companies on Instagram often posted photos with more sexual content and nudity, "You see girls all the time in less, but I think there are a lot of homophobic people that like to just bash on my @dapperdykes page." She heeded Instagram's warning and removed the photo rather than risking the platform closing her account and losing hundreds of followers.

Queenie similarly felt as though Instagram's moderation processes targeted women. She saw them as constraining both her self-representations and promotion of her burlesque dancing: "You can only get so nude on Instagram." Her frustration reflects the sentiments of feminist artists who, as Olszanowski (2014) observes, highlight with their images how Instagram censors women's bodies regardless of context and according to gender discourses that deny women the agency to display their bodies on their own terms. Crawford and Gillespie (2014) assert that while platforms employ flagging systems to appear neutral in processes of content moderation, such systems function according to multiple embedded influences, including corporate strategies and values. Participants managed these refractions through self-censorship and relocating their self-representations to platforms with different policies. Queenie posted her nude modeling portraits and burlesque photos to her "not safe for work" Tumblr account to avoid Instagram's moderation. While this accords with Instafamous approaches that maintain their self-representations in accordance with platform policies and conventions, it also provides a view of how users manage microcelebrity across platforms.

Conclusion

These stories and experiences from queer women about their Instagram use show how sexual identity can play a key role in the production of networked self-representations that adopt platform-specific microcelebrity practices. Aligning with long-standing themes of microcelebrity practice, participants reflected their sexual identity in intimate displays to connect with audiences, tailored their self-representations reflexively according to audience feedback, and managed refraction by targeting specific audiences. They combined these practices with Instafamous techniques, following platform trends of using popular hashtags, shouting out accounts with many followers, producing highly stylized images, and referencing shared LGBTQ and popular culture. These findings build upon Marwick's (2015) recognition of popular users' Instafamous practices by identifying similar approaches in the self-representations of everyday users. Further, they highlight how an identity category, particularly sexual identity, can serve as a form of personal expression and a reference that affiliates individuals with recognizable and glamorized lifestyles.

While Instafamous practices stem from Instagram's platform architecture and user conventions, queer women's experiences show how the platform both afforded and constrained aspirational labor toward personal and/or economic goals. Instagram's hashtags and @mentions enabled individuals to declare their affiliation with particular identities and users while also connecting with others over these shared affiliations. Filters and features for adjusting images, along with compatible third party apps, allowed queer women to produce stylized images while the platform's emphasis on visual imagery made intertextual references to celebrities and popular culture salient for audiences. However, participants also resisted platform features that converged audiences, such as automatic cross-posting to Facebook, in order to produce targeted self-representations. Other users' practices, employing pseudonymous accounts to harass and send unsolicited sexual messages, also added to queer women's daily labor of blocking and reporting accounts. Ignoring these comments and working around Instagram's limited space for textual address, participants shifted dialogue with audiences into private messages or to other platforms. Instagram's content moderation policies and user flagging system required some participants to self-censor their self-representations or risk losing the audiences they cultivated through Instafamous practices. Although the women in this study used platform-specific means of gaining attention for their business, talent, or reputation, they also developed work-arounds and engaged with multiple platforms when Instagram limited their microcelebrity practices.

When speaking with these women, it was difficult to gauge the actual outcomes of their Instafamous approaches to microcelebrity. Participants who employed a range of microcelebrity practices across platforms tended to have more followers than others but it was not clear if this could be directly linked to financial or personal outcomes. Duffy (2016) notes that the reward system for aspirational labor is highly uneven since laborers' creative production is often mired in gender expectations and overshadowed by the consumption of branded goods as part of their self-promotion. Participants in my study struggled against gender discourses applied to queer women. This was evident in the lengths they went to not to be rendered invisible, attempting to "look gay" or countering a "straight look" with queer hashtags, fighting assumptions that queer women are actually attracted to men or are always heteroflexible. Their labor also involved continuous deflection of heterosexualizing messages and dick pics following from popularized lesbian fantasies in broadcast media. In order to be recognizable as queer, participants referenced popular culture, commodities (e.g. fashion items), and celebrities branded or associated with LGBTQ lifestyles. Such references tended to highlight the white, upper-class, commercialized, and normatively gendered representations of LGBTQ people and associated celebrities that already dominate broadcast media. These dominant gendered and heteronormative representations complicate queer women's microcelebrity practices and reinforce the existing concentration of attention on popular and celebrity culture.

At the same time, queer women's self-representation on Instagram does make a difference. In the broad media landscape, queer women's microcelebrity strategies bring visibility to a range of identities that are generally absent from broadcast media. From the dance videos of an African-American woman to the wilderness photos of a translesbian woman and her family, the women in my study represented diverse ethnic, gender, and class identities in many different ways. Individually, their Instagram use factored into broader strategies for reflecting a sense of identity, connecting with others, and realizing their aspirations. Together, with thousands of other LGBTQ Instagram users, their individual stories told through visual content and networked through platform technology provide a collective depiction of queer community and solidarity. As demonstrated by participants' decisions regarding microcelebrity practices, they exercised agency in harnessing Instagram's affordances for their personal, economic, and social purposes. This involved developing creative self-branding practices, managing self-representations, and engaging with multiple platforms to include sexual identity as an element of their networked selves.

Acknowledgments

Thank you to Jean Burgess, Elija Cassidy, and Frederik Dhaenens for your insights into earlier drafts of this content. Thanks also to colleagues at the Queensland University of Technology for your support and input into these findings. I would very much like to thank all of the women who discussed their Instagram use with me.

Notes

1 I adopt Mary Gray's (2009) definition of "queer" as "the action of identity work" (p. 26), which involves "the collective labor of crafting, articulating, and pushing the boundaries of identities" (p. 26)—a process that was evident in participants' self-representations. I refer to "women" or "female" individuals in alignment with how participants identified their gender, which includes trans and androgynous women. For lack of a neutral umbrella term for people of diverse sexual and gender identities (Barker et al., 2009), I refer to lesbian, gay, bisexual, trans, and queer people in aggregate as LGBTQ people.
2 See for example, the "Rainbow Dash" fan wiki: http://mlpfanart.wikia.com/wiki/Rainbow_Dash
3 See www.autostraddle.com/style-thief-achieve-hannah-harts-hartosexual-style-for-your self-312851/
4 See https://lesbianswholooklikejustinbieber.tumblr.com/
5 The practice of re-posting another user's photos into one's photo feed, similar to retweeting on Twitter or sharing a post on Facebook.

References

Abidin, C. (2016). "Aren't these just young, rich women doing vain things online?": Influencer selfies as subversive frivolity. *Social Media + Society*, April–June, 1–17. doi: 10.1177/2056305116641342

Allen, L. (1997). *The lesbian idol: Martina, kd and the consumption of lesbian masculinity*. London: Cassell.

Barker, M., Richards, C., & Bowes-Catton, H. (2009). "All the world is queer save thee and ME . . .": Defining queer and bi at a critical sexology seminar. *Journal of Bisexuality*, 9(3–4), 363–379.

Bayley, L. (2017). 20 couples that give us major #relationshipgoals. *Glamour*, March 29. www.glamourmagazine.co.uk/gallery/cute-celebrity-couples-on-instagram-relationship-goals

Brickman, B.J. (2016). This charming butch: The male pop idol, girl fans, and lesbian (in)visibility. *Journal of Popular Music Studies*, 28(4), 443–459. doi: 10.1111/jpms.12193

Castle, T. (1993). *The apparitional lesbian*. New York: Columbia University Press.

Cauterucci, C. (2016). Lesbians and key rings: A cultural love story. *Slate*. www.slate.com/blogs/outward/2016/12/21/the_lesbian_love_of_key_rings_and_carabiners_explained.html

Ciasullo, A.M. (2001). Making her (in)visible: Cultural representations of lesbianism and the lesbian body in the 1990s. *Feminist Studies*, 27(3), 577–608.

Citron, D. K. (2009). Law's expressive value in combatting gender harassment. *Michigan Law Review*, 108, 373–416.

Collins, D. (1999). "No experts: Guaranteed!": Do-it-yourself sex radicalism and the production of the lesbian sex zine "Brat Attack." *Signs*, 25(1), 65–89.

Crawford, K., & Gillespie, T. (2014). What is a flag for? Social media reporting tools and the vocabulary of complaint. *New Media & Society*, 18(3), 410–428. doi: 10.1177/1461 444814543163

Cunningham, S., Craig, D., & Silver, J. (2016). YouTube, multichannel networks and the accelerated evolution of the new screen ecology. *Convergence: The International Journal of Research into New Media Technologies*, 22(4), 376–391. doi: 10.1177/1354856516641620

Dhaenens, F. & Van Bauwel, S. (2012). The good, the bad or the queer: Articulations of queer resistance in *The Wire*. *Sexualities*, 15(5/6), 702–717. doi: 10.1177/1363460712446280

Diamond, L. M. (2005). "I'm straight but I kissed a girl": The trouble with American media representations of female-female sexuality. *Feminism & Psychology*, 15(1), 104–110. doi: 10.1177/0959353505049712

Duffy, B. E. (2016). The romance of work: Gender and aspirational labour in the digital culture industries. *International Journal of Cultural Studies*, 19(4), 441–457. doi: 10.1177/1367877915572186

Duguay, S. (2016). Lesbian, gay, bisexual, trans, and queer visibility through selfies: Comparing platform mediators across Ruby Rose's Instagram and Vine presence. *Social Media + Society*, 2(2), 1–12. doi: 10.1177/2056305116641975

Gray, M. L. (2009). *Out in the country: Youth, media, and queer visibility in rural America*. New York and London: New York University Press.

Hearn, A. (2008). "Meat, mask, burden": Probing the contours of the branded "self." *Journal of Consumer Culture*, 8(2), 197–217. doi: 10.1177/1469540508090086

Himberg, J. (2014). Multicasting: Lesbian programming and the changing landscape of cable TV. *Television & New Media*, 15(4), 289–304. doi: 10.1177/1527476412474351

Hoff, V. D. (2015). 10 times Justin Bieber and Ruby Rose were twins. *Elle*, August 13. www.elle.com/fashion/celebrity-style/g26657/justin-bieber-ruby-rose-twins/

Jackson, S. & Gilbertson, T. (2009). "Hot Lesbians": Young people's talk about representations of lesbianism. *Sexualities*, 12(2), 199–224. doi: 10.1177/1363460708100919

Jagose, A. (2002). *Inconsequence: Lesbian representation and the logic of sexual sequence*. Ithaca and London: Cornell University Press.

Jane, E. A. (2014). "Back to the kitchen, cunt": Speaking the unspeakable about online misogyny. *Continuum*, 28(July), 558–570. doi: 10.1080/10304312.2014.924479

Light, B., Burgess, J., & Duguay, S. (2016). The walkthrough method: An approach to the study of apps. *New Media & Society*. doi: 10.1177/1461444816675438

Marwick, A. & boyd, d. (2011). I tweet honestly, I tweet passionately: Twitter users, context collapse, and the imagined audience. *New Media & Society*, 13(1), 114–133. doi: 10.1177/1461444810365313

Marwick, A. E. (2015). Instafame: Luxury selfies in the attention economy. *Public Culture*, 27(1), 137–160. doi: 10.1215/08992363-2798379

Marwick, A. E. (2016). You may know me from YouTube: (Micro-)Celebrity in social media. In P. D. Marshall & S. Redmond (Eds.), *A companion to celebrity* (pp. 333–350). Malden, MA: Wiley.

McBean, S. (2016). The "gal pal epidemic." *Celebrity Studies*, 7(2), 282–284. doi: 10.1080/19392397.2016.1165005

McKee, A. (2003). *Textual analysis: A beginner's guide*. London: Sage.

Morris, M. & Anderson, E. (2015). "Charlie Is So Cool Like": Authenticity, popularity and inclusive masculinity on YouTube. *Sociology*, 49(6), 1200–1217. doi: 10.1177/003803 8514562852

Ng, E. (2013). A "post-gay" era? Media gaystreaming, homonormativity, and the politics of LGBT integration. *Communication, Culture & Critique*, 6(2), 258–283. doi: 10.1111/cccr.12013

Olszanowski, M. (2014). Feminist self-imaging and Instagram: Tactics of circumventing sensorship. *Visual Communication Quarterly*, 21(2), 83–95. doi: 10.1080/15551393.2014.928154

Raun, T. (2014). Video blogging as a vehicle of transformation: Exploring the intersection between trans identity and information technology. *International Journal of Cultural Studies*, 18(3), 365–378. doi: 10.1177/1367877913513696

Senft, T. M. (2008). *Camgirls: Celebrity and community in the age of social networks*. New York: Peter Lang.

Senft, T. M. (2013). Microcelebrity and the branded self. In J. Harley, J. Burgess, & A. Bruns (Eds.), *A companion to new media dynamics* (pp. 346–354). Malden, MA: Blackwell.

Smith, K. M., & Tyler, I. (2017). Lesbian brides: Post-queer popular culture. *Feminist Media Studies*, 1–17. doi: 10.1080/14680777.2017.1282883

Sport, K. (2007). Below the belt and bleeding fingertips. *Australian Feminist Studies*, 22(53), 343–360. doi: 10.1080/08164640701364703

Walters, S. D. (2001). *All the rage: The story of gay visibility in America*. Chicago: University of Chicago Press.

8

AFFECTIVE MOBILE SPECTRES

Understanding the Lives of Mobile Media Images of the Dead

Larissa Hjorth and Kathleen M. Cumiskey

> From accessing Facebook tribute pages during public disasters to the linger-
> ing digital traces on a smartphone of someone deceased, mobile media are
> both extending earlier memorial practices such as photography and creating
> new ways in which death and loss manifest within our daily lives.
> *(Cumiskey and Hjorth, 2017, p. 3)*

Mobile media practices are inextricably part of the mundane rhythms of everyday life and in the cultivation of a networked self within affective publics. Discursive devices such as hashtags not only frame themes to events but provide
"affective attunement" that drives these publics to be mobilized (Papacharissi,
2015). For Papacharissi (ibid.), affective publics are networked publics mobilized. As the affective nature of the digital becomes increasingly framed by platforms, which, in turn creates more intense forms of what Papailias (2016) calls
"affective witnessing" (i.e. where witness and mourner distinctions blur), it can
be argued that we are moving from networked societies (Van Dijck, 2013;
Castells, 1996) toward a "networked self." And so how does this "networked
self" manifest within the particular context of mobile media as a constellation
of platforms? In particular, what is the life of the networked self when dealing
with mobile media death?

Mobile media provide a lens onto our intimacies, rituals, and experiences—
amplifying the joys whilst magnifying the despairs. Camera phone practices, in
particular, are entangled within the constructions of self in a variety of ways. They
entangle play, work, and politics and affect and provide insight into contemporary media practices. The camera phone broadens the usual tropes and genres of
photography and ultimately now shapes how people, events, and places are experienced, shared, and remembered (Palmer, 2012; Zylinska, 2015; Frohlich et al.,

2002; Kindberg et al., 2005; Whittaker et al., 2010; Van House et al., 2005; van Dijck, 2007; Hand 2013). Camera phone image taking and sharing has become an integral part of how we move and know the world and how we know ourselves and others—an integral part of the digital wayfarers' toolkit whereby embodied experiences of moving through spaces are intimately entangled with the digital and with our various social identities (Hjorth and Pink, 2014).

As Graham and colleagues argue, new media are affording emergent modes for life to be "extended, prolonged, and ultimately transformed through the new circulations, repetitions, and recontextualizations on the Internet and other platforms" (2013, p. 133). This is especially the case with mobile media as a witness, repository, disseminator, and magnifier of events. As this chapter will reveal, as a vehicle for, and of, our intimacies, identities, and networked publics, mobile media become a space, practice, and tool in which everyday lives and deaths are interwoven. Images of deceased loved ones become entangled with images of dead strangers, creating textures of mourning, affectivity, and witnessing that can be hard to extricate from.

The latest global forecast in *Info Trends*'s *2016 U.S. Digital Camera End User Study* predicted that mobile devices would capture over 1.1 trillion photos in 2016. This number is expected to grow to over 1.4 trillion in 2020. Beyond the unfathomable challenge of what is to be done with that much digital data, it becomes evident that our networked selves are documented and catalogued, hashtagged and shared. Candid and more personal photos may be stored and revisited in moments of solitude. The meaning-making process of loss often requires solitude. The ability of mobile devices to provide users with access to stores of visual representations of others takes on unique significance when grieving (Cumiskey and Hjorth, 2017). Grief distorts our identity. It may be the digital data and the remnants of our networked self that help users put the pieces back together.

This chapter seeks to sketch some of the ways new mobile media visualities are shifting how we experience images in, and of, death. In this phenomenon, death as a distortion of self-identity is juxtaposed against the distortions of identity that mobile visualities create. As a tool for, and of, intimacy, mobile media create a particular relationship and mode of affect. Through mobile media, death, dying, and grieving are being recalibrated as a dynamic tension between existing rituals and the ways in which co-presence—temporal and geographic distance being overcome by electronic proximity—plays out.

In order to understand this contingent and emergent area, we explore a few key themes. In the next section we outline mobile visuality, followed by a section on "mobile memories." We then turn to the notion of the "mobile-emotive" (Cumiskey and Hjorth, 2017) as a lens in which to understand some of the ways in which mobile media are playing out in, and through, our networked selves, entangling intimacy, affect, and death in remediated ways. Lastly, we turn to consider some future provocations related to what it means to live in an age that Papailias (2016) defines as "affective witnessing." We explore the ways in which witnessing can impact how people make meaning and extend notions of performativity.

This chapter considers how mobile media shape, and are shaped by, particular affordances and affects related to death (Cumiskey and Hjorth, 2017). We begin by locating the role of "mobile visuality" in framing and contextualizing particular forms of reception, interpretation, and affective witnessing. We then turn to the idea of "mobile memories"—that is, how mobile media align and render particular forms of intimacy and loss. We argue that mobile visuality and mobile memories are informed by "mobile-emotive" processes—namely, the adaptation of culturally specific, affect-laden rituals in, and around, mobile media practices. This understanding of how loss is framed by and through mobile media, as we have argued elsewhere (Cumiskey and Hjorth, 2017), can be defined as a "mobile spiritualism"—a phenomenon whereby the mobile device can become haunted, digitally and materially, by the dead, and contribute to the building of an occulture (Partridge, 2013) not readily recognized or acknowledged by mobile users. This chapter also considers the role of ethics in studying this type of phenomenon—not only in terms of responsibilities managing the representations of dead people's data and its effect upon families but also the impact upon the researcher.

Mobile Visuality

The "selfie" can be used as a prime vehicle through which media, memory, and death can be explored, especially as it relates to the growing synergy between intimacy, affect, mobile media, etiquette, and identity (Cumiskey and Hjorth, 2017; Senft and Baym, 2015; Walker Rettberg, 2014; Frosh, 2015; Gibbs et al., 2015a, 2015b). While selfies are often simplistically spoken about as vehicles for narcissism (Senft and Baym, 2015), the true bastion of a networked self, this escapes the fact that, as Brooke Wendt (2014) argues, they are often about a misrecognition—or an attempt at *apperception*—of the moment and its subject. Channelling Marshal McLuhan, Wendt argues we photograph and share ourselves in the hope to gain clarity and confirmation. The selfie can serve as a kind of placeholder and evidence of experience—even if absent of meaning or significance. Selfies reflect different cultural genealogies of camera phone practices specific to particular locations (Hjorth, 2017). They can also be vehicles for not just personal sociality or augmented self-representations but also be transformed into sites of political mobilization—"affective publics"—as demonstrated in the Sewol ferry disaster (Hjorth, 2017; Cumiskey and Hjorth, 2017). This mobilization often de-personalizes the subject in the particular while at the same time broadcasting a readily consumed, almost collective, networked self to others.

Sharing photos via social media can privilege the input of others, especially when hashtags are used and the "crowdsourcing" of personal and affective content can allow for that content to become categorizable and reduced to representational features (Juliano and Srinivasan, 2012). Sharing photos with others can serve as a means of self-validation and self-construction: the marking of existence. It can broadcast to others aspects of one's social identity and serve to ameliorate some of the effects of loss when those social identities and the networked self become disrupted through death (Cumiskey & Hjorth, 2017). Death has played a key role in photograph history (Barthes, 1981; Sontag, 1977; Deger, 2008). In some cultures, like Australian indigenous culture, it is viewed as disrespectful to view images of the dead (Deger, 2008). And yet for many cultures, the sacred and the profound are now entangled within multiple mobile feeds (Cumiskey & Hjorth, 2017).

Images of the dead, the dying, and the bereaved populate our mobile media. Auto-play features of digital content may subject us to graphic and violent content against our will. The role of the viewer versus the subject challenges how we consume these images and videos. As the sharing of affect-laden digital images and videos is often meant to agitate and instigate action, debate over the true purpose of posting and sharing this content still rages on. Most recently these debates have centered on whether or not to share videos of police killings, terrorist acts, suicides, global crimes against humanity, and crimes committed by minors.

In this way, mobile visuality ontologically breaks with previous photographic traditions (Chesher, 2012; Palmer, 2014). The affect of the camera phone image—with its attendant forms of embodied visuality (i.e. the mobile as an extension of one's subjectivity and intimate practices)—plays a particular rhythm in the texture of connecting to death with, on the one hand, the ephemeral, and, on the other, the enduring. For example, it is not uncommon for someone to take a picture in and around a deceased or dying loved one with their mobile phone with the proposal of not sharing (against the typical logic of camera phone practices whereby the default is often to put it online and share) (Cumiskey and Hjorth, 2017). While the etiquette around this practice is questionable (Gibbs et al. 2015a, 2015b), it also highlights that as one of the most intimate devices (that extends our sense of self and expression), mobile media are also a repository for intimate visuality that is never shared and instead physically accompanies its subject as part of a process of mementoes that can be linked back to photograph albums or worn lockets (Cumiskey and Hjorth, 2017). This moves the construction of self beyond a networked self to a purely digital "un-shared" self. Indeed, the act of unsharing—as a movement against the default function of sharing and the networked self—is an emergent area in need of more consideration and research.

The networked nature of much of mobile visuality and of the self does inform some of the complex ethical dilemmas in and around the unimagined futures of what we do with the data of the dead. Once we sorted through loved ones' material artifacts, now data trails—some of which are owned by corporations (i.e. Facebook owning copyright of user uploaded images)—will create more complex narratives that will be harder to curate. This phenomenon sees the rise in what Brubaker and colleagues (2014) call "stewarding"—namely, the informal curation of dead people's digital data.

Sharability takes on ethical dimensions when the content can be viewed as objectionable and when the content is out of the hands of the originator of the content. Beyond etiquette, if the subject of such content is dead, what responsibility to that subject do we have if we continue to share it or merely consume it? With mobile media, the politics of networks and image ownership comes into play. As Bollmer has eloquently noted (2015), we are yet to fully understand the implications of digital data when the owner or subject dies. In "Fragile storage, archival futures," Bollmer (2015) considers the paradoxes around "the specific material conditions required to preserve and maintain digital storage, which is too often imagined as both ephemeral and everlasting" (n.p.). The tensions around the ephemeral and enduring are playing out across multiple levels—epitomized by the visual diarization and aestheticization of everyday life and the networked self in Instagram to the anti-archive of spontaneous visuality in the form of Snapchat. They highlight fundamental paradoxes around the lives and death of mobile media images and the subject of those images themselves.

As Refslund Christensen and Gotved note, digital media not only redefine death and its processes in terms of "*mediation* (the representation of something through media)" and "*remediation* (the representation of one medium in another)" but also "*mediatization* (the process through which core elements of a social or cultural activity assume media form)" (2015, p. 1). This process of multiple mediations is heightened in the case of mobile media and the networked self. Mobile media progressively become embedded within place-making and memorial culture. There are now trends in how to memorialize loved ones online—such as cultural iconography related to mourning rituals—that have become electronic alongside the virtual participation in funeral rituals that now often take place online (Cumiskey and Hjorth, 2017).

As Papailias (2016) notes, the viral database creates a procedural assemblage between mourning and witnessing. Rather than a divide between the mourner and those that witness, affective viral media shape new types of witnesses–mourner interpellations. In this process, Papailias signals to Judith Butler's (2009) work around the unevenness of mournable bodies in media whereby some bodies are more affective and grievable than others. In this work we need to understand the uneven landscape of not only cultural intimacy (Herzfeld, 1997) but also digital intimate publics (Hjorth and Arnold, 2013). What does it mean for researchers in terms of the ethics of studying affective witnessing and its impact on individuals? What is the responsibility of the researcher in terms of studying images of the dead and contacting their families? As data of the dead becomes more imploded and less contained, what are our ethics as researchers? We reflect upon these issues, which will complicate the future of mobile media increasingly.

Mobile Memories

The ways in which the digital interweaves the online and offline into everyday experience now means that "digital shadow haunts death and after-death processes, rituals and representation . . . This quotidian placement of death is amplified in the rhythms of mobile media within everyday life" (Cumiskey and Hjorth, 2017, p. 6). The ubiquitous nature of mobile media has led to what Andrew Hoskins has called "post-scarcity memorial media boom" (2011, p. 27). As Refslund Christensen and Gotved (2015) observe, "media are materialities that allow us to communicate with the dead or about the dead over the gaps between the world of the living and whatever spatial and temporal sphere the dead may reside without being absorbed into these gaps ourselves" (p. 1). The visual labor of social media resides in what at times feels metaphoric or unreal or timeless and yet digital afterlife roles such as "stewarding" (or managing online media and identities of a posthumous loved one) are increasingly serving to shoulder or perhaps extend some of the psychological labor around grief and loss (Brubaker et al., 2014; Cumiskey and Hjorth, 2017).

As mentioned in the previous section, the capabilities of the mobile device itself can allow for the user to view it as an extension of their individual psychological *space* and a site where they constitute their sense of self. Mobile memories have the potential to influence what is ultimately remembered. Social media profiles are representations of one's self that are constructed in collaboration with others. Facebook in recent years has been heavy handed in its desire to assist users in the construction of self-narratives, in mapping the significance of others in users' lives and in helping users "remember" events of the past. Moreover, with personal shared data becoming increasingly hard to own, how our lives will be created after our death is still yet to be fully understood.

Beyond engagement via social media—as companion, witness, repository, and disseminator—the mobile phone serves to enhance the affect surrounding the experience of events (Cumiskey and Hjorth, 2017). Diverse registers of "memory capital" (Reading, 2009a, 2009b; Bourdieu, 1979) are linked to national citizenship and transnational human value chains. Mobile media are used to construct types of memory knowing and knowledges that afford specific forms of intimacy within a networked public and in the construction of a networked self. Mobile media both continue and remediate older forms of memory practices such as photography, letter writing, and rituals of representation.

The contextualized and content-driven nature of mobile media is required to best understand the mobile witnessing phenomenon. Mobile witnessing is moving the platform beyond its original intention and beyond any one specific platform, especially when it comes to social media use. The overlay of multiple platforms of engagement, whether they be synchronous or asynchronous, still impacts mobile media use and this "polymedia" serves to compartmentalize different types of intimacies, identities, and publics (Madianou and Miller, 2012;

Cumiskey and Hjorth, 2017). These tapestries of use take on heightened affect when engagement shifts to the spontaneous witnessing of events, especially those associated with grief and horror.

As one of the most emotionally investigated and intimately charged devices, mobile media can provide us insight into contemporary moral, cultural economies, and values that are being shaped, and are shaping, changing processes in how we communicate, share, memorialize, and understand ourselves within the context of loss:

> Grief, like mobile media, is inherently informed by the social and by widely varying communal rules. It is inextricably interwoven within the social as it is within the cultural. It is indicative of intimate publics. The experience of mourning, while at times a private experience, is one that is unique to the individual; and as such it becomes an experience that is constituted through reflection, individualized through the interpretations of events, and understood in conversation with others.
>
> *(Cumiskey and Hjorth, 2017, p. 10)*

Mobile media, as companions to daily life events, become involved and entangled in how users form emotional bonds with others. Traces of these bonds survive beyond the physical loss of the loved one. The mobile device then becomes a vehicle through which the grief experience is processed and understood. This then further complicates the relationship between these modern practices, grief traditions, and private moments of grief not so readily shared (Cumiskey and Hjorth, 2017; Gibbs et al., 2015a; Haverinen, 2014). Mobile visuality and mobile memories can, in turn, inform a reconceptualizing death, afterlife, and notions of selfhood after death (Cumiskey and Hjorth, 2017). In the next section we discuss the idea of "mobile-emotive" as a way in which to understand how intimacy and affectivity are framed by mobile media practices.

Mobile-Emotive: Reframing Intimacy and Affectivity

Mobile intimacy overlays the electronic with the social, the emotional with co-presence, and allows the device itself to be transformed into a portable memory box. With the rise of mobile social media, different forms of individual and public participation can be intertwined with ways of communicating that are personalized, embodied, and emplaced, and that can generate a sense of intimacy and closeness (Cumiskey and Hjorth, 2017, p. 15).

The nature of mobile communication is one of an open channel. Users' connection to others, through SMS, digital photos, and social media posts is never ending and the impact of remote others creates an ongoing rhythm of seamless and seamful moments in everyday life. These connections are occurring simultaneously in the intimate realm of the networked self that the personal device affords while being broadcast publicly in online platforms. As Berlant (1998) observed, in an article published before social media had become an integral part of everyday worlds, intimacy has taken on new geographies and forms of mobility, most notably as a kind of "publicness" (p. 281). The boundaries of intimacy are blurred in digital mediated environments and relationships. Since the inception of mobile phones, this tension between taking what was private behavior (i.e. sharing personal details over a telephone located in your home) into the public realm has moved mobile media users' abilities beyond mere code switching to a hybrid experience and psychological adjustment toward blending private and public behavior (Sheller, 2014). This blending also complicates the negotiation of masked and unmasked representations of self—highlighting that all versions of intimacy are ultimate mediated.

Hjorth and Arnold (2013) have argued that we can use this framework to understand the competing histories, identities, and practices within the Asia-Pacific region. Here there is a need to think about intimacy as something that is not just amongst individuals but also in terms of what Michael Herzfeld calls "cultural intimacy." Herzfeld (1997) notes that the "intimate seeps into the public spheres that have themselves been magnified by the technologies of mass mediation" (p. 44). Here cultural intimacy takes three forms: historical, institutional, and geographical. Through a notion of cultural intimacy we can reconfigure intimate publics as they move in and out of the digital practices.

Intimate publics are now inescapable from "mobile intimacy" (Hjorth and Lim, 2012); that is, the ways in which intimacy and our various forms of mobility (across technological, geographic, psychological, physical, and temporal differences) infuse public and private spaces through mobile media's simultaneous mediation of both intimacy and space. This kind of intimacy is often also now embodied within the user's identity and the device becomes inseparable and entangled between the virtual, the material, the affective, and the corporal and spiritual (Cumiskey and Hjorth, 2017; Farman, 2012). This inescapable intimacy between self and device is evident when one is populating public space and people are engaged and interacting with their devices more than with others that are physically present.

There is something to be said about the affective power of the intimacy created between the user and those that they are connecting with through their devices. The ways in which intimate space is generated within the devices themselves are harder to observe but there is a growing interest in exploiting how meaningful it is to have the technological capability to psychologically shrink the physical distance between the user and their communicative partner. For example, the website letsgaze.com provides the ability to have a "long distance movie night" where users can simultaneously watch a movie online together. This website includes the use of a webcam so that users can actually see their viewing partner's reactions to the film and hear their commentary. This sense of co-presence is heightened by virtual connection and the sharing of online experience. An intimacy that only networked selves get to experience.

In our fieldwork on mobile media and loss, co-presence played a key role (Cumiskey and Hjorth, 2017). Co-presence was first popularized by Erving Goffman in his seminal work, *Presentation of Self in Everyday Life* (1959). The Internet and mobile communication fields now use this term to represent the symbolic and psychological sense of presence that occurs when mobile media users feel a connection to remote, networked others despite their lack of physical presence (Licoppe, 2004; Ito, 2003; Sconce, 2000; Hjorth, 2005). Co-presence can be understood as "the degree to which geographically dispersed agents experience a sense of physical and/or psychological proximity through the use of particular communication technologies" (Milne, 2010, p. 165). This form of co-presence still impacts the behavior of users and can sometimes have more influence over users' behavior than physically co-present others.

Co-presence emphasizes the device's ability to assist the user in formulating an intensely emotional and affective ever-present augmented reality that is not dependent on a stable relationship with physical structures (outside of the necessary infrastructure for mobile communication—the device itself, cell towers, power sources, satellites, etc.) (Cumiskey and Hjorth, 2017, p. 26).

We use the term "mobile-emotive," here and in our book *Haunting Hands* (2017), to represent how engagement with mobile media mediates all intimate connections and that intimate connections with others may no longer be context or proximity dependent. Mobile-emotive practices center on the ways in which mobile media users engage their devices as extensions of their social and emotional selves. These practices are affective in nature and an extension of *electronic emotions* (Vincent and Fortunati, 2009; Vincent, 2010; Cumiskey and Hjorth, 2017). The ever-presence of mobile devices and the ensuing attachment to those devices primes them as vehicles through which users constitute a self and process all experiences including those related to grief and loss.

Having outlined mobile visuality, mobile memories, and mobile-emotive, we will now turn to some thoughts about provocations around studying mobile media and loss in an age of "affective witnessing." For example, should researchers show images of the dead? Should they contact families (risking upsetting the grieving process)? What are the ethical limits? With mobile media increasingly becoming a repository for all the data trails of the dead, what are the limits of affective witnessing?

Mobile Futures: Provocations and Expectations

In this concluding section we consider some of the provocations and expectations around the contested role of the life of mobile media death as a vehicle for networked self. We return to our initial question in the introduction—what is the life of the networked self when dealing with mobile media death? And how does the life of digital data propose to take on different afterlives of the networked self?

Increasingly we will see the significant role of mobile media in the life, death, and after-life processes (Brubaker et al., 2014). For loved ones, mobile media become a crucial embodied part of that passage from life to death and afterlife. As many scholars such as Bollmer, Brubaker, and others note, the life of digital data after death takes on particular textures and politics that we are only just beginning to understand. The role of the online and mobile in accelerating the sharing and dissemination processes has been noted by many including Reading and Gotved. In the case of death, this creates a haunting infinite regress. For researchers, the role of dealing with these difficult images means thinking through the methods and politics of the digital. For example, what does it mean to do digital ethnography when the subject is dead? How does this challenge the reflexivity and power relations?

Many industries within the digital have faced the need to address this growing phenomenon—understanding an ethics for research integrity in and around our treatment of images of the dead. It is up to researchers to set the standards for how we treat, contextualize, and understand online images of the dead. Is this an ethics of the networked self? This practice also asks us to consider the role of the researcher in terms of advocacy or activism. Where is the line between research, engagement, and impact? Facebook has started its own compassion area of research to comprehend what it defines as the aforementioned stewarding and through the work of Brubaker and Lingel (2015) we are beginning to understand some of the ways in which loved ones can help to create images and post-mortem digital identities of the deceased.

Facebook also now has to contend with how it handles user-generated content that depicts violence and death. Is censorship important in these instances or is there value in the free exchange of content? The role of circulation takes precedence here. Social media generate a culture of circulation in that it is through reposting and the recirculation of digital content that representations of death and suffering are not just transmitted but the circulation itself becomes a constitutive act (Lee and LiPuma, 2002). While the desire to respond to tragedy may emerge from a mobile-emotive space, the circulation of affective content may be stripped of meaningfulness as it gets reinterpreted and reimagined through a wide range of lenses and contexts. The content itself can become manipulated and changed and unrecognizable to the subject. In many of these contexts, whether we are researchers or users, we are often idle consumers of disturbing content and become non-intervention bystanders absolving ourselves of any moral or ethical responsibility for what we are witnessing. Reports about the ways in which social media users may engage in encouraging violent acts and acts of self-destruction are dark territory worthy of investigation. How we "witness" and how we participate in events online is an important area of research that highlights an oscillation between the networked self and affective publics.

Let us return to Papailias's powerful "affective witnessing" notion. In this work we need to understand the uneven landscape of not only affective witnessing and cultural intimacy but also the role of the research in this circulation culture. Should researchers intervene? Should we contact families of the deceased? What types of responsibilities should researchers take on board in terms of their research giving back to the community? And so how do we, as researchers, reconcile the affective witnessing of the deceased with the life of those loved ones? What are the politics and ethics of intimacy when dealing with mobile intimacy? What methods should we be recalibrating? What are we missing? As death online takes more and more complex cartographies and genres we need to ensure we as researchers have robust methods as well as understanding its impact upon the deceased families.

Increasingly, new etiquette and practices are emerging in and around mobile media grief. From selfies at funerals (Gibbs et al., 2015a; Cumiskey and Hjorth, 2017) to industries around digital legacy and memorialization (Gibbs et al., 2015a), the role of mobile media is playing a key role in the transformation of boundaries and limits related to the cultural norms surrounding death. Future studies into this area of mobile media and loss will need to negotiate these particular mobile-emotive forms of co-presence and ritual not only in terms of tradition versus social change but also in relation to more longitudinal comparative research. If we are truly to understand the relationship between death and the rituals of grief, we need to monitor these cycles beyond old Western "limits" of the funeral. For example, how do mobile media help people deal with their bereavement processes a decade after they have lost a loved one?

Moreover, there will be a need to interrogate the role of data and its haunting as digital traces of ourselves increasingly grow. Once upon a time, the family of the deceased would have to deal with the material traces left behind—the clothes, the house, the books, and the printed photographs. With material increasingly becoming entangled with the immaterial, the closing down of online accounts and the limiting of digital traces will become harder to control. How will the impact of "big data" shape how mobile media memorialization plays out? For example, what happens to all the qualified self data of the deceased? And what stories do these data tell? How will this phenomenon impact upon the role of "stewarding" by loved ones of the deceased.

The frequency with which we are now exposed to faces of death, impending global annihilation, news of imminent destruction, the aftermath of disasters, and the worrying reality of maniacal demagogues with high powered weapons, one would think that our own mortality would be constantly salient to us. This phenomenon is shaping how we understand, experience, and ritualize death and destruction. As we suggest in this chapter, understanding the life of mobile media death can help us frame more complex and paradoxical modes of what it means to be present and co-present.

While we do engage with digital content that depicts death, often images of the dead are ones in which they are pictured alive. Whether it is conscious to us or not, through these images the subject has the potential to exist forever, barring any extensive purging of data. Our faith in our devices also works to allow us to deny the death of the devices themselves. From a dead battery and broken screen to a non-degradable device "put to rest" in a landfill, we do discard devices when they fail us or when a newer version is released. This throwaway tendency further underscores the paradoxical ways in which we may make emotional investments in technology that then become undermined by the business of the mobile communication industry and our vulnerability toward consumption.

Here we see some of the paradoxes of the networked self in an age of Anthropocene—we invest deeply emotionally in technology only to be in an accelerated cycle of dilapidation. We constantly yearn for new technology while nostalgically desiring the past—highlighted by the nostalgic (analogue-looking) aesthetic of camera phone apps such as Instagram. It is this sense of compulsive consumption that distracts us and at times burdens us. Nostalgia, looking back, holding on, and letting go are all activities that we engage in around digital media, meaning-making, and grief. As researchers we are left with the question, in what ways does our networking assist us in understanding ourselves and those whom we are intimate with and in what ways does the uploading of our lives to our devices disconnect us from accepting our corporeal existence and the realities of death?

Acknowledgment

This chapter condenses some of the ideas explored in Cumiskey and Hjorth's *Haunting Hands* (Oxford University Press, 2017).

References

Barthes, R. (1981). *Camera lucida*. New York: Farrar, Straus and Giroux.
Berlant, L. (1998). Intimacy: A special issue. *Critical Inquiry, 24*(2), 281–288.
Bollmer, G. (2015). Fragile storage, archival futures. *Journal of Contemporary Archaeology, 2*(1), 66–72.
Bourdieu, P. (1979 [1984)]). *Distinctions*. Cambridge, MA: Harvard University Press.
Brubaker, J. R., Dombrowski, L., Gilbert, A., Kusumakaulika, N., & Hayes, G. R. (2014) Stewarding a legacy: Responsibilities and relationships in the management of post-mortem data. *Proc. CHI 2014*. Toronto, Canada. April 26–May 1.
Butler, J. (2009) *Frames of war: When is life grievable*. London: Verso.
Castells, M. (1996). *The rise of the networked society*. Oxford: Blackwell Press.
Chesher, C. (2012). Between image and information: The iPhone camera in the history of photography. In L. Hjorth, J. Burgess, & I. Richardson (Eds.), *Studying mobile media: Cultural technologies, mobile communication, and the iphone* (pp. 98–117). New York: Routledge.
Cumiskey, K. & Hjorth, L. (2017). *Haunting hands: Mobile media practices and loss*. New York: Oxford University Press.
Deger, J. (2008). Imprinting on the heart. *Visual Anthropology, 21*(4), 292–309.
Farman, J. (2012). *Mobile interface theory*. London: Routledge.

Frohlich, D., Kuchinsky, A., Pering, C., Don, A., & Ariss, S. (2002) Requirements for photoware. In *CSCW'02: Proceedings of the 2002 ACM conference on Computer Supported Cooperative Work* (pp. 166–175). New York: ACM Press.

Frosh, P. (2015). The gestural image: The *selfie*, photography theory, and kinesthetic sociability. *International Journal of Communication*, 9. http://ijoc.org/index.php/ijoc/article/view/3146

Gibbs, M., Meese, J., Arnold, M., Nansen, B., & Carter, M. (2015a). #Funeral and instagram: death, social media, and platform vernacular. *Information, Communication & Society*, 18(3), 255–268. doi: 10.1080/1369118X.2014.987152

Gibbs, M., Kohn, T., Nansen, B., & Arnold, M. (2015b). (DP140101871) *Digital commemoration*. ARC Discovery.

Goffman, E. (1959). *The presentation of self in everyday life*. Harmondsworth: Penguin Books.

Graham, C, Gibbs, M., & Aceti, L. (2013). Introduction to the special issue on the Death, Afterlife, and Immortality of Bodies and Data. *The Information Society*, 29(3), 133–141, doi: 10.1080/ 01972243.2013.777296

Hand, Martin. (2013). *Ubiquitous photography*. New York: John Wiley & Sons.

Haverinen, Anna. (2014). Death and mourning rituals in online environments. PhD dissertation. Helsinki, Finland.

Herzfeld, M. (1997). *Cultural intimacy: Social poetics in the nation-state*. New York: Routledge.

Hjorth, L. (2005). Postal presence: The persistence of the post metaphor in current SMS/MMS practices. *Fibreculture Journal*, 6. http://journal.fibreculture.org/issue6/

Hjorth, L. (2017). Visual afterlife: Posthumous camera phone practices. In A. Kunstman (Ed.), *Selfie citizenship* (pp. 119–126). New York: Springer.

Hjorth, L. & Arnold, M. (2013). *Online@Asia-Pacific*. London: Routledge.

Hjorth, L. & Lim, S.S. (2012). Mobile intimacy in the age of affective mobile media. *Feminist Media Studies*, 12(4), 477–484.

Hjorth, L. & S. Pink (2014). New visualities and the digital wayfarer: Reconceptualizing camera phone photography. *Mobile Media & Communication*, 2(1), 40–57.

Hoskins, A. (2011). Media, memory, metaphor: Remembering and the connective turn. *Parallax*, 17(4), 19–31.

Ito, M. (2003). Mobiles and the appropriation of place. *Receiver 8*. http://academic.ever green.edu/curricular/evs/readings/itoShort.pdf

Juliano, L. & Srinivasan, R. (2012). Tagging it: Considering how ontologies limit the reading of identity. *International Journal of Cultural Studies*, 15(6), 615–627.

Kindberg, T., Spasojevic, M., Fleck, R., & Sellen, A. (2005). The ubiquitous camera: An in-depth study of camera phone use. *IEEE Pervasive Computing*, 4(2), 42–50.

Lee, B. & LiPuma, E. (2002). Cultures of circulation: The imaginations of modernity. *Public Culture*, 14(1), 191–213.

Licoppe, C. (2004). Connected presence: The emergence of a new repertoire for managing social relationships in a changing communication technoscape. *Environmental and Planning D*, 22(1), 135–156.

Lingel, J. (2013). The digital remains: Social media and practices of online grief. *The Information Society: An International Journal*, 29(3), 190–195.

Madianou, M. & Miller, D. (2012). *Migration and new media: Transnational families and polymedia*. London: Routledge.

Milne, E. (2010). *Letters, postcards, email: Technologies of presence*. New York: Routledge.

Palmer, D. (2012). iPhone photography: Mediating visions of social space. In L. Hjorth, J. Burgess, & I. Richardson (Eds.), *Studying mobile media: Cultural technologies, mobile communication, and the iphone* (pp. 85–97). New York: Routledge.

Palmer, D. (2014). Mobile media photography. In G. Goggin and L. Hjorth (Eds.), *The Routledge companion of mobile media* (pp. 245–255). New: Routledge.

Papacharissi, Z. (2015). *Affective publics: Sentiment, technology, and politics*. New York: Oxford University Press.

Papailias, P. (2016). Witnessing in the age of the database: Viral memorials, affective publics, and the assemblage of mourning. *Memory Studies*, 1–18. doi: 10.1177/1750698015622058

Partridge, C. 2013. Haunted culture: The persistence of belief in the paranormal. In O. Jenzen & S.R. Munt (Eds.), *The Ashgate research companion to paranormal cultures* (pp. 39–50). Burlington, VT: Ashgate.

Reading, A. (2009a). Memobilia: Mobile phones making new memory forms. In J. Garde-Hansen, A. Hoskins, & A. Reading (Eds.), *Save as . . . digital memories* (pp. 81–95). Basingstoke: Palgrave Macmillan.

Reading, A. (2009b). Mobile witnessing: Ethics and the camera phone in the war on terror. *Globalizations*, 6(1), 61–76.

Refslund Christensen, D. & Gotved, S. (2015). Online memorial culture: An introduction. *New Review of Hypermedia and Multimedia*, 21(1–2), 1–9.

Sconce, J. (2000). *Haunted media: Electronic presence from telegraphy to television*. Durham, NC: Duke University Press.

Senft, T. & Baym, N. (2015). What does the selfie say? Investigating a global phenomenon. *International Journal of Communication*, 9, 1588–1606.

Sheller, M. (2014). Out of your pocket. In G. Goggin and L. Hjorth (Eds.), *The Routledge Companion to Mobile* (pp. 197–205). New York: Routledge.

Sontag, S. (1977). *On photography*. New York: Farrar, Straus and Giroux.

Van Dijck, J. (2007). *Mediated memories in the digital age*. Stanford: Stanford University Press.

Van Dijck, J. (2013). *The culture of connectivity*. Oxford: Oxford University Press.

Van House, N., Davis, M., Ames, M., Finn, M., & Viswanathan, V. (2005). The uses of personal networked digital imaging: An empirical study of cameraphone photos and sharing. *CHI 2005*, April 2–7, Portland, Oregon, USA.

Vincent, J. (2010). Living with mobile phones. In J.R. Höflich, G.F. Kircher, C. Linke, & I. Schlote (Eds.), *Mobile media and the change in everyday life* (pp. 155–170). Berlin: Peter Lang.

Vincent, J. & Fortunati, L. (2009). *Electronic emotion: The mediation of emotion via information and communication technologies*. Interdisciplinary Communication Studies, 3. Oxford: Peter Lang Verlag.

Walker Rettberg, J. (2014). *Seeing ourselves through technology*. London: Palgrave Pivot.

Wendt, B. (2014). *The allure of the selfie*. Amsterdam: Institute of Networked Cultures.

Whittaker, S. E., Bergman, O., & Clough, P. (2010). Easy on that trigger dad: A study of long term family photo retrieval. *Personal and Ubiquitous Computing*, 14(1), 31–43.

Zylinska, J. (Ed.). (2015). *Photomediations*. New York: Open Press.

9

CLEAVAGE-CONTROL

Stories of Algorithmic Culture and Power in the Case of the YouTube "Reply Girls"

Taina Bucher

YouTube is the world's largest platform for creating, sharing, and watching video content. Each day, users watch a billion hours of videos, and as of July 2015 more than 400 hours of video content were uploaded to YouTube every minute. Launched in 2005, the video-hosting platform was bought by Google only a year into its existence, and is now, twelve years later, one of the most visited websites overall. Given its popularity, YouTube has become something of a cultural phenomenon. As of 2016, YouTube is the most popular social media site in the United States based on penetration, reaching 72% of the population. In the northern European context, YouTube has seen a massive growth in popularity in recent years, particularly amongst the younger population. In 2016 the number of children and teens in Denmark who consumed YouTube content on a daily basis almost doubled from 2014, reaching over 70% of young people between 7 and 12 years of age. As Jean Burgess and Joshua Green write, "YouTube clearly represents a disruption to existing media business models and is emerging as a new site of media power" (2013, p. 5). While YouTube has certainly challenged the existing business models of the television industry in particular, less visible is the way in which YouTube is constantly challenging the existing dynamics of its own industry from *within*.

At the heart of these disruptions are the platform's recommendation and ranking algorithms responsible for "selecting and filtering content, guiding users in finding and watching certain videos out of the million of uploads" (Van Dijck, 2013, p. 113). As stated in one of the few papers describing YouTube's algorithms on a higher level, the recommendation system "is extremely important for YouTube as a product" (Covington et al. 2016, p. 193). For content creators this means that the visibility of their videos is tightly controlled by an algorithmic system that is less than transparent in terms of the criteria it uses to make that selection. Not only is it hard to know *how* the algorithm works to select certain videos over others but also these algorithmic systems constantly change. For YouTubers—people who frequently use the site, particularly by producing and starring in videos—these continued changes make it difficult to know how to effectively reach their audiences. As Taryn Southern, a popular YouTuber, put it in an interview with *Business Insider*, the need to cater to mechanisms that constantly change makes "you just feel like a slave to the algorithm" (Munsterman, 2017). While it might appear as if YouTube's recommender system favors likes and comments one day, the next day it might seem as if it is all about how much time people spend watching those videos that suddenly counts more. Despite the availability of some (if every sparse) public information about how YouTube's algorithms work such as company blogs and community guidelines, YouTubers can only ever guess as to what the algorithm is and whether their videos are more or less likely to be regarded as good enough for the recommendation systems to be promoted.

The purpose of this chapter is to disentangle some of the messiness that changing algorithms entail. Specifically, this chapter considers the stories that algorithm changes tell with regards to what is valuable—how value is governed, generated, and negotiated in and through algorithmic social media platforms like YouTube. This chapter contributes to the conversation on the relationships between social media platforms and content producers by focusing on the algorithm as an arbiter of power and resistance.

The YouTube recommendation and ranking algorithms are far from neutral intermediaries connecting users to the right content. As this chapter argues, algorithms both shape and are shaped by specific sociomaterial practices. Audiences are entangled in algorithms insofar as user practices influence the ranking and recommendations that are provided. By the same token, algorithms also influence the kind of content that gets uploaded as content creators are responding to the incentives of attention and potential revenues. If you want your videos to be noticed, Taryn Southern suggest, the "only way to feed the beast" is to post daily and in very particular ways (Munsterman, 2017). As Derek Muller, another popular YouTuber, suggests, what gets uploaded to YouTube in many cases depends on how the platform treats content. Muller, who is a trained physicist with a PhD in making films to teach physics, runs several acclaimed science channels on YouTube. Similar to Southern, Muller thinks content creators are adapting their videos to fit with the available mechanisms of the platform. These adaptations, however, are far from straightforward. Sociomateriality offers a relational approach to the question of algorithms, emphasizing how "agents, things, or concepts cannot be understood as having determinate boundaries, properties, or meanings prior to their encounters" (Orlikowski and Scott, 2015, p. 205). From this perspective, algorithms are "contextually situated and performative" in the sense that they do not cause anything to happen in and of themselves but rather "materialize in particular times and places through particular practices" (ibid.).

To illuminate how algorithms materialize in practice, this chapter considers the case of the YouTube "Reply Girls," a group of young women who rose to a brief moment of YouTube fame in 2012 for using their cleavage-baring bodies as thumbnails to drive traffic. During a period stretching from summer 2011 to spring 2012, the YouTube Reply Girls emerged as something of a cultural phenomenon. These women had found a way of exploiting the YouTube algorithm for related and suggested videos, combining it with an age-old attention-grabbing technique—their cleavage-baring bodies—to make money gathering clicks and votes. In this chapter, I am not concerned with passing judgments about the normative aspects of enticing clicks by posting thumbnail pictures of cleavages. Instead, I want to ask: what can such practices tell us about algorithms and their cultural forms?

My understanding of the case is informed by Lauren Berlant's "thinking about the ordinary as an impasse shaped by crisis in which people find themselves developing skills for adjusting to newly proliferating pressures to scramble for modes of living" (2011, p. 8). Drawing on the idea of a "situation," defined by Berlant as "a state of things in which something that will perhaps matter is unfolding amid the usual activity of life" (ibid., p. 5), I approach the case of the Reply Girls as a situation that helps us to discern claims about power relations in the algorithmic media landscape. I begin by telling the story of the Reply Girls, and how this group of YouTubers became entangled in one of the biggest algorithm changes in YouTube's history.

"We have a situation": The Rise and Fall of the Youtube "Reply Girls"

> It is 2:50 am in the morning, and I can't sleep. What can I say. The YouTube algorithms are going to change on March 14th, meaning that replies are no longer to appear in the related section anymore. So, I'm kinda worried, to be honest. I don't know if I'm wrong, but after all this time I've been reluctant to surrender to all this hatred; to all of these attacks; to all of the threats. But I think the reply saga is over. Or at least, it will be very soon. Will I keep on doing replies? I don't know. I'm a bit worried, cuz I don't know what is going to happen.

Meet TheReplyGirl, a twenty-something Canadian girl who rose to something amounting to YouTube fame a few years ago by posting daily video replies to already popular YouTube videos using sexually suggestive thumbnails to solicit views.[1] In a video posted on her YouTube channel in early March 2011, TheReplyGirl talks to her viewers about an upcoming algorithm change that YouTube had apparently just announced. In the video she is clearly distressed, talking in a low whispering voice. She says she is worried about what the announced algorithm changes imply, the impact it will have on her video views and the business that she has been developing for the past seven months. In the video she seems to be in an emotionally distraught state, and not just because it is 2:50 am in the morning. TheReplyGirl, who turned to YouTube as a means of rising above the poverty line and counting on it for basic income, acknowledges that her cleavage-baring practices have not been particularly well received by the YouTube community (O'Neill, 2012). Categorized as spam, the YouTube community quickly made her and other young women engaging in similar practices the target of numerous threats and hateful comments.

The phenomenon of the Reply Girls came to public scrutiny in early 2012, at a time when their cleavage-baring thumbnails had become an increasingly prevalent sighting on the right-hand side of popular YouTube videos, a section known as related or recommended videos. Making video replies to popular videos has been a common fan-practice on YouTube since the platform's inception. YouTube used to offer a feature known as "video responses," placed in the comment section of every video. This way, users could not only write comments, but also upload their own video replies. This feature allowed users to indicate a thematic relationship between the original video and the reply video by using metadata.[2] If the reply video reached a certain popularity threshold, the algorithm would display it more prominently as part of the related and recommended video section.

The Reply Girls had found a way of exploiting the recommendation algorithm by employing various engine optimization tactics to drive traffic to their videos. Megan Lee Hart, one of the Reply Girls, explains the process: first she realized that YouTube's algorithm seemed to prioritize reply videos when creating the list of "suggested videos" that appear on every page. Then she noticed, by watching reply videos and observing the behavior of users that breasts were a pretty good indicator for which videos gathered the most clicks. Hart adapted by adding suggestive graphics to her thumbnails, and bright colored all-caps words to attract more clicks. These videos did not just attract numerous clicks, but also massive down-votes by frustrated users who felt deceived or irritated by the proliferating cleavage-baring images popping up in the related feed. Instead of treating these down-votes as negative signals, the algorithm was computing them as tokens of engagement. Paradoxically, the many "thumbs down" drove the videos higher up—not down—the ranking (Read, 2012). To the agony of the many YouTubers who continued to down-vote the cleavage-baring videos, the Reply Girls only seemed to become even more prevalent as part of the related video section.

The Reply Girls started to catch the attention of Google after months of concerned YouTubers leaving forum posts, making videos, signing petitions, and raising awareness about the issue. The phenomenon also attracted considerable press coverage with technology and Internet news sites like *Daily Dot*, *Gawker*, and *Huffington Post* regularly reporting on the Reply Girls "controversy." The controversy solidified in February 2012, with a Change.org petition gathering over 4000 supporters in their quest for better user tools to combat spam as part of what they called the "uprising of the Anti-ReplyGirls movement."[3] Moreover, several high-profile YouTubers lashed out against the Reply Girls, with Yogcast, the well-known Minecraft video-game commentators on YouTube, launching on a personal crusade against the girls. As journalist Fruzina Eördöugh, who covered the case extensively for *Daily Dot*, pointed out, the massive backlash against the Reply Girls resulted in much bullying, hate, and even death threats.[4] As indicated in the TheReplyGirl's last reply videos quoted above, the hateful comments were clearly wearing on a real person, something she also mentioned to me in an email exchange as a reason for not wanting to be involved with YouTube anymore. The day after posting the video reflecting on the upcoming algorithm change, TheReplyGirl posted another one. This time, her tone of voice was calmer and she said she had had a chance to reflect a bit more on the supposed changed. Although she reckoned the "reply saga" would have come to an end, she was also more optimistic. After all, YouTube had made similar threats about changing its algorithm without anything major happening. But something did indeed happen as YouTube went on to significantly change its algorithms.

On March 9, 2012, YouTube announced they would update the related and recommended videos, favoring "watch time" over the numbers of clicks videos receive. As YouTube reasoned, "clicks aren't always the best way to predict whether you'll be interested in a video. Sometimes thumbnails don't paint the whole picture, or a video title isn't descriptive" (YouTube, 2012b). The new algorithm would better reflect viewer engagement, understood by how long people would spend watching a particular video. While not explicitly referring to the Reply Girls as the reason for the major overhaul, the algorithm change appeared only a week after a YouTube manager had tweeted saying that their engineers were working on tackling the issue of the Reply Girls. By "regularly tweaking the system," YouTube had discovered that "time watched is one of the best indicators of a viewer's engagement." While clicks would still be a measure, engagement would become "the leading indicator for serving these videos" (ibid.). Instead of rewarding videos that were successful at attracting clicks, shifting to watch time meant rewarding videos that "increase the amount of time that the viewer will spend watching videos on YouTube," but also the likelihood that users will spend time watching successive videos (YouTube, 2012b).

The transition to watch time was by no means a small change. In subsequent years it was repeatedly described as a major change in the company's entire philosophy, a calculated decision to change how YouTube measured its own success (D'Onfro, 2015). If the old way produced lots of clicks, but also increasingly frustrated users, the new way produced an arguably better user experience, but also aggravated content creators. As Cristos Goodrow, Vice President Engineering at Google and responsible for Search & Discovery on YouTube, recalls, the aftermath of the algorithm change that led to the decline in the Reply Girls produced in a massive backlash in terms of angry content creators calling to complain that they were now out of business. For years, YouTube had seemed to favor clicks above all else; creating a culture that encouraged the production of clickable and shareable videos. With the introduction of watch time, however, YouTube seemed to abandon their prevailing philosophy of clicks, "burying videos that people clicked away from quickly, and surfacing those that people watched for a long time" (ibid.).

While it may be easy to dismiss the change toward watch time as corporate strategy, and the Reply Girls simply as spam, this would be an all too easy way out. Borrowing from Berlant, we might rather be saying: "we have a situation here" (2011, p. 5). Instead of seeing the Reply Girls as a singular thing, a brief rupture or happening back in time, I want to suggest that the case shows something much more general. There are some lessons to be learned. In the remainder of the chapter I will trace what this more general lesson to be learned amounts to, by tracking how the Reply Girls resonate across many different scenes, including the changing logics of algorithms, the professionalization of user-generated content, and algorithmic cultures of resistance. As Kathleen Stewart suggests, describing a situation may sometimes require "a digressive detour and a slowing and de-dramatization of analytic frames" (2012, p. 366). This is to say that there is not necessarily a right order to the story, nor will all components be covered or connections be traced. Of all the possible stories that could be told about the Reply Girls, the following three offer a way of understanding the culture of algorithms as the intimate connections between platforms and the networked self.

First Story: The Cruel Optimism of Aspirational Labor

The first story to be told about the situation of the Reply Girls is that the case is neither isolated nor exceptional. In order to understand how the YouTube Reply Girls are not exceptional but ordinary, our first "digressive detour" takes us back to the business model and value of cultural production on YouTube. Although social media platforms have typically been hailed as democratic and participatory spaces where user-generated content flourishes and everyone can participate, "there is no evidence" says Patrick Vonderau, "that YouTube was, at any point in its history, an underdetermined space without commercial purpose" (2016, p. 363). For YouTube, the central challenge has always been to find a feasible business model from the linking of cultural production to value creation. One of the most important steps in the commercialization of video-generated content was the introduction of YouTube's Partner. Launched in 2007, the Partner program offered a shared advertising revenue solution whereby YouTubers could generate revenue from their videos and access YouTube's specialized analytics and content management tools. Initially this program was only eligible for producers of very popular content. In April 2012, however, the program opened up to anyone who could document at least one successfully monetized piece of content. While early inquiries showed that advertisers preferred their ads to be placed next to legal and professional content, years of encouraging users to broadcast themselves had made amateur content the real market contender (Cunningham, 2012, p. 419).

Having come a long way from its original tagline of "Broadcast yourself" and *Time* magazine voting the "You" in YouTube person of the year in 2006, the distinction between amateur and professionally produced content on YouTube has become ever more blurry. Researchers have noted how YouTube has gradually been "professionalized" and more "formalized" over the years (Burgess and Green, 2009; Cunningham, 2012; Jakobsson, 2010; Morreale, 2014; Van Dijck, 2013). It is not just that YouTube, being a commercial platform, has brought market mechanisms into spheres traditionally considered non-market (household, everyday), but that YouTube more generally has spurred "the professionalization and formalization of amateur media production" (Burgess, 2012, p. 54). As Peter Jakobsson writes: "the function of [open production] on YouTube is not only or primarily aimed at an egalitarian and democratic culture of production, but also to generate an entrepreneurial desire that is aligned with the commercial interests of the company" (2010, p. 116).

If the early days of YouTube were mainly about getting as many users to participate and to upload their videos to the site, as the platform became more popular various initiatives, including the Partner program and the YouTube Creators hub, were introduced to professionalize amateur content to work alongside copyright protection policies and advertisers' interests (Burgess, 2012, p. 56). More recently, the rise of multichannel networks (MCN), intermediary firms that operate in and around YouTube's advertising infrastructure, have professionalized the space of amateur content production even further. MCNs, more commonly referred to as YouTube networks, act as talent management companies of sorts, working "to push their most promising YouTubers up the value chain and make them stars in the offline world" (Lobato, 2016, p. 352). According to Romano Lobato we are witnessing a new phase in the history of YouTube, where content creators are no longer encouraged to broadcast themselves but to "sign up with an agent" to become even better versions of themselves (ibid., p. 358).

Important to these transitions is the rise of the so-called YouTube Star fueled by new models of media entrepreneurialism. YouTube stars are hugely popular YouTubers, who have developed their own personal brands by reaching massive audiences. Perhaps the biggest star of them all is the 27-year-old Felix Kjellberg who is better known for his gaming vlogs (video diaries and commentaries) under the username PewDiePie. Since 2013, PewDiePie has been the most subscribed user on YouTube with over 56 million subscribers as of August 2017. Having made a hugely lucrative career out of commenting and reacting to video games as he plays through them, PewDiePie was the highest paid YouTube star in 2016 with a reported paycheck of $15 million. PewDiePie is of course an exception with regards to such figures. Most content producers do not become stars, attract huge audiences, or earn much money. What matters, however, is the *promise* of potential stardom and economic revenue. This was also the case for the Reply Girls and for the many other "entrepreneurial vloggers" (Burgess and Green, 2009).

While the rise of the YouTube Star in the league of PewDiePie represents one end of the entrepreneurial spectrum, the economic potential of "amateur" content has been an important part of YouTube from the very beginning. As Burgess and Green suggest, "For YouTube, participatory culture is not a gimmick or a sideshow; it is absolutely core business" (2009, p. 6). One of the first to effectively activate this participatory culture for commercial gain was the video blogger *LonelyGirl15*, a girl named Bree who rose to YouTube fame in 2006 by posting personal diary entries from her bedroom. As it later turned out, Lonely-Girl15, was really an actor named Jessica Lee Rose who had found the casting call Bree on Craigslist (Bakioğlu, 2016). As controversial as the unveiling of Bree as a manufactured vlogger was, it also introduced the idea of broadcasting yourself to fame and fortune.

Much important work has been published on the "entrepreneurial spirit" and the idea of self-branding pervading the cultural industries and social media platforms today (Duffy, 2017; Marwick, 2013; Neff, 2012; Postigo, 2016; Ross, 2009). What this body of work helpfully demonstrates is the ways in which platforms like YouTube encourage users to engage with their services in an entrepreneurial way by perpetuating neoliberal discourses that emphasize the importance of self-investment. As Neff and colleagues have shown, there is certain "coolness" attached to a career in the culture industries, a rhetoric that essentially compels workers to glamorize employment risk (2005, p. 331; see also Duffy and Hund, 2015). Regardless of whether the Reply Girls saw themselves as entrepreneurial vloggers on the career path in the cultural industries, riding the attention economy in this way certainly managed to secure some of them YouTube partnerships and a decent living. In the case of the Canadian girl whose channel was called TheReplyGirl, the videos were anything but wilful pranks but rather meticulously produced for clicks and subscribers. During her relatively short time of YouTube-reign, TheReplyGirl reportedly earned up to $15,000 a month on a tight production cycle that included up to twenty videos a day (Eördögh, 2012; McMahon, 2012). As said, for TheReplyGirl operating a YouTube channel became a way to get above the poverty line. Far from "cool" or "glamor," TheReplyGirl worked a ten-hour day to make the reply videos, a production cycle that also involved monitoring popular YouTube videos and trying to predict which ones would be going viral, and figuring out the right keywords and tags to use.

Situated somewhere in between meaningless spam and legitimate vlogging, the Reply Girls can also be understood as an example of what Berlant (2011) has termed *cruel optimism*. Through this notion, Berlant directs us to consider the rise and fall of the "Reply Girls" as a complex nexus of desire, cultural production, and differential relations of precarity that have emerged in response to continued fantasies of "the good life." For Berlant, "a relation of cruel optimism exists when something you desire is actually an obstacle to your flourishing" (2011, p. 1). Optimistic relations only become cruel when they actively impede the aim that drew the subject to the object of desire. To a certain extent we might think of the "aspirational labour" (Duffy, 2017) performed by entrepreneurial vloggers as relations of cruel optimism in the sense that the fantasy of a "good life" through fame and fortune is rarely realized. Although TheReplyGirl indeed managed to rise above the poverty line (at least temporarily), the trolling, continued threats, and hateful comments she received as a result of her click-bait techniques indeed made her initial optimism seem somewhat cruel.

Second Story: The Algorithm Change as Event

The second story to be told about the situation of the Reply Girls is how the case usefully reveals the power and politics of algorithm in the event of its change. In a blog post from 2012, YouTube claimed about 100 changes to the suggested and recommended video algorithms during their seven years of existence (YouTube, 2012a). As part of a major infrastructure overhaul at YouTube in 2012, the company changed its recommender system from a regression-based algorithmic approach to neural networks and deep learning. One of the biggest confusions around algorithms is the notion of *the* change. Algorithms do not change occasionally but are continuously tweaked and shaped to accommodate new and incoming data streams. In the age of machine learning, systems that learn to solve a computational problem from examples without being explicitly programmed to do so (Domingos, 2015), algorithms, or more accurately the models they generate, are changing by default. With the venture into machine learning techniques that hinge on progressive learning and constant change, the idea of a singular algorithm change seems hard to sustain.

Yet, the idea of the algorithm change lingers. People frequently talk about changing algorithms and entire blogs and professions (SEO, anyone) are dedicated to the idea of the algorithm change. Christian Sandvig (2015) notes how, in an attempt to make algorithms more intelligible to the public, we are seeing an epistemic development in which "algorithms now have their own public relations." While Google reports changing its algorithms almost twice a day, only a handful of "major" changes become publicly known. Panda, Penguin, and Hummingbird are all the names of major updates, each represented by cute animal logos, press releases, and public speculation. As Google engineers explained in a blog post announcing the Panda update that was designed to reduce rankings for "low-quality sites":

> Many of the changes we make are so subtle that very few people notice them. But in the last day or so we launched a pretty big algorithmic improvement to our ranking—a change that noticeably impacts 11.8% of our queries.
>
> *(Singhal and Cutts, 2011)*

While YouTube is less explicit than its parent company when it comes to nam-
ing its updates after endearing animals, the rate at which it tweaks and updates its
systems has fast-tracked too. As Cristos Goodrow explains, the Search & Discovery team at YouTube works on at least ten different changes at any given time,
which may take somewhere between a few weeks to several months to finally
launch. The process typically involves some analysis and intuition, followed by
implementation and changes to the code as well as a high degree of experimentation and evaluation.[5] In Goodrow's estimate, this implies about fifty to one
hundred changes to the recommendation algorithm a year.

Given this perpetual change it might seem somewhat of a paradox to zoom
in on the algorithm change as an event. Yet, some changes are more visible
and more fundamental than others. The case of the Reply Girls is particularly
interesting because it helped spur one of the most significant changes in the history of YouTube. As such it offers a rare glimpse into the politics of platforms
as it manifests in changing algorithms. The prolific cleavage-baring thumbnails
and reply videos produced by a handful of YouTubers played an important role
in YouTube changing focus from favoring clicks and view counts to maximiz-
ing for "watch time" and sustained attention instead. While the Reply Girls
had done nothing wrong per se as they had simply built their businesses and
practices around the existing culture of clicks and reply videos, there had come
a time when the legitimate use of the platform had crossed the line and become
bothersome. Akin to Sarah Ahmed's notion of a "feminist killjoy" who "stops
the smooth flow of communication" and upsets the usual order of things (2017,
p. 37), the Reply Girls were doing more than exploiting the recommendation
algorithm—they were getting in the way of something. By using the platform on
their own terms, the Reply Girls disturbed the anticipated uses of the platform—
the ways in which it was supposed to be. Although YouTube never publicly
blamed the Reply Girls for *causing* the platform to change directions, more infor-
mally these girls were often mentioned as one of the main reasons for devaluing
the importance of view counts and clicks. Not only had the Reply Girls sparked
huge protests from within the YouTube community, but they had also become
bothersome in another very important way. Frustrated users also meant frustrated
advertisers. Although Goodrow said in an interview that he felt bad for upsetting content creators, he knew that watch time would ultimately be better for
users. Importantly, it would be "better from an ad perspective, too: The longer
someone watched a video, the more likely YouTube could insert an ad during
it" (D'Onfro, 2015).

Changing algorithms are fundamentally linked to the economic interests
of platforms and need to be understood as important arbiters of power in the
mobilization of various stakeholders and affected actors. YouTube's relationship
to advertisers has always been one of the main reasons for changing existing
policies and practices. When advertisers in the early days preferred their content
shown alongside professionally produced content, YouTube made sure to launch

programs and initiatives to make amateur content more professionalized. With the introduction of watch time, YouTube made sure to offer production help to channels specializing in lengthy commentaries such as gaming and review channels. More recently, YouTube revamped its ad policies after experiencing a major backlash from advertisers starting to pull out of Google and YouTube over ads displayed alongside extremist or hateful content. As a result, YouTube changed its rules regarding ad revenue for users in spring 2017 and enforcing them by algorithmically removing ads from videos that were in any way deemed hateful or offensive. Although YouTube claims they are not telling the user *what* to create, after all, "each and every creator on YouTube is unique and contributes to the vibrancy of YouTube [. . .] advertisers also have a choice about where to show their ads" (YouTube Help, 2017). The "adpocalypse" as this incident was colloquially called, did not only grant advertisers the ability to opt out of videos that fell into vague and broadly definable categories such as "sensitive social issues" or "sensational and shocking," it also continued to demonize certain users. For many YouTubers the "adpocalypse" meant a radical drop in ad revenues, not because they were actually sympathizing with terrorism or the extremist content, but because the many channels featuring satire, political commentary, and game reviews often cover controversial and sensitive topics that the algorithms pulling the ads are able to differentiate from "real" hate speech.

In order to improve their analytics for advertisers, Cunningham and colleagues suggest, "YouTube routinely changes their algorithms, which has resulted in the mysterious—mysterious, that is, to creators who depend on the constant connectedness to their viewers—disappearance of millions of subscribers overnight for some creators" (2016, p. 381). During autumn 2016, for example, speculations abounded about another perceived YouTube algorithm change as several well-known YouTubers started to complain about drops in subscribers and views on their otherwise popular channels, sparking conversations about a major new algorithm change. The controversy culminated when PewDiePie announced that he would be deleting his channel as a result of YouTube's lack of transparency. Several other YouTubers followed suit, claiming they had noticed significant drops in viewers despite getting *more* subscribers. Take the Canadian crafts vlogger Jackie, who runs several channels including NerdECrafter and NerdEJackie, in a video tellingly titled "LESS IS MORE! Thinking out loud about Youtube algorithm and changes 2016" she speculates how she has noticed the algorithm changing and affecting her channels in a negative way. She explains to her viewers how the YouTube algorithm is "frozen" and that "it will be fixed in late October" but that it will be difficult to predict what impacts the new implementations will have. In several of her videos Jackie openly speculates how she is going to deal with the supposed changes, not just talking about crafts, but also crafting out new strategies for circumventing any negative impacts that the new algorithm may have. As I have discussed elsewhere (Bucher, 2017), whether the changes are factual or not, may not always matter to the people seemingly affected, as their practices are often times affected by what they imagine the algorithm to be.

Algorithm changes do not just show the contested nature of algorithms, but also the difficulty in navigating a perpetually changing algorithmic landscape. For YouTubers this means grappling with the question of what it is that You-Tube *wants*. In practice this means staying on top of what YouTube seems to optimize for at any given time. There are at least two sides to this guessing game. On the one hand, content creators need to adhere and adapt their practices to the existing and ever-changing policies of platforms. In terms of guessing what the platform wants, multiple available documents exist to give content creators a sense of what kind of content and behavior is valued, including terms of service documents, community guidelines, advertising-friendly content guidelines, and AdSense Program policies. The platform generally prohibits sexual, dangerous, graphic, or hateful content. Uploaders also have to respect copyright and "things like predatory behaviour, stalking, threats, harassment" may result in being permanently banned from the site. To be eligible for advertising, videos must comply with the AdSense rules. For example, it is not permitted to inflate impressions or clicks artificially, even when done manually. Moreover, the community guidelines make clear that users are not allowed to "create misleading descriptions, tags, titles, or thumbnails in order to increase views." If these are the rules, algorithms are used to enforce them. On the other hand, the guessing game may help to foster new creative practices and productive engagement with the platform that are not always in agreement with the platform's own visions. In the next and final story, the condition of changing algorithms is discussed with regards to such resistive and tactical practices.

Third Story: Algorithmic Cultures of Resistance

While it might be easy to dismiss the YouTube Reply Girls as spam and mind-less click-bait behavior, the third story to be told asks us instead to consider these girls as social media experts who cleverly exploited and hacked the system to their own benefit. Here, the notion of a "hack" refers to a way of taking advantage of and exposing weaknesses of an existing system. So far this chapter has con-sidered the ways in which algorithms can be used strategically by platforms to encourage practices of "entrepreneurial vlogging" whereby content creators are trying their best to make themselves "algorithmically recognizable" (Gillespie, 2014). Although YouTube claims not to interfere with the kind of content users upload, in practice, the algorithm governs content production in the sense that certain kinds of signals reward some content over others. When YouTube started to optimize for watch time, channels that were built around clicks and view counts lost while gaming channels, for example, had a clear advantage because of their length. In other words, algorithms govern by encouraging certain kinds of behavior and practices. What gets uploaded to YouTube largely depends on how the site treats that content. The story of watch time, then, is not just a story of the demise of the Reply Girls but also the story of the condition of possibility for the success of YouTubers like PewDiePie. The story, of course, does not stop here. What the notion of sociomateriality teaches us is precisely how algorithms should not be considered a causal factor. Instead, algorithms materialize in practice as a result of different actors coming together. If we understand algorithms as an assemblage or arrangement "endowed with the capacity of acting in different ways depending on their configuration" (Callon, 2007, p. 320), we cannot be content with a story that positions YouTube or *the* algorithm as an all-too dominant force of power. Like the feminist killjoy mentioned earlier, the power of the Reply Girls lies in their disruptive and productive force. Like the "difficult" person who speaks inappropriately at the dinner table upsetting the idea of a happy family meal, the Reply Girls brought important things into view, including the arrangements necessary for the otherwise invisible operation of platforms.

While it may be tempting to frame resistance in opposition to a pre-established dominant force, this is not what I would like us to consider. Following Michel Foucault, resistance is not the opposite of power, but ontologically related. As Foucault asserts, "where there is power, there is resistance" (1978, p. 95). Subjects are not victims to power, but part and parcel of its modes of operation. Users are never simply controlled or determined by algorithmic systems. Power, as Foucault understood it, is a relation, a capacity to produce and transform a certain state of affairs. If power is simply the "actions brought to bear upon possible actions" (Foucault, 1982, p. 789), the question then is: how and with what effects does this capacity get exercised by different actors in the algorithmic assemblage, including users like the Reply Girls?

We already know from a broad range of work within media sociology, audience studies, and cultural studies (Hirsch and Silverstone, 2003; Fiske, 2002) how audiences and media users are never simply passive but have always appropriated and used media on their own terms, sometimes in clear opposition to the perceived hegemonic positions of the media industry (Hall, 2001). In somewhat related terms, the sociology of technology, or more specifically, the social construction of technology (SCOT) perspective, sees user agency as central to the development of technology (Bijker et al., 1987; Pinch and Bijker, 1984). Work on media resistance of different kinds also points out how the refusal to accept or comply with the ways in which media operate is always historically and politically contingent (Portwood-Stacer, 2013; Syvertsen, 2017). While this body of literature usefully illuminates the longer history of media resistance and the active power of audience, they also tend to emphasize resistance as a negation of power as if these were opposites. For the same reason I also think Michel de Certeau's (1984) influential concepts about everyday tactics and institutional strategies fall short in understanding algorithmic cultures of resistance. Lev Manovich (2009) observes something similar when he notes that the consumer economy today is quite different from the one de Certeau described, where strategies look more like tactics and vice versa. While I am sympathetic to the idea of tactics as the constant manipulation of events in order to turn them into "opportunities" (de Certeau, 1984, p. xix), the co-creative processes characteristic of the media industries today and the feedback loops of machine learning suggest that the event is not something to be seized by the "weak" and "subordinate," but something made and remade by constituents that co-become.

Where does this leave us in terms of theorizing algorithmic cultures of resistance? One more digressive detour first as we need to address the question of when the algorithmic becomes culture. Many scholars have noted how we are living in an algorithmic culture (Galloway, 2006; Hallinan and Striphas, 2016; Kushner, 2013; Roberge and Melançon, 2017; Seyfert and Roberge, 2016; Striphas, 2015). For Hallinan and Striphas algorithmic culture denotes the increased use of computational processes "to sort, classify, and hierarchize people, places, objects, and ideas" and the kinds of expressions that arise from those processes (2016, p. 119). Analyzing the specific case of the Netflix Prize, the authors observe how "questions of cultural authority are being displaced significantly into the realm of technique and engineering" (ibid., p. 122). In considering Google as a culture of search, Roberge and Melançon suggest that algorithms are not just making their mark on culture and society but have to a certain extent also become culture: "algorithms *do* cultural things, and they are increasingly active in producing meaning and interpreting culture" (2017, p. 13).

On a fundamental level, following Alexander Galloway (2006), we might say that interacting with algorithmic cultural objects like games or YouTube videos means *operating* them as well. As users are becoming intimate with a complex informatics environment, they are also more likely to try to figure out how algorithmic systems work. To a certain extent this is where I see the Reply Girls, not necessarily in opposition to or caught by the "Googleplex," but in an intimate relation to changing forces. If, as Hallinan and Striphas claim, "engineers now speak with unprecedented authority on the subject, suffusing *culture* with assumptions, agendas, and understandings consistent with their disciplines" (2016, p. 119), then ordinary users like the Reply Girls are starting to permeate algorithms with assumptions, agendas, and understandings that are consistent with their own specific backgrounds and life worlds.

In trying to be recognized by the YouTube algorithms, content creators get creative, find new and innovative uses of the platform, challenge the existing order of things, disrupt how things are supposed to be, make certain arrangements more visible and thus open for inspection, expose the unstable nature of power relations between platform owners, engineers, advertisers, content creators and audiences, and make us question and revisit what it means to be a legitimate user of the platform to start with. Thus, this third and final story urges us to consider the Reply Girls alongside similar practices of "gaming the system" that we know from other platforms such as "Googlebombing" (Bar-Ilan, 2007), "hashtag-jumping" on Twitter (Christensen, 2013) or tactics of obfuscation

(Brunton & Nissenbaum, 2015). As Tarleton Gillespie suggests, such "efforts to face the algorithm . . . anticipating its workings and designing contributions so as to be recognized by it" usefully reveal "how an algorithmic system works, how it is imagined to work, and how users believe it should work" (2017, p. 75). What the case of the Reply Girls shows is how algorithmic culture is not merely about algorithms doing cultural things, or things to culture, but how people's practices and ways of doing in everyday life also do things with and to these algorithmic systems.

Conclusion

The Reply Girls and their cleavage-baring thumbnails are but one instance of the kinds of cultural forms that emanate in response to algorithmic systems today. This chapter has argued that despite the seemingly mindless and "spammy" behavior these YouTubers displayed there is much value in looking beyond such first appearances. Far from representing a simple disturbance in the chain of content distribution between a platform provider and an audience, the case of the Reply Girls entails a set of complicated and dynamic power relations that illuminate the differential configuration of the algorithmic space of YouTube. As content creators wanting to reach an audience, being in algorithmically controlled spaces entails trying to figure out how the algorithmic mechanisms of the platforms they use work. As the case of the YouTube Reply Girls shows, these girls were not just attuned to these mechanisms to the extent that they certainly qualify as social media experts, but they also managed to figure out *too much*. While the Reply Girls did not do anything wrong in the sense that the platform did encourage the production of clickable content at that time, the case usefully highlights how desired behavior can turn into undesired behavior when it no longer benefits or contributes value to the platform. By exploiting the system in ways that took advantage of the quirks in the algorithm and the reputation system that rewarded down-votes just as much as it did up-votes, the Reply Girls turned from valuable users to *ab*users of the system. From the perspective of YouTube and other users who did not appreciate the click-bait, the Reply Girls became something that had to be responded to. The Reply Girls might or might not be the primary reason for YouTube's change in its algorithmic philosophy, but the events of spring 2012 that saw the introduction of watch time and the weakened power of clicks and votes nonetheless need to be understood against the backdrop of the situation. As we are reminded, a situation changes the ordinary into something that will perhaps come to matter, something that compels thought and action.

The case, however, also shows that who or what is responding or responded to is not always clear. If one side of the story entails content creators having to monitor the systems while feeling like a "slave to the algorithm" as the YouTuber Taryn Southern suggests, the flipside is that platform providers have to be alert as well. Power and resistance are part of the same operation and the question is: how and with what effects they are exercised by different actors in the algorithmic assemblage? While algorithms have the power to shape practice (e.g. videos created to optimize for certain signals such as clicks or watch time), people's practices have the power to shape how algorithms are designed, change, and evolve (e.g. how YouTube introduced watch time partly as a response to clicks gone awry). Dynamic power relations configure users differently as respected, useful, annoying or harmful, while users in turn see algorithms and platforms variously as business opportunities, helpful, discriminatory, or detrimental.

How or when users and platforms become one or the other might not always be easy to tell. In this chapter the case of the Reply Girls was used as a methodological device to identify such moments of subtle transitions by allowing us to understand how the algorithm change as event is used strategically to configure the conditions of participation. The algorithm change says: "Here, this is how the world turns now, spin in the right direction and you will be rewarded." The algorithm change does not merely encourage certain practices or foreclose others, it also opens up a valuable space for understanding the often quite complicated and convoluted power relations in networked modes of being.

The point of any digressive detour, including the one we have been on in this chapter, is not necessarily the destination or conclusion. The stories and scenes encountered along the way do not always add up and each and every one may take us in a new direction altogether. There is a story about aspirational labor and the ways in which platforms such as YouTube have gradually become more professionalized to steer user-generated content in the "right" direction. There is the story about how the "right" direction materializes in changing algorithms but might indeed be upset by the inconvenience of those who trouble the usual order of things. There is also the story of playing YouTube as if it were an algorithmic game and in doing so letting others see things they may otherwise not have been able to see. The rest of the stories are up to you.

Notes

1 Although her name is publicly known, I am not going to refer to it here, as she in private communication has stated that "given the opportunity again I would never have used my name." Therefore, I will only refer to her by the YouTube handle she used then, TheReplyGirl.
2 The "video response" feature was dismantled in September 2013 due to a "minuscule .0004% click-through rate" (Panzarino, 2013).
3 www.change.org/p/google-youtube-give-youtube-users-tools-to-combat-video-spam
4 Some of Eördöugh's articles include: www.dailydot.com/news/youtube-reply-girl-algo rithm-thereplygirl; www.dailydot.com/news/reply-girls-youtube-yogscast-machinima-response; www.dailydot.com/business/youtube-reply-girls-spam-return-will-hyde
5 Interview with Cristos Goodrow, Vice President Engineering at Google and responsible for Search & Discovery on the YouTube channel Computerphile (published on April 24, 2014): www.youtube.com/watch?v=BsCeNCVbd8&index=8&list=FLQJyA P44hZwB4N_ZtlaG6Gw

References

Ahmed, S. (2017). *Living a feminist life*. Durham, NC: Duke University Press.

Bakioğlu, B. S. (2016). Exposing convergence: YouTube, fan labour, and anxiety of cultural production in Lonelygirl15. *Convergence*, "https://protect-us.mimecast.com/s/yGx0Cqx V2vt8LB3yEtQC4Rk?domain=doi.org" https://doi.org/10.1177/1354856516655527.

Bar-Ilan, J. (2007). Google bombing from a time perspective. *Journal of Computer-Mediated Communication*, 12(3), 910–938.

Berlant, L. G. (2011). *Cruel optimism*. Durham, NC: Duke University Press.

Bijker, W. E., Hughes, T. P., & Pinch, T. J. (1987). *The social construction of technological systems: New directions in the sociology and history of technology*. Cambridge, MA: MIT Press.

Brunton, F. & Nissenbaum, H. (2015). *Obfuscation: A user's guide for privacy and protest*. Cambridge, MA: MIT Press.

Bucher, T. (2017). The algorithmic imaginary: Exploring the ordinary affects of Facebook algorithms. *Information, Communication & Society*, 20(1), 30–44.

Burgess, J. E. (2012). YouTube and the formalisation of amateur media. In D. Hunter, R. Lobato, M. Richardson, & J. Thomas (Eds.), *Amateur media: Social, cultural and legal perspectives* (pp. 53–58). Abingdon: Routledge.

Burgess, J. E. & Green, J. B. (2009). *The entrepreneurial vlogger: Participatory culture beyond the professional-amateur divide*. Stockholm: National Library of Sweden/Wallflower Press.

Burgess, J. & Green, J. (2013). *YouTube: Online video and participatory culture*. Chichester: John Wiley & Sons.

Callon, M. (2007). What does it mean to say that economics is performative. In D. MacKenzie, F. Muniesa, & L. Siu (Eds.), *Do economists make markets* (pp. 311–357). Princeton: Princeton University Press.

Christensen, C. (2013). Wave-riding and hashtag-jumping: Twitter, minority "third parties" and the 2012 US elections. *Information, Communication & Society*, 16(5), 646–666.

Covington, P., Adams, J., & Sargin, E. (2016). Deep neural networks for YouTube recommendations. Paper presented at the Proceedings of the 10th ACM Conference on Recommender Systems. RecSys '16, September 15–19, Boston, MA, USA.

Cunningham, S. (2012). Emergent innovation through the coevolution of informal and formal media economies. *Television & New Media*, 13(5), 415–430.

Cunningham, S., Craig, D., & Silver, J. (2016). YouTube, multichannel networks and the accelerated evolution of the new screen ecology. *Convergence*, 22(4), 376–391.

D'Onfro, J. (2015). The "terrifying" moment in 2012 when YouTube changed its entire philosophy. July 3. www.businessinsider.com/youtube-watch-time-vs-views-2015-7?r= US&IR=T&IR=T

de Certeau, M. (1984). *The practice of everyday life*. Berkeley: University of California Press.

Domingos, P. (2015). *The master algorithm: How the quest for the ultimate learning machine will remake our world*. New York: Basic Books.

Duffy, B. E. (2017). *(Not) getting paid to do what you love: Gender, social media, and aspirational work*. New Haven: Yale University Press.

Duffy, B. E. & Hund, E. (2015). "Having it all" on social media: Entrepreneurial femininity and self-branding among fashion bloggers. *Social Media + Society*, 1(2). doi: 10.1177/ 2056305115604337

Eördögh, F. (2012). Confessions of a reply girl: Alejandra Gaitan bares all. www.dailydot. com/society/alejandra-gaitan-reply-girl-interview

Fiske, J. (2002). *Television culture*. London: Routledge.

Foucault, M. (1978). *The history of sexuality: An introduction. Vol. 1*. New York: Vintage.

Foucault, M. (1982). The subject and power. *Critical Inquiry*, 8(4), 777–795.

Galloway, A. R. (2006). *Gaming: Essays on algorithmic culture*. Minneapolis: University of Minnesota Press.

Gillespie, T. (2014). The relevance of algorithms. In T. Gillespie, P. Boczkowski, & K. Foot (Eds.), *Media technologies: Essays on communication, materiality, and society* (pp. 167–194). Cambridge, MA: MIT Press.

Gillespie, T. (2017). Algorithmically recognizable: Santorum's Google problem, and Google's Santorum problem. *Information, Communication & Society*, 20(1), 63–80.

Hall, S. (2001). Encoding/decoding. In M. G. Durham & D. M. Kellner (Eds.), *Media and cultural studies: Keyworks* (pp. 166–176). Malden, MA: Blackwell.

Hallinan, B. & Striphas, T. (2016). Recommended for you: The Netflix Prize and the production of algorithmic culture. *New Media & Society*, 18(1), 117–137.

Hirsch, E. & Silverstone, R. (2003). *Consuming technologies: Media and information in domestic spaces*. Abingdon: Routledge.

Jakobsson, P. (2010). Cooperation and competition in open production. *PLATFORM: Journal of media and communication*, 12, 106–119.

Kushner, S. (2013). The freelance translation machine: Algorithmic culture and the invisible industry. *New Media & Society*, 15(8), 1241–1258.

Lobato, R. (2016). The cultural logic of digital intermediaries: YouTube multichannel networks. *Convergence*, 22(4), 348–360.

Manovich, L. (2009). The practice of everyday (media) life: From mass consumption to mass cultural production? *Critical Inquiry*, 35(2), 319–331.

Marwick, A. E. (2013). *Status update: Celebrity, publicity, and branding in the social media age*. New Haven: Yale University Press.

McMahon, T. (2012). How reply girl's videos make her mounds of cash. www.macleans.ca/society/technology/how-reply-girl-makes-mounds-of-cash/

Morreale, J. (2014). From homemade to store bought: Annoying Orange and the professionalization of YouTube. *Journal of Consumer Culture*, 14(1), 113–128.

Munsterman, R. (2017). YouTube star Taryn Southern explains the demanding new reality of being famous on social media. www.businessinsider.com/youtube-star-taryn-southern-explains-the-demanding-reality-of-social-media-fame-2017-6?r=US&IR=T&IR=T

Neff, G. (2012). *Venture labor: Work and the burden of risk in innovative industries*. Cambridge, MA: MIT Press.

Neff, G., Wissinger, E., & Zukin, S. (2005). Entrepreneurial labor among cultural producers: "Cool" jobs in "hot" industries. *Social Semiotics*, 15(3), 307–334.

O'Neill, M. (2012). YouTube responds to reply girls, changes related & recommended videos algorithm. March 13. www.adweek.com/digital/youtube-reply-girls

Orlikowski, W. J. & Scott, S. V. (2015). The algorithm and the crowd: Considering the materiality of service innovation. *Mis Quarterly*, 39(1), 201–216.

Panzarino, M. (2013) Google dumps video responses from YouTube due to dismal .0004% click-through rate. August 27. https://techcrunch.com/2013/08/27/google-dumps-video-responses-from-youtube-due-to-dismal-0004-click-through-rate/

Pinch, T. J. & Bijker, W. E. (1984). The social construction of facts and artefacts: Or how the sociology of science and the sociology of technology might benefit each other. *Social Studies of Science*, 14(3), 399–441.

Portwood-Stacer, L. (2013). Media refusal and conspicuous non-consumption: The performative and political dimensions of Facebook abstention. *New Media & Society*, 15(7), 1041–1057.

Postigo, H. (2016). The socio-technical architecture of digital labor: Converting play into YouTube money. *New Media & Society*, 18(2), 332–349.

Read, M. (2012). Weird internets: How the Reply Girl's breasts earned her YouTube death threats. http://gawker.com/5889759/weird-internets-how-thereplygirls-breasts-earned-her-youtube-death-threats

Roberge, J. & Melançon, L. (2017). Being the King Kong of algorithmic culture is a tough job after all: Google's regimes of justification and the meanings of Glass. *Convergence*, 23(3), 306–324.

Ross, A. (2009). *Nice work if you can get it: Life and labor in precarious times*. New York: New York University Press.

Sandvig, C. (2015). Seeing the sort: The aesthetic and industrial defense of "the algorithm." *Journal of the New Media Caucus*, 10(3), 1–21.

Seyfert, R. & Roberge, J. (2016). *Algorithmic cultures: Essays on meaning, performance and new technologies*. Oxford: Taylor & Francis.

Singhal, A. & Cutts, M. (2011). Finding more high-quality sites in search. https://google-blog.blogspot.no/2011/02/finding-more-high-quality-sites-in.html

Stewart, K. (2012). Pockets. *Communication and Critical/Cultural Studies*, 9(4), 365–368.

Striphas, T. (2015). Algorithmic culture. *European Journal of Cultural Studies*, 18(4–5), 395–412.

Syvertsen, T. (2017). *Media resistance: Protest, dislike, abstention*. Cham, Switzerland: Springer.

Van Dijck, J. (2013). *The culture of connectivity: A critical history of social media*. Oxford: Oxford University Press.

Vonderau, P. (2016). The video bubble: Multichannel networks and the transformation of YouTube. *Convergence*, 22(4), 361–375.

YouTube Content Creators (2012a). A note about recent changes. https://youtube-creators.googleblog.com/2012/05/note-about-recent-changes.html

YouTube Content Creators (2012b). Changes to related and recommended videos. https://youtube-creators.googleblog.com/2012/03/changes-to-related-and-recommended.html

YouTube Help (2017). Advertiser-friendly content guidelines. https://support.google.com/youtube/answer/6162278?hl=en

10

FROM NETWORKED TO QUANTIFIED SELF

Self-Tracking and the Moral Economy of Data Sharing

Aristea Fotopoulou

The formation of identity in digital media has been a central concern for media studies and other scholars in the last decade. The networked self is performed through interaction, connection, display, and management of visibility through privacy. Self-representation in this context is always a conversation between written, visual, and quantitative forms (Rettberg, 2016). Tampering with the affordances of social networking platforms, it is constructed in relation to the management of sociality, and as Papacharissi (2010) explains, this construction entails performances of the self across platforms and for a variety of audiences. Self-representation in social media largely relies on experiencing online platforms as spatial environments—the self moves through "imagined geographies of place" (ibid., p. 306).

As self-tracking technologies and practices (Lupton, 2014; Neff & Nafus, 2016) such as apps and gadgets become ordinary however, for example, with the inclusion of pedometers in mobile phones, it becomes increasingly evident that the construction of the "quantified self" is not merely another form of self-representation in digital culture, or just another aspect of the networked self. It requires special attention not least because cultural understandings of quantification and data link to wider questions of power relations. The quantified self is a cultural trend whose pioneers are people from the Quantified Self community (with capital QS), who undertake a range of practices of self-monitoring, data collection, management and analysis, with the use of wearable sensors and mobile technologies, in order to produce knowledge about the self.

Although sociological and other theoretical frameworks of the quantified self have largely done so through analysis of governmentality, surveillance, and self-monitoring, here my interest is with the values that shape and are shaped by the emerging culture of quantification and personal informatics, and the cultural understandings of data "sharing"—the sharing of personal data in the form of life logs, medical data, or just public records. In this chapter, I suggest that new practices of gathering data, through personal informatics, active self-tracking or passive and ubiquitous monitoring, are changing how people understand the Self, their personal and social responsibility. In what follows, I outline the key characteristics of the shift from networked to quantified self. I draw from ethnographic and media research that examined understandings of personal data amongst digital health start-up entrepreneurs and self-quantifiers in the San Francisco Bay Area.[1] Reflecting on this research, I frame self-tracking as a ritualistic performance of the self, and argue that contemporary cultural understandings of self-tracking and data sharing are underpinned by a moral economy. Its values prescribe new ways of connecting with others and enacting "good citizenship" through data practices, and normalize these practices as our means to an altruistic sociality. In other words, sharing data and self-quantifying operate as ritualistic performances of the "good citizen."

First, I revisit contested notions of Big Data and the implications that the intensification of data monitoring presents for identity, sociality, and citizenship. Then I move on to trace values of data longevity, permanence but also the right to self-erasure, as they manifest both in cultural texts, such as the fiction novels *The Circle* and *Super Sad True Love Story*, and in legal schemes such as the Right to be Forgotten. Third, I consider the moral undertones in the framing of personal data disclosure as "sharing" by apps and platforms such as *PatientsLikeMe*. Using some key examples from my ethnographic study, I next outline the delicate dance between commercialization and self-knowledge in the Quantified Self community. Finally, I discuss the performative and material aspects of the quantified self, and the centrality of ritual. These five sections work together to explicate the construction of the quantified self in digital media and with self-tracking technologies.

The Imagination of Data

Big Data are changing the shape of the social fabric; they change the ways in which people connect and the ways in which commons and the public good are defined. Jamie Sherman (2015) has sketched an application of Walter Benjamin's essay on *Art in the Age of Reproduction* in today's data quantification and tracking practices by drawing a parallel between the proliferation of images—about which Benjamin wrote—and the proliferation of data today. There are indeed important reasons to study the proliferation of data, and particularly how both the active and the willing, as well as the passive collection and sharing of personal data alters how individuals and populations perceive themselves. First, there are privacy concerns that relate to the ability to share and collect data with the use of ICTs, especially mobile devices, and a clear need for new regulation of monitoring and surveillance (Andrejevic, 2014). Although there are important differences with the American legal framework, in Europe the controversial EU Data Retention Directive (2006/24/EC), for instance, allows telecommunications companies to store customer metadata for six months (Brown, 2013). Beyond legal frameworks, devices and interfaces often allow self-tracking by default—for example, the operating system on iPhones iOS/10 performs location tracking and ad tracking by default, whereas older versions (iOS/8) did not offer a feature for turning off distance tracking. Therefore questions arise about how far existing legal frameworks that guide design and companies can effectively protect our constitutional rights as democratic citizens. Then, there are ethical and social concerns that link to the sharing of health data and the new meanings of surveillance in everyday life settings, in the context of care (French and Smith, 2013). The ubiquity of mobile devices and sensors allows close observation of behavioral change in a gamified way, which even makes self-surveillance pleasurable (Whitson, 2013). Such significant changes in what we allow to be monitored, how we participate in the monitoring and how we benefit from data, as individuals and as communities, need critical exploration.

Users, consumers, and patients play an active part in the process of collecting personal data: they track, obtain data, interpret infographics, determine their meaning, and attempt behavioral changes.[2] The vision of agency and empowerment of the quantified self is linked to these everyday practices of active self-tracking (Fotopoulou and O'Riordan, 2016). But as noted, self-tracking and data sharing is complemented by passive tracking, performed by collecting information even when the user does not purposefully do the tracking. The estimate of 50 billion devices and objects (buildings, roads, household appliances) will be connected online by 2020, which reminds us how we all contribute data in some way or another, even when we do so unintentionally. As Internet users we are of course becoming increasingly used to such unintentionality, as social media data mining becomes ordinary (Kennedy, 2016). Allowing users only limited degrees of manual adjustment, social media platforms that count and sort online data, such as Google and Facebook, work automatically via algorithm (Van Dijck, 2013). If controlling one's own visibility online is an important right to self-knowledge (Couldry et al., 2016), the question then is how can we think about the self in relation to self-tracking, passive data tracking and the ways in which data may be shared or publicly disclosed? Can we trust data to tell the whole story about who we are, to make us aware of ourselves as individuals and as collectivities?

Self-tracking practices are inexorably linked to a turbulent and fast-forming landscape demarcated by the digital health and biosensor industry. In the United States, the Affordable Care Act (ACA) has encouraged the specialization of accelerators (companies that help start-ups) according to ownership, purpose, or affiliation. Most health care accelerators such as Rock Health, Blueprint Health, Healthbox, Janssen Labs, and Start-Up Health are focused on digital health, which also intersects with biotechnology/pharma, medical technology, health care services, health care IT, and genomics, whereas the vast majority of those are based in California (Suennen, 2014). In the UK, NHS England envisions online portals and mobile phone apps where patients can access click-and-collect services for health and social care (Blog.zesty, 2015). Academic researchers, particularly in the medical sciences, also turn to the Internet as a huge collection of datasets. And many start-up Internet companies are also entering the field of tracking personal data for use in research or for commercial use, and they offer a new form of Internet service provision in the fields of digital health and biomedical research.

One may argue that this sheer volume, velocity, and variety of data, what is called Big Data, is in itself a good reason for trusting measured data (Anderson, 2008). Big Data is, however, still a contested term (Bassett, 2015), and indeed "data" more generally operate as a powerful discursive tool (Thornham and Gómez Cruz, 2016). Big Data changes the definition of knowledge. By privileging large-scale quantitative approaches, it sidelines other forms of analysis and limits the kinds of questions that can be asked: this has important normative and political consequences (Stephansen and Couldry, 2014). As boyd and Crawford also note, Big Data loses its meaning when taken out of context (2012, p. 670). Personal data are not just numbers, they are culturally produced and interpreted (Gitelman, 2013). "Data need to be imagined as data to exist and function as such, and the imagination of data entails an interpretive base" (ibid., p. 2). In other words, *data* only ever become *information* when they are interpreted in a context that is defined relative to the interests of particular actors (Kallinikos, 2009). Therefore the implications of data for identity, sociality, and citizenship relate to how such data will be interpreted and analyzed, and how and what kinds of knowledge are being made from these data. With smart, wearable, and other self-tracking technologies, we are experiencing a fundamental shift from previous forms of mediated self-disclosure and identity performance: it is the shift to quantity rather than form or content (what have been understood as the traditional generic aspects of digital and non-digital cultural products) from which meaning is being made.

All these Emotions, All these Yearnings, All these Data

Lenny Abramov, the main character in Gary Shteyngart's satirical romance *Super Sad True Love Story* exclaims:

> My hair would continue to gray, and then one day, it would fall out entirely, and then, on a day meaninglessly close to the present one, meaninglessly like the present one, I would disappear from the earth. And all these emotions, all these yearnings, all these data, if that helps to clinch the enormity of what I'm talking about, would be gone. And that's what immortality means. It means selfishness. My generation's belief that each one of us matters more than you or anyone else would think.

This sense of permanence, of data outliving physical bodies and lives, permeates Shteyngart's book, but also Rucker's *The Lifebox, the Seashell and the Soul*—where the Lifebox stores immortality and the world is largely computational.[3] Most interesting though is Dave Eggers's exploration of ranking, status, and sociality in a world where all personal information is made public and where data are constantly being generated. *The Circle* is the story of Mae, a naive and easily manipulated character, who makes it into a dream Google-like job situated in transparent buildings. A story about a Silicon Valley utopia that turns into a dystopia, *The Circle* introduces some of the key ideas that illustrate a shift from networked to quantified self. Participating in social networks is not really an option for the main character. Mae wants to remain inside the elite circle of trend-setting visionaries. In this world, the activity of rating is tantamount to the public performance of the self—a presence to be rated and evaluated, and to be self-sustained. Her encounter with data in social profiles, and as we learn from her, *our* encounters with personal analytics acquire, as Sherry Turkle has pointed out, potentially *existential* importance (2011). Data and measuring, quantifying everything, seem to give a sense of permanence, of longevity—a proof of existence. "Data—It will be here next year and next century," as one of the characters in the book concludes.

This understanding of personal data as permanent and of self-tracking as a way of life that could secure access to a person's *real* and immortal self is also widely prevalent in policy documents at European and U.S. level. Here, however, we can recognize a different cultural anxiety—the negotiation between disclosure and transparency, as well as the anxiety about the centrality of memory in the construction of both personal and collective identity. In an era that has been described as the "end of forgetting" (Bossewitch and Sinnreich, 2013), informational disclosure to unspecified, future audiences makes the concept of "context collapse" (Marwick and boyd, 2011) even more problematic. Resisting a self that becomes "transparent" (Lanzing, 2016) presupposes finding ways to navigate between, on the one hand, the conflicting demands for visibility and openness, and, on the other hand, the "Right to be forgotten."

Openness has expanded from sociocultural vision of knowledge commons in computer software to electronics hardware (Powell, 2015), to a necessary component of creating and governing commons. The flip side of this coin is the right to oblivion (or "Right to be forgotten"), which forms part of the data protection regulation by the European Commission. It aims to oblige public and private organizations to destroy or anonymize personal data in every format, paper or electronic, once the purpose for which they were created and gathered is achieved. But as it has been observed, an effective right to oblivion means that we need to move to a multidimensional conceptualization of the right to privacy (Xanthoulis, 2012). In addition to control over what can be measured and how it can be shared, here the concern and the control over visibility is associated with what can be erased and forgotten. It is a way of controlling self-representation and future profiling by escaping our algorithmic past. Met with substantial resistance in the United States, the regulation has been seen to limit how the internet operates as a global system of sharing information, and even as a great threat to free speech (Rosen, 2011). We could say that, as our identities are becoming increasingly dispersed and shared through multifaceted digital presence, autonomy and privacy are not preconditions of having a self any more. To even have a self, individuals needs to be able to manage their personal data and all those digital traces that inform predictive algorithms and construct different future instances of that self, quantified and networked.

But what happens with public records and the self-concept of communities, individual citizens, and societies? It is often said that those who control the past control the future. There are different versions of the past, which can be told as stories without being claimed as objective facts. Public administration changes give us vital information about the self-concept of that society and its interaction with the state. Such changes entail access of citizens to public archives for personal or for research reasons. But when individuals have multiple versions of identity, spread over social media platforms, genomic profiling, and self-tracking devices and apps—and when the state moves many of its responsibilities to private corporations—the matter of who has access to social memory and in what ways becomes more complex.

"Secrets are Lies. Sharing is Caring. Privacy is Theft"

In *The Circle*, through a series of manipulative mind games, Mae Holland reaches the three quotes that distil the essence of this dystopian world-within-a-world: "Secrets are Lies, Sharing is caring, Privacy is theft." This uncanny play with words signifies a re-attribution of, not property as Engels and Marx would hope, but of data access and information. Alluding to Proudhon's slogan that "property is theft," and the call for the abolition of private property that Marx and Engels advocated, the novel invites us to consider the idea that *privacy and property* have similar value. This proposition may not be after all that far-fetched. Without doubt we already know how Facebook sells our data to advertisers and how data is a new form of capital. The current vision communicated by large corporations, especially in the digital health industry, concurs with Mae Holland's principles. For instance, in "5 Insights in Digital Health" (Baum, 2014), big CEOs state that those who control capital control the data and vice versa.

Just like property rights, questions of data ownership, privacy rights, personal informatics flows, and disclosure are infused with moral significance. Hacking, identity theft, and piracy are considered violations of intellectual ownership and, as such, they are inevitably deemed as immoral acts. But when it comes to personal data ownership, the motto "privacy is theft" alludes to a reversal of this existing moral order: the violation here is the owners' *exclusivity* to their own data. The quote is certainly an oxymoron but it gives us a flavor of the paradoxical aspects

FIGURE 10.1   Screenshot of meforyou.org

of datafication and digital culture more generally, where personal information disclosure is being reframed as "sharing."

One of the many websites advocating the sharing of personal data for the common good and for the advancement of scientific research is *Meforyou.com* (Figure 10.1). The video featured on the website is a close shot of the face of little white girl called Georgia, while the narrator explains that she is not a statistic but a person with hopes, and a risk of developing breast cancer. The discourse of "all in this together" and dedicated action that concludes the video and saturates the website overall, calls for a contribution to the commons, and makes a case for a moral obligation to contribute to the repository. Similarly, the military *Million veteran program* recruits participants without requiring consent.[4] The project *Health Data Exploration* in their report "Personal Data for the Public Good" (HDE, 2014) articulate a vision of transforming public health with personal data provided voluntarily by self-trackers, in order to complement more traditional clinical or public health data collection. Emil Chiauzzi, Research Director of *PatientsLikeMe*, notes that there are vast opportunities afforded by the collection of passive data when it comes to inferring patient behavior. The video *Data for Good*, featured on the *PatientsLikeMe* website, invokes the dream of turning patient experience into voice (Figure 10.2). We see a manifestation of this same vision in many examples of online platforms inviting personal data sharing directly with researchers in clinical experiments[5] or platforms for open user-donated genetic data, such as *OpenSNP*.

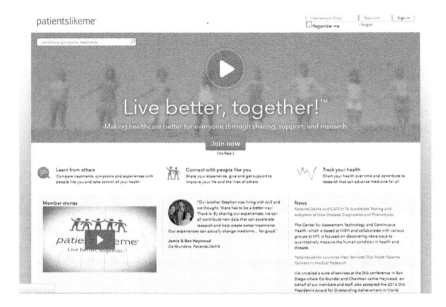

FIGURE 10.2   Screenshot of patientslikeme.com: Live better, together!

Beyond health data, the collection of passive data such as real-time traffic data is also advocated as a means to the greater social good. For example, in the article "Would you share private data for the good of city planning?" (Grabar, 2015) location data collection from individuals is thought to help understanding city planning and therefore understanding people. The question posed here is "How can data utopians convince the hoi polloi to share their comings and goings?" Although there are clear answers to this question,[6] it is the posing of the question that remains problematic. The rhetoric of the common good in smart and sustainable city projects is sticky because it may in fact give rise to distinct material–political arrangements and practices that recast who or what counts as a citizen (Gabrys, 2014, p. 7). The distinction between early adopters of innovative technology and ordinary people is a hierarchical one. Citizenship then becomes less about the enactment of rights and more about governance through self-monitoring and other data practices.

Although the value system that imbues data practices is predominantly a code of moral behaviors that pertain to sociality and community, it is supported by and is based on financial imperatives. For example, insurance companies provide attractive incentives of lower premiums to customers who share personal data (Lupton, 2016). In some platforms, users rely on paid subscriptions for punishment if they do not train enough or overeat (Cederström & Spicer, 2015). The "tracked self" is hence faced with increasing challenges of navigating through conflicting sets of values around technological innovation—those prescribed by communities of users such as the Quantified Self, and those of commercial enterprise (Barta & Neff, 2016).

People's Understandings of Data Sharing

California and Silicon Valley are hubs of activity. The Quantified Self (QS) is a phenomenon born in the San Francisco area, and can be best understood in the context of Californian techno-utopianism.

The quantified self is a dynamic identity that is produced by a community through interpretations of its own self-tracking activity, while its guiding premise remains to enable self-knowledge through self-tracking and large-scale data gathering. This production of meta-narratives about the meaning of self-tracking and practices in technoscientific capitalism make the QS a particularly interesting community (Fotopoulou, 2014). The QS is a dynamic media culture that constantly reinvents itself and its position in existing social structures through the narratives that it produces and circulates in the media. *Wired* is central to how ideas and definitions about the QS have disseminated since 2006 (Ruckenstein and Pantzar, 2015).

My research showed that people who use self-tracking for health or well-being purposes in their everyday life are often inclined to share their personal data with

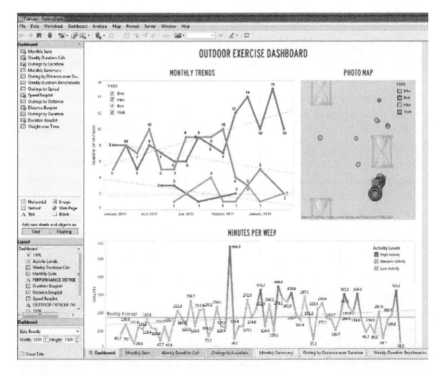

FIGURE 10.3   Screenshot showing the custom analysis developed by a runner to better understand their personal data. (Image provided by Mike McDearmon (2014), a product designer I interviewed who also logs his running creatively in a photoblog.)

others. Social media (Twitter, weblogs) are predominantly used for sharing visualizations and reports of data, whereas increasingly new social spaces are created, such as forums and specialized online platforms, where users exchange information about hacking into personal data (e.g. Fitbit, Quantified Self discussion forum, *PatientsLikeMe*). Interviews and participation in various events during my research made it clear that the motivation behind sharing information with others is often to learn (see Figure 10.3). Sharing personal concerns and data enables the production of knowledge about shared medical conditions and shared interests, and it also enables the development of technical skills (self-hacking). This finding is consistent with the wider framing of commercial wearable devices and fitness tracking in the media; as the hype of "big data is the new gold" calmed down after 2013, those technologies and practices have been framed with discourses of self-responsibility, empowerment, and agency (Fotopoulou and O'Riordan, 2016; Lupton 2016). Self-knowledge through sharing dovetails with all the above, although sharing over ownership of data seems to have become a new mode of user experience.

The Quantified Self community has been thought to enact a form of "soft resistance" to the hegemony of Big Data, and self-quantifiers have been understood as DIY actors who create and hack smaller, fragmented databases (Nafus and Sherman, 2014). However, as Whitney Erin Boesel (2014) noted in our conversation, users do not consciously enact "resistance"; they do not necessarily challenge existing hierarchies within science and technology when they are using a product such as a tracking app. They rather aim at improving their lives but by aligning themselves with the aims of the start-up or bigger company which sells the product for profit. What is more, nothing stops the industry from using smaller scale databases—in fact wearable sensors, fitness and medical companies mainly harvest these kinds of data. Individuals who tracked and self-quantified in my study were skeptical about the use of their personal data by companies and third parties without their consent, and were wary about who will have access to their data in the future. They had concerns about the collection, ownership, and sharing of data that were derived from tracking for fitness, pleasure, and self-improvement, but, interestingly, these concerns were significantly played down when it came to tracking for health by patients and caregivers.

This delicate dance between the commercial goals of companies and developers, and the aims for self-determination and self-knowledge of self-quantifiers manifests explicitly in the medical sector. Here, medical professionals and companies encourage the adoption of self-tracking tools in a top-down manner; sharing data with both is compulsory. In his attempt to release his personal data collected by his pacemaker company, one of my informants, Hugo Campos (2014) entered a long-lasting exchange with the industry (those who sell the pacemaker and own the data it records) and the medical establishment. Since medical professionals would only grant him a health report, and not the original data-log, self-tracking became for him a practice of life and death significance, as he called it. The user even attempted to hack the pacemaker, with the help of a programmer, in order to gain access to his own health data. This case indicates not only how much user control versus corporate control over data is a political issue, but also how the emerging communities of data tracking represent trust in data-logs as a means of knowing oneself.

Of course not everyone is a "data junkie," obsessed with access to huge amounts of their raw data—something that in any case requires advanced programming skills in order to make sense. And not everyone I talked to was a "genetic exhibitionist" either, as is the case with those who share genetic profiles in the social network *OpenSNP* (Hernandez, 2015). This is a key reason why developers of apps such as *Human*, a pedometer software that aims to motivate 30 minutes of minimum daily physical activity in users, are moving toward minimal interface design and a simple form of self-tracking. As the CEO told me, "instead of assuming that throwing immense amounts of data will change their behavior, we focused on distilling" (Olmos, 2014). At the same time, start-ups are becoming more alert to how privacy-sensitive personal data are. In response, they anonymize everything in the backend, so that it is impossible even for them to individualize single cases. Apps like *Human* are targeted to a more average user demographic, who is not necessarily interested in how the app works or what is inside the box.

Data Subjectivity: Ritual, Performativity, and Labor

In digital culture, practices of sharing, reconfiguring, and copying have been promoted with models such as mash-ups,[7] and have been understood as paradigmatic shifts to the idea of the modern individual. These practices celebrate how the cultural product remains unfinished, and a non-linear production process, with contributions from the collective, across time and space (Sinnreich, 2016). At its extreme, the moral and ethical dimensions of these practices have been even rendered into a recognized religion, Kopimism, as a way of reinstating the fallacy of copyright and of navigating questions of agency, power, and identity in networked society (ibid.). When it comes to self-tracking and data collection, the unfinished, fragmented product is the self, emerging through an endless process of reconstruction across shared datasets and statistical analyses. The quantified self is thus not merely another form of representation, a "data-double" (Harding, 2015) or a cultural Other that results from dataveillance. Its performative and material nature is based, on the one hand, in the vision that data can be infinitely recycled, repurposed and "correlated" (Mayer-Schönberger and Cukier, 2013), and that our future selves, social lives, and personal experiences can be predicted. On the other hand, it is performative because it is enacted through the telling of stories and re-enactments of identity in spaces of sharing such as the community meetings of the Quantified Self meet-ups, where meaning about technology is being made.

Indeed, self-tracking and sharing data are practices that are framed as pre-emptive: they come with the promise that risk can be eliminated in the future, as long as we get our acts together and collect more accurate data. Digital technologies that involve tracking personal behavior and quantified data are becoming central in discourses of patient empowerment not only in the United States, but also increasingly in U.K. and E.U. contexts. As noted elsewhere, mundane applications such as FitBit operate to anchor big visions of such low-risk futures and an innovation-led society (Fotopoulou and O'Riordan, 2016).

Collective knowledge production, such as crowdsourcing in cultural and museum projects, has been thought to feed into "communicative capitalism" (Dean, 2009). Indeed, in models of collective ownership and production that relate to the sharing of personal data, what is uncritically advocated and celebrated is the unpaid or free labor (Terranova, 2004) of a body that is productive and works around the clock, during sleep, work, and leisure. Everyday, all day, activity is being tracked for the extraction of statistical data/value, under the premise of the greater "common good." Although the work that this entails appears simple and automated, it requires multiple modes of engagement from the user; for example, in the case of FitBit, interpreting data graphs, responding to motivational messages and sharing stories, techniques and data via social networking. What we see here, as I have argued elsewhere is the formation of a distinct *data subjectivity* for which continuous productivity in all aspects of everyday life is essential (Fotopoulou and O'Riordan, 2016). The monitoring of such productivity operates as a rewarding practice that provides reassurance about being an ideal, proactive neoliberal citizen and good consumer who enacts self-responsibility and self-awareness.

Although the repetition of logging of information or checking of graphs and stats is a mundane activity, it is at the same time a ritualistic performance of the self. We may think here the repetitive practices of letter and journal writing (Rettberg 2016; O'Riordan, 2017) and logging information on an everyday basis, but importantly, how publicizing and sharing such information introduces elements from dogmas, such as self-confession and self-revelation. Accounting publicly for everyday activities and measures resembles giving an account to the higher order in confession; here of course it is not a religious institution, but closer to what Shapin (1990) calls "regimes of scientific knowledge assurance," and the scientific societies of gentlemen. In the era of big data and citizen science, shaped by discourses of empowerment, self-responsibility, and data-collectivism, this regime of knowledge assurance is being transferred to the Crowd (or the smaller, controlled crowd of the QS show-and-tell meet-up setting). The invitation to share what was previously conceived as personal is a performance of the "good citizen" and responsibility to others. And in contrast to the traditional representational forms of the diary or the journal, the public space and context of this ritualistic performance and self-disclosure is undefined.

Conclusion

I started this chapter with the question: how is our engagement with self-tracking technologies, such as apps and devices, changing the ways we perform and enact identity? Drawing from analysis of cultural texts, and on fieldwork with communities and individuals who practice self-tracking, I have examined the key aspects that indicate a shift from the networked to the quantified self, and explored the construction of the quantified self. The fast-forming landscape of tracking devices and data collection appears like a "data-topia," where citizens share information and empower themselves through data sharing, whilst contributing to the "common good." I suggested that our cultural understandings of collecting and sharing personal data are underpinned by a set of moral values.

First, we can identify a belief in the permanence and immortality of data, and a trust in their legitimacy. Navigating through the conflicting demands of visibility and openness, and the "right to be forgotten," to erase the past, is a key task, as our identities become increasingly dispersed and shared through self-representations in social media platforms, self-tracking apps, genomic and algorithmic profiling. The self here is less about autonomy and more about efficient management of this major undertaking.

Second, the framing of personal data disclosure as "sharing" by apps and platforms such as *PatientsLikeMe*, as well as location data in smart city projects, indicates a reversal of the existing moral order (where someone has exclusive ownership of their personal information, eloquently expressed in the motto "Privacy is theft"), and is particularly problematic. What is more, data sharing and self-quantifying normalize dataveillance and ubiquitous computing as our key access points to sociality and citizenship. At a time when public spaces and commons are vanishing, and for lack of other processes and spaces for meaningful sharing, sharing personal data becomes a key means of manifesting altruism.

Apart from the moral values of sharing for the common good however, I have underlined how the values of self-awareness and "knowledge through numbers," as well as those of technological innovation and marketization are shaping the Quantified Self community. These values are not necessarily moral but they delineate acceptable sociality within the community.

Who we are, and how we perceive and enact identity, citizenship and belonging, as our societies become progressively enmeshed with data-driven technologies and communication systems, is not merely another form of representation, or a case of "data-doubles." The Self in times of quantification is performative and material because data can be recycled and repurposed, to tell different stories about us, about the past and the future. The stories we tell about the data we collect, and the meanings we make by interpreting these data, are performative re-enactments of our identities. We read ourselves as texts through our data-stories, and this loop of reading and adjusting ourselves through technologies is always performative. But data-stories are not always interesting—the self is in fact performed in the mundane acts of repetition and continuous productivity, which are highly ritualistic as they introduce elements from dogmas such as self-confession. And it is by attending particularly to the ritualistic performances of the ideal, neoliberal "good," sharing citizen that manifest in the practice of self-tracking and public self-disclosure, that we can unravel how power operates. As is the case with previous instances of technological change, understanding the operation of power remains a key critical task for us, at the intersections of digital culture with data.

Acknowledgments

This chapter is based on research that received funding from the RCUK Digital Economy NEMODE network (2014). Research Placement at the Centre for Science and Justice, University of California, Santa Cruz, for the project Tracking biodata: sharing and ownership.

Notes

1 During the research a series of interviews was conducted that addressed questions of sharing, ownership, and value of personal data with a number of organizations, companies, and individuals. The project was funded by the Research Council UK Digital Economy Theme, New Economic Models in the Digital Economy Network (NEMODE).
2 Active tracking usually involves devices that contain a pedometer and accelerometer (measuring speed and distance traveled), temperature sensor, and some even include heart rate sensor. Some recognized first-generation quantified tracking devices and applications are Fitbit, myZeo, BodyMedia, MapMyRun, RunKeeper, MoodPanda, Nike Fuelband, The Eatery, Luminosity's Brain Trainer, and the NeuroSky and Emotiv brain-computer interfaces (BCI).
3 See Bossewitch and Sinnreich (2013) for other examples of fictional texts that examine the link between memory and identity.
4 The project suggests that only when researchers link to profiles (names and other identifying information) is there a need for protection.
5 See Van Dijck and Poell (2016) for a detailed analysis of health apps.
6 The proposed solution is anonymization of data before they are channeled into governmental projects, and promoting the value of open data for the common good.
7 Mash-ups blend pre-recorded sound tracks, usually by overlaying the vocal track of one song seamlessly over the instrumental track of another.

References

Andrejevic, M. (2014). Surveillance in the big data era. In K.D. Pimple (Ed.), *Emerging pervasive information and communication technologies (PICT): Ethical challenges, opportunities and safeguards* (pp. 55–69). Dordrecht, Netherlands: Springer.
Anderson, C. (2008). The end of theory: The data deluge makes the scientific method obsolete. *Wired magazine*, 16(7).
Barta, K. & Neff, G. (2016). Technologies for sharing: Lessons from quantified self about the political economy of platforms. *Information, Communication & Society*, 19(4), pp. 518–531.
Bassett, C. (2015). Plenty as a response to austerity? Big Data expertise, cultures and communities. *European Journal of Cultural Studies*, 18(4–5), 548–563.
Baum, S. (2014). 5 insights from digital health CEOs at JP Morgan Healthcare conference. *MedCity News*, January 14. https://medcitynews.com/2014/01/5-interesting-points-raised-digital-health-roundtable/

Blog.zesty (2015). NHS England outlines 5 year drive for "Digitised Healthcare." |*blog.zesty.co.uk.* http://blog.zesty.co.uk/nhs-englands-chief-outlines-5-year-drive-digitised-healthcare/

Boesel, W.E. (2014). Skype interview by Aristea Fotopoulou, March 20, San Francisco.

Bossewitch, J. & Sinnreich, A. (2013). The end of forgetting: Strategic agency beyond the panopticon. *New Media & Society*, 15(2), 224–242.

boyd, d. & Crawford, K. (2012). Critical questions for big data: Provocations for a cultural, technological, and scholarly phenomenon. *Information, Communication & Society*, 15(5), 662–679.

Brown, I. (2013). Lawful interception capability requirements. *Computers & Law*, 24(3), 14–16.

Campos, H. (2014). Skype interview by Aristea Fotopoulou, March 7, San Francisco.

Cederström, C. & Spicer, A. (2015). *The Wellness Syndrome*. London: Polity Press.

Couldry, N., Fotopoulou, A., & Dickens, L. (2016). Real social analytics: A contribution toward a phenomenology of a digital world. *The British Journal of Sociology*, 67(1), 118–137.

Dean, J. (2009). *Democracy and other neoliberal fantasies: Communicative capitalism and left politics.* Durham, NC: Duke University Press.

Fotopoulou, A. (2014). The quantified self community, lifelogging and the making of "smart" publics. *openDemocracy.* www.opendemocracy.net/participation-now/aristea-fotopoulou/quantified-self-community-lifelogging-and-making-of-%E2%80%9 Csmart%E2%80%9D-pub.

Fotopoulou, A. & O'Riordan, K. (2016). Training to self-care: Fitness tracking, biopedagogy and the healthy consumer. *Health Sociology Review*, 26(1), 54–68.

French, M. & Smith, G. (2013). "Health" surveillance: New modes of monitoring bodies, populations, and polities. *Critical Public Health*, 23(4), 383–392.

Gabrys, J. (2014). Programming environments: Environmentality and citizen sensing in the smart city. *Environment and Planning D: Society and Space*, 32(1), 30–48.

Gitelman, L. (2013). *Raw data is an oxymoron*. Cambridge, MA: MIT Press.

Grabar, H. (2015). Would you share private data for the good of city planning? *Next City, Science of Cities,* January 27. http://nextcity.org/daily/entry/traffic-data-privacy-sharing-city-planning

Harding, J. (2015). Data doubles and the specters of performance. In S.E. Wilmer & A. Žukauskaitė (Eds.), *Resisting biopolitics: philosophical, political and performative strategies* (pp. 173–188). London: Routledge.

Health Data Exploration. (2014). Personal Data for the Public Good Report. California Institute for Telecommunications and Information Technology. http://hdexplore. calit2.net/wp-content/uploads/2015/08/hdx_final_report_small.pdf

Hernandez, D. (2015). The social network for people who want to upload their DNA to the Internet. *Fusion.net.* http://fusion.net/story/40034/the-social-network-for-people-who-want-to-upload-their-dna-to-the-internet

Kallinikos, J. (2009). On the computational rendition of reality: Artefacts and human agency. *Organization*, 16(2), 183–202.

Kennedy, H. (2016). *Post, mine, repeat*. Basingstoke: Palgrave Macmillan.

Lanzing, M. (2016). The transparent self. *Ethics and Information Technology*, 18(1), 9–16.

Lupton, D. (2014). Self-tracking modes: Reflexive self-monitoring and data practices. doi: 10.2139/ssrn.2483549.

Lupton, D. (2016). *The quantified self*. Chichester: John Wiley & Sons.

Marwick, A.E. & boyd, d. (2011). I tweet honestly, I tweet passionately: Twitter users, context collapse, and the imagined audience. *New Media & Society*, 13(1), 114–133.

Mayer-Schönberger, V. & Cukier, K. (2013). *Big data: A revolution that will transform how we live, work, and think.* Boston, MA: Houghton Mifflin Harcourt.

McDearmon, M. (2014). Skype interview, March 25, San Francisco.

Nafus, D. & Sherman, J. (2014). Big data, big questions | this one does not go up to 11: The quantified self movement as an alternative big data practice. *International Journal of Communication*, 8, 11.

Neff, G. & Nafus, D. (2016). *The self-tracking.* Cambridge, MA: MIT Press.

Olmos, R. V. (2014). Skype interview by Aristea Fotopoulou, March 25, San Francisco.

O'Riordan, K. (2017). *Unreal objects: Digital materialities, technoscientific projects and political realities.* London: Pluto Press.

Papacharissi, Z. (Ed.). (2010). *A networked self: Identity, community, and culture on social network sites.* Abingdon: Routledge.

Powell, A. B. (2015). Open culture and innovation: Integrating knowledge across boundaries. *Media, Culture & Society*, 37(3), 376–393.

Rettberg, J. W. (2016). *Seeing ourselves through technology: How we use selfies, blogs and wearable devices to see and shape ourselves.* Berlin: Springer.

Rosen, J. (2011). The right to be forgotten. *Stanford Law Review. Online*, 64, 88.

Ruckenstein, M. & Pantzar, M. (2015). Beyond the quantified self: Thematic exploration of a dataistic paradigm. *New Media & Society*, 14(7), 1164–1180. doi: 10.1177/1461444815609081

Shapin, S. (1990). Science and the public. In R. Olby, N. Cantor, J. R. R. Christie, & M. J. S. Hodge (Eds.), *Companion to the History of Modern Science* (pp. 990–1007). London: Routledge.

Sherman, J. (2015). How theory matters: Benjamin, Foucault, and Quantified Self—Oh my! *Epic*, January 28. www.epicpeople.org/how-theory-matters/

Sinnreich, A. (2016). Sharing in spirit: Kopimism and the digital Eucharist. *Information, Communication & Society*, 19(4), 504–517.

Stephansen, H. C. & Couldry, N. (2014). Understanding micro-processes of community building and mutual learning on Twitter: a "small data" approach. *Information, Communication & Society*, 17(10), 1212–1227.

Suennen, L. (2014). Survival of the fittest: Health care accelerators evolve toward specialization, California Health Care Foundation. www.chcf.org/~/media/MEDIA%20LIBRARY%20Files/PDF/S/PDF%20SurvivalFittestAccelerators.pdf

Terranova, T. (2004). *Network culture: Politics for the information age.* London: Pluto Press.

Thornham, H. I. & Gómez Cruz, E. (2016). Hackathons, data and discourse: Convolutions of the data (logical). *Big Data & Society*, 3(2), 1–12. doi: 10.11/2053951716679675

Turkle, S. (2011). *Alone together: Why we expect more from technology and less from each other.* New York: Hachette.

Van Dijck, J. (2013). *The culture of connectivity: A critical history of social media.* Oxford: Oxford University Press.

Van Dijck, J. & Poell, T. (2016). Understanding the promises and premises of online health platforms. *Big Data & Society*, 3(1), 99–107. doi: 10.1177/2053951716654173

Whitson, J. R. (2013). Gaming the quantified self. *Surveillance & Society*, 11(1/2), 163–176.

Xanthoulis, N. (2012). Conceptualising a right to oblivion in the digital world: A human rights-based approach. http://ssrn.com/abstract=2064503

11

"DOING" LOCAL

Place-Based Travel Apps and the Globally Networked Self

Erika Polson

> My personal pet hate is travelers who DO things. Did you DO Angkor Wat, nope I went there but I didn't do it. How do you DO a city? If anyone knows can they please tell me.
>
> *(James, Bordersofadventure.com, 2013)*

> Don't go to Paris. Don't tour Paris. And please, don't *do* Paris. Wherever you go—don't *go* there, *LIVE* there.
>
> *(Airbnb, 2016)*

In the first quote above, James is using a post on an adventure travel blog to engage in a common traveler's ritual: complaining about the discursive practices of other travelers. In this case, his objection is to those who would see travel as a series of must-dos—lists of sites one must visit and practices one must engage in, as if checking off a series of boxes, to have properly "done" their trip. Although this competitive travel-*doing* seems to stem from an effort by cultural experience seekers to differentiate themselves from mass tourists—frequenters of all-inclusive resorts, tour busses, cruises—the usage has recently become *lingua non grata* in a continuously evolving economy of traveler cool,[1] and James's complaint reflects a shift away from a type of travel that celebrates the overt consumption and exploitation of cultural sites.

Spurred by innovations in the peer-to-peer sharing economy, as well as by developments in location technology that connect networked users to place-based people and services, many companies targeting the new global traveler have moved away from portraying travel destinations as exotically "other," and now emphasize immersion into everyday life while abroad. The purpose of this chapter is to explore this shift in travel practices, and to understand how it connects to the growing use of location-based social media platforms that link people to place—reflecting efforts to produce "insider" experiences of alternative lives, and changing what counts as cultural capital among those who travel. In a world of travel made more accessible by low-cost airlines, a hyper focus on finding a unique experience has become more pronounced, and more challenged, by a social media culture where images of travel circulate continuously. The travel industry has sought to keep up by tailoring offerings to individual and niche desires, and intrepid wanderers have sought new ways to distinguish their experiences. One answer, provided by technology companies and embraced by users, has been an attempt to collapse the travel genre into the domestic space, by connecting travelers to everyday life situations (or simulations) involving home, friendship, cooking, and other daily routines through networked travel applications. The common promise of these apps is that they will allow the visitor to "feel like a local."

Of the many tech companies that work to connect travelers to local life, perhaps none has been more successful at capitalizing on this new exoticism of the everyday than Airbnb—the web-based home rental service that bills itself as a way to get away from the tourist zones and into "real local neighborhoods." A recent ad airing on television in the United States is illustrative: the ad opens with a view of the Eiffel Tower; as a hand comes up to photograph it with a selfie-stick, a young narrator's admonishing voice advises the following, "Don't go to Paris. Don't tour Paris. And please, don't *do* Paris." This last phrase is spoken derisively as the frame cuts to a tour group rolling by the Arc de Triomphe on Segway scooters. Cue a change of music, and the next scene shows a hip female traveler arriving alone at the door of a local residence, warmly welcomed inside by a friendly French man. The ad goes on to juxtapose scenes of mass tourists all taking the same photo of the same attraction with their smartphones, against those of people joyfully cooking, socializing, napping, playing sports, riding a bicycle, and even enjoying a public bath surrounded by newfound friends, and commands the viewer, "Wherever you go—don't *go* there. *Live* there."

Building on its claim to the local immersion market, Airbnb has recently launched an "Experiences" section of its app, where extroverted locals can sell hanging out, dinner parties, and excursions to travelers, creating a part-time tour operation in the same way that Uber drivers may use their own cars to become part-time taxis. The company recruits hosts by encouraging them to "Organize an art walk or a picnic with friends, so travelers can see how locals live." Other companies in the sector offer similar access to local experiences, local meals, and local parties—all with local people. Meanwhile, online publications have gotten the picture, and the Internet is full of lists of the "Top 10 ways to travel like a local anywhere" (e.g. Padykula, 2015), and related advice for eating, dressing, and behaving like a local.

In this chapter, I draw from theories of the middle classes and leisure/travel to reflect on new developments in location-based social travel apps, linking the globalizing middle classes to the web-based tools enabling travelers to put emerging identities as "networked global citizens" into practice by connecting them to knowledge, service, and comfort offered by "local" people around the world. The overall argument presented here is five-fold: 1) social media are sites for the performance and circulation of travel experience, and such performances of a "globally networked self" can be valuable cultural capital for upwardly mobile middle classes in a global economy; 2) however, as travel experiences pass repetitively through social media channels, they seem increasingly staged or cliché, and thus travelers seek new ways of obtaining "authentic" or unique experiences; 3) such authentic travel experiences are increasingly sought through efforts to "live like a local"; 4) localization apps provide users with a means to enact the fantasy of the "global citizen"; and 5) in a globally networked context where outwardly focused middle classes from a variety of nations will share increasing comfort and familiarity with each other, the emerging economy for localization platforms becomes a channel for capitalizing on and reproducing these affinities—raising questions about who is counted as an outsider or insider, who is counted as a "local." After a brief history of how travel has evolved as a middle-class status asset, the chapter will explore how the emergence of web-enabled services and apps dedicated to connecting networked travelers to local places and people is one indicator that for the globalizing middle classes, the networked self has a growing global component.

Status (Updates) through Travel

Although travel originated through trade, by the late nineteenth century it had become a bourgeois leisure pursuit associated with self-cultivation through the consumption of new and foreign experiences, marking it as an arena for the development of middle-class cultural capital. Bourdieu conceived that social mobility within the middle classes came from "discovering the powers or forms of capital which are or can become efficient, like aces in a game of cards" (1987, p. 4), and used the notion of "cultural capital" to connote status-bearing competencies gained through experiences that yield familiarity with knowledge, practices, lifestyles, and customs considered of value in a particular culture (1984). For aspirational middle classes, travel has been employed as a means to self-improvement (Soica, 2016), and "pursued as a status asset, as well as an enjoyable and exciting experience" (Rojek, 1993, p. 120). As such, travel, and its various virtues or lack of them, has become a contested discursive field.

In *The Tourist: A New Theory of the Leisure Class*, MacCannell (1976, 1999) noted that by the mid-twentieth century, the spirit of bourgeois competition characterizing a middle-class work ethic had extended into the realm of leisure, and attitudes began to shift toward judgment and derision of the figure of "the tourist." He found tourists were being "reproached for being satisfied with superficial experiences of other peoples and places" and, in this newly contested arena, a growing chorus of voices asserted that a better tourism must be "based on a desire to go beyond the other 'mere' tourists to a more profound appreciation of society and culture" (1999, p. 10). The underlying goal of these endeavors was the pursuit of "authentic" experience—an effort MacCannell saw as counter to the alienation of modern life, something to be found in non-Western cultures with "simpler" lifestyles where people lived off the land and in concert with community and tradition. However, such desires were easily coopted by tourist sites, where access to inner worlds and real life was reproduced through what MacCannell referred to as "staged authenticity" (p. 98).

An example of staged authenticity can be seen in Bruner and Kirshenblatt-Gimblett's (1994) ethnography of a British expatriate family's tourism operation in Kenya, where visitors are treated to performances of life in a traditional Maasai homestead set up on their defunct family ranch (followed by tea). Tour brochures promise the chance to see "legendary Maasai" in their natural habitat, enacting warrior and tribal dance scenes of their "proud past" (p. 440); the ethnographers noted that, to provide a "simulation of realism" the ranch owners "did not permit the Maasai to wear their digital watches, T-shirts, or football socks" and electronic music and kitchen equipment had to be "locked away and hidden from the tourist view" (p. 457). Considering that the consumption of the tourist experience occurs mainly through the production of visual media (Lofgren, 1999)[2] and these photographic representations are important for helping tourists to organize and authenticate their experiences (Urry, 1990), it is unsurprising that Bruner and Kirshenblatt-Gimblett found the daily Maasai performance amounted mainly to a series of "tableaux vivant, designed for a live photographic encounter" (p. 450).

Azariah (2016) has pointed out that the very notion of tourism as something staged "attributes an illusory quality to tourist experience that suggests it is defined against something more genuine" (p. 940). For middle-class subjects seeking distinction through more "authentic" travel experiences, that more genuine option was pursued through a division that emerged between the "traveler" and the "tourist" (Munt, 1994).[3] For some, *travel* involved eschewing the comforts of the resort or the organized tour and embracing the uncertainty and chaos of the unplanned itinerary. The self-improvement ethic of this move can be seen in the essay, "Why we travel," where Pico Iyer (2000) wrote that when traveling, he was "searching for hardship" as part of his own moral character development (para. 3). Overall, travel is portrayed as more authentic than tourism because it is considered "adventurous, spontaneous, and involving some degree of hardship," while tourism, "is perceived as being superficial, passive, devoid of any real risk, and commercially motivated" (Azariah, 2017, p. 4). In addition to authenticity, distinction is achieved by pursuing the more "unique" experience. Zuelow (2016) has stressed that the form of cultural capital acquired through tourism is made more difficult to achieve when "everybody is touring the same places and seeing the same sites" and pointed out that discerning travelers continuously seek new ways to go off the beaten track; he noted the growth of tourism to Antarctica as an example (p. 175).

As travelers seek more unique and authentic experiences in the places they visit, a variety of new travel practices and genres have developed that attempt to do more to provide meaningful engagement with some aspect of "local culture." For tourists who are weary of the commodification of culture seen through the growing presence of the multinational brands dotting travel routes, local food and drink can become the site of authentic experience (Sims, 2009). In recent years, Schnell (2011) noted an "enormous expansion in promotion of local food and agriculture to tourists," finding that food was used as a means of "experiencing the 'authentic' or 'true' nature of a place" (p. 281). This "agritourism" sees its counterpart in the growth of "wine tourism," through which Quadri-Felitti and Fiore (2012) have claimed tourists link authenticity to such site-specific interactions as meeting the wine maker, purchasing regional wines, or going for a hike on private lands. While these examples show how the quest for authenticity is directed toward "consuming the local," other efforts focus on accessing the local through participatory experiences. This is seen, for example, in the rise of "voluntourism," where organizations offer travelers an opportunity to participate in an excursion that "has a volunteer component, as well as a cultural exchange with local people" (Brown, 2005, p. 480)—although the actual benefit to local communities has been called into question (see Simpson, 2004). Jansson (2007) has noted the development of an "immersive" travel ethos among some backpackers, where they might seek to "be on the same level" as locals by attempting to connect to local social networks and avoiding expressions of the "tourist gaze"—for example, by not taking photographs (p. 17). This positioning of authenticity as something residing in "the local" is one of the issues underlying the rise of apps aimed at helping travelers to feel like, act like, or connect to local life.

Interestingly, this shift toward "the local" in tourism practices finds its parallel in a shifting focus by researchers toward understanding the "everyday life" of tourists. In much of the literature discussed above, tourism and travel have been symbolically constructed by researchers as the opposite of everyday life, something that functions through the differentiation of the traveler from the "hosts," and the accessing of alternative realities in terms of location, routines, food, and so on (e.g. see MacCannell, 1976, 1999). It has been characterized by "uniqueness, for being an escape from routine, and so being something out of the ordinary" (Azariah, 2017, p. 7). However, a recent move in tourism studies has begun to critique the over-simplified contrasts produced by seeing tourism as an escape from real life, with "a reconsideration of the distinctiveness of tourism from everyday life experiences" (Uriely, 2005, p. 200). This intervention acknowledges the embodiment of the traveler, and the importance of ordinary practices and routines used to feel comfortable or at home while away (Pons, 2003).

Larsen (2008) argued that the problem with thinking of tourism as a dualism between home and away is that "everyday life and tourism end up belonging to different ontological worlds, the worlds of the mundane and the exotic" (p. 22). He pointed to Urry's (1990) transformation from *The Tourist Gaze*, in which he portrayed tourism as formed in opposition to the everyday, to his exploration in *The Tourist Gaze 3.0* (Urry & Larsen, 2011) of how tourism and everyday life were becoming de-differentiated. Researchers have realized that, rather than leave themselves and their real lives behind when they travel, the daily routine—everyday practices, routines, and relationships—becomes a part of the "traveler's baggage . . . no longer an escape from everyday life but also a way of performing it" (Larsen, 2008, p. 22). This turn, which seeks to highlight the "everyday and habitual nature of much tourism life" (ibid., p. 26), corresponds to the emerging local trend among tourists themselves, where alternative versions of everyday life are celebrated by picturing (and posting) oneself as a natural inhabitant of multiple locals. Networked digital media are central to this development.

Digital Media and Travel

Digital media and communications have greatly impacted why, where, and how people travel. Decisions about where to go, as well as lodging, dining, and other activities are now heavily influenced by online user-generated reviews and photographs, which are considered more reliable than information provided by tourism businesses and organizations (Litvin et al., 2008). Although written travel narratives told through fictional and non-fiction accounts, photography, guidebooks, postcards, and so on have a long history (Azariah, 2017), online and social media have been increasingly taken up by users eager to share their own travel stories and experiences in a collaborative way (see Leung et al., 2013). In fact, today, travel content is among the most viewed content on social media (Watson, 2015).

The digital transformation of travel centers heavily on two areas: the live, networked nature of traveler communication capabilities, and the advent of digital photography. While travel before the Internet was associated with narratives of leaving the world behind, maintaining only intermittent connection with loved ones through letters posted to predetermined stops, today's leisure travelers now use a variety of mobile devices to stay in touch with geographically dispersed friends and family members (Germann Molz, 2012). The ability to remain connected to social networks (via email, texting, Skype or other web-based video-calling platforms, and social networking sites [SNS]) is associated with what Jansson (2007) has called the "decapsulation" of tourist experience, where the gap between home and away, between the ordinary and extraordinary, is compressed through uses of digital media. Jansson argued that the portability of digital media expands the access that foreigners have to new terrain (e.g. through navigation technologies) and impacts representations of the travel experience, through the immediate ability to share and receive feedback on images and narratives. Such immediacy has been said to create a sense that people's social networks are actively traveling with them during a journey (Germann Molz, 2012), which may provide comfort for travelers. However, although a study by Kim and Tussyadiah (2013) found real-time travel-related posting or photo-sharing on SNS led to social support as well as a more "enjoyable tourism experience," they noted this was particularly true when tourists used self-presentation strategies to "*selectively* present their travel stories" (p. 87, emphasis added).

One of the most significant ways of framing and sharing travel memories is through photography, and the transition to digital photography has impacted travel in terms of both how tourists take photos and what they do with them. For example, Larsen (2014) illustrated how the ability to delete and retake photographs allows for more experimentation and provides more "control over how people and places are represented" (p. 103). Affordances for sharing travel pictures via networked media mean these photos are more visible than ever before (Rubinstein & Sluis, 2008), inviting questions about how the sense of distinction and uniqueness of travel experiences might be impacted by the increasing circulation (and reproduction) of travel imagery.

On the one hand, sharing similar images can play a role in producing collective experiences and identities around travel. Visual imagery may help us to organize our ideas about things before we see them, and, moreover, the "touristic experience involves not merely connecting a [visual] marker to a sight, but participation in a collective ritual, in connecting one's own marker to a sight already marked by others" (MacCannell, 1999, p. 137). In this way, by taking and posting a photo of a familiar site, or by replicating a popular pose or technique, travelers position themselves as among others who have visited these places and engaged in these rituals. This can be seen, for example, in "Pisa pushing"—in which the photographic subject poses in the foreground of Italy's Leaning Tower of Pisa with arms outstretched from a position where, in the resulting two-dimensional photo, their hands seem either to hold up or push over the tower. Through photographs and hashtags posted to social networking sites—popular tags include #travel, #athomeintheworld, #letsgoeverywhere, and #wanderlust—users connect their experiences to those of others through similar visual representations and emotional responses to travel.

However, as travel images pass through a variety of social media channels that privilege the visual, and their archival presence is compounded by the use of shared hashtags, posts about experiences projected as unique may seem instead to become rather ordinary. In her essay, "A thousand words: A writer's pictures of China," Alice Walker (1989) leaves her camera at home and instead creates a journal of written snapshots about a trip to China, with each "picture" describing scenes through a combination of context, thoughts, backstories, tangential musings, and feelings. Among Walker's reasons for renouncing travel photography was as a response to the mainstreaming of personal meanings attached to travel: "When the TV commercial declares Kodak 'the nation's storyteller,' I shudder, because I realize our personal culture is about to become as streamlined as our public" (p. 99). Such concerns seem amplified by today's social media environment, where, as Jacob Silverman (2015) opined in *The Guardian*, "nuance, difference, and complexity evaporate as one scrolls through these endless feeds, vaguely hoping to find something new or important but mostly resigned to variations on familiar themes" (para. 1).

Reflecting a growing reflexivity about this issue among millennials, college student Elizabeth Lepore used a blog post entitled "Doing it for the gram: A semester abroad according to Instagram" (2017) to critique how she and her friends used the study abroad program to amass a series of experiences across multiple European cities that felt in hindsight like they were simply staged for Instagram. She wrote about a photo taken early on with some friends at the monastery in Monserrat, noting that, "by the end of the semester, I don't think a single one of my friends did not take identical photos perched on the edge of the mountain" (para. 7). During the semester, Lepore's social media contained the posts of her friends, many of whom were simultaneously studying in different cities across Europe, as well as their own networks of study abroad friends, so that her feed was a continual stream of travel imagery. She soon realized she was seeing the exact same photos posted on Instagram from a list of places considered cool and must-dos among study abroad peers (e.g. the John Lennon wall in Prague, the baths of Budapest) and lamented, "I started to feel like I was a walking cliché" (para. 11).

Silverman (2015) has argued that digitally shared travel photos have become more about communicating an experience to others than about creating a memory of the moment for oneself. Master's students in the University of Amsterdam's New Media and Digital Culture program took their critique of such self-promotion via social media-shared travel photos to a satirical level, by creating an app called "Been There, Done That" that allows people to insert their photographs into popular travel backgrounds, in order to "fake their way around the world" and share it on social media (Kersten, 2015, para. 1).

Central to the convergence of travel photography and networked communications is the emergence of the "selfie"—a photo "characterized by the desire to frame the self in a picture taken to be shared with an online audience" (Dinhopl & Gretzel, 2016, p. 130)—which has become so prominent that many hotels and popular tourist attractions now provide (or sell) "selfie sticks" to visitors (Paris & Pietschnig, 2015) while some over-touristed areas have banned use of the sticks (Coldwell, 2017). Dinhopl and Gretzel (2016) argued that selfie-taking has altered the "tourist gaze," so that now the tourists themselves become objects of the gaze, with an audience made up of distant others on social media. They noted that, in framing and presenting themselves through selfies, tourists shift the focus away from "fetishizing the extraordinary at the tourist destination" and instead "seek to capture the extraordinary within themselves" (p. 126).

Performances of self-as-traveler are strengthened by the ability to broadcast locations, whether through check-ins, place-based hashtags, or the automatic geo-tagging that can be enabled on many SNS apps. Schwartz and Halegoua (2015) created the notion of the "spatial self" (where the self is displayed on social media using geo-coded markers of offline physical activities) to understand a growing tendency for individuals to "document, archive and display their experiences and/or mobility within space and place" in order to perform aspects of their identities to others (p. 1644). This concept of location performance is highly relevant to the context of networked travel, and particularly so considering how travel can be a means to accrue and project cultural capital, as noted in the previous section.

Accessing a Local "Experience"

A recent *Time* magazine article on the subject of how to travel like a local began with this assessment: "No one wants to feel like a tourist. And these days, people don't even want to feel like travelers, but want to *experience* a place like a *local*" (Hoeller, 2015, para. 1, emphases added). A series of such articles now dominates the travel advice publishing genre, with suggestions for how to dress, eat, and move through space like a local in order to blend in and have a more connected experience, while also suggesting that such experiences will be more meaningful and unique than those of other tourists. The value of "looking" like a local as the first step to gaining access to these experiences is highlighted by many travel bloggers, seen for example in a post advising readers to "carry yourself with confidence" so that people will think you know "what you are doing and where you are going . . . even if you don't have a clue" (Hewitt, 2010, para. 19). An article on *Life Hack* suggests putting your tourist map away and just stumbling around the local area, as you may find a "trail that leads to an overlook of the ocean that no one has ever captured photographs of before" (Klein, 2016, para. 10), and shares other recommendations for distinguishing oneself from other tourists by doing as the locals do, such as climbing to the top of a cliff, even if afraid of heights, in order to find hidden gems that "other tourists never even know of" (para. 12). Although the idea that some "locals" might also be too afraid of heights to climb that cliff may not have occurred to the author, it is beside the point—the "local" here functions not as an actually attainable subjectivity but as a discursive tool to propel the search for authentic travel experiences, and evaluate such experiences vis-à-vis those of other travelers.

A range of mobile and web-based applications has emerged to both enable and drive the travel-like-a-local trend. Among the most successful platforms are those that connect visitors to either free or paid "local" lodging. Airbnb increasingly dominates the for-profit local housing marketplace, but has been critiqued for talking up its community/sharing aspect when in fact most often people are renting an entire (unoccupied) home that entails very little interaction with local hosts (see "New Airbnb," 2017). Using a less consumption-oriented model, the social networking community Couchsurfing connects members with beds through a free guest-and-hosts matching service that promises users they can "meet and stay with locals all over the world," and extends its commitment to creating connections among visitors and locals through community gatherings and dinners.

Considering that hanging out with people ("new friends") may be more likely to make strangers feel like they are living a local life than if they have simply taken over someone's home for a few days, a range of apps promises to connect travelers to locals through eating together or sharing "experiences." The commodification of "experience" has become central to the tourism industry (Andersson, 2007), and the organizing concept of most travel apps is on providing access (mostly for a fee) to local experiences. For example, consider the promotional language of some of this sector's emergent brands: the Spanish company, Vayable,[4] offers the chance to "discover and book unique experiences with local insiders"; WithLocals,[5] a Netherlands-based company, connects travelers to home dining and other excursions in Europe and Asia, promising users will "enjoy a city like a local" by being connected to locals "through food and experiences"; and VizEat, a French company, enables people to sell in-home dining and promises travelers they can "taste the city with locals" and "enjoy immersive food experiences with locals in 110 countries."[6]

Reflecting a growing awareness that the local experience is more valuable when involving a personal connection to place, Airbnb's CEO Brian Chesky has acknowledged that "the future of Airbnb isn't about spaces . . . It's about hosts" (in Chafkin & Newcomer, 2016, para. 7). In fall 2016, the company launched the new Experiences[7] section of the app and website, with a highly curated set of excursions led by local hosts who are expected to perform the affective labor of producing a local feeling in the guests. This mandate is clear through Airbnb's guidelines for hosting an experience: proposals must demonstrate that the host is "credible," "genuine," and "empathetic," and the experience must provide "access," "participation," and "perspective" that carries a "personal meaning" ("Become an experience," n.d.). In advertisements for the site's experiences and lodging functions, still and video formats are used to insert the viewer into the local scene, literally encouraging the traveler to picture herself in an alternate life, yet to consider it as real.

The use of experiences to produce a fantasy of being local is the central concept taken up by connective media in the travel sector, and this fantasy relies on the perception that one is doing "real-life" things—whether eating, going for a walk, or hanging out with "new friends," or sleeping in a bedroom in a real neighborhood. That there is very little "local" about these companies' goals can be noted in Vayable's stated mission "to become the *global platform* for real-life experiences" ("How this works," n.d., para. 1, emphasis added).[8] Indeed, to have access to just one "local" place would do very little for the middle-class traveler—it is the access to a globally networked series of locals that builds value, as these localization apps provide users with a means to act out emerging global identities, promising the ability to safely embody multiple worlds. Rosen and colleagues (2011) have demonstrated how this works with the worldwide Couchsurfing community. Through participation in the online networking aspect of the organization, people form social network ties that make them feel a connection not only to the individuals with whom they interact, but also to the groups and communities of which those members are a part. In providing those ties to users, the Couchsurfing community "specifically allows people to locate, negotiate, and establish *new* social network ties in *any* geographic location, as opposed to existing ties in a finite cache of locations" (p. 984, emphasis in original). Rosen and colleagues found that through this network, travelers, often considered to be isolated and without connections, were able to feel as though they had "a social support network and friends in otherwise unknown locations" (p. 984).

Although Couchsurfing is mainly free to users, the newer, for-profit apps discussed above seek to provide a similar form of access on a more drop-in, fee basis as opposed to requiring the social labor of participation in the online community. This scaling up of the localization business indicates the extent to which the ability to perform the self as a local, rather than a tourist, increasingly sets the terms for the cultural capital associated with travel. For the discerning global traveler, the new thing to *do* is "local."

A Globally Networked Self

This chapter has explored how networked digital media are reshaping travel through the rise of apps that promise to help people travel like a local. Considering the history of travel as a middle-class status asset, I connected these developments to a drive for distinctive travel—where distinction may be challenged by an oversaturation of travel images shared on social media—to demonstrate how the moving target around what counts as a valuable travel experience currently finds its locus in "the local" as the site for authenticity. Networked media facilitate these experiences in various ways, in particular those apps enabling direct communication and exchange between "hosts" and guests, as well as cross-platform social media posts where companies, bloggers, and travelers circulate discourses extolling the benefits of being local.

In a context where social mobility for the middle classes is increasingly attached to amassing "global cultural capital" (see Polson, 2016), localization apps and their associated social media tools allow for the accrual of experiences and connections for performing a "globally networked self." In laying out the contours of the "networked self," Papacharissi (2011) pointed out that social network sites provide "a stage for self-presentation and social connection" (p. 304) by both enabling public displays of one's connectivity as well as promoting the "exchanges and ties" (p. 307) that help foster such connectivity. For those who include travel as a tool for self-presentation, social media allow for placing oneself as a traveler in relation to a network of friends and family, larger social networks, and other travelers. Increasingly, these connective media also allow for making "local" connections that have global resonance through their presence on platforms that connect users to geographic locations around the world.

In conclusion, it is worth considering how the platforms explored here— and their accompanying discourses of "the local"—might be thought of in relation to questions about "who they connect, who they disconnect, and how" (Papacharissi, 2011, p. 309). On the one hand, as middle classes from a variety of nations share increasing comfort and familiarity with each other, these localization platforms become a channel for capitalizing on and reproducing these affinities, connecting people and growing their global networks. However, a fixation with being able to easily and temporarily access "the local" clearly has its counterpoint in the anti-immigrant rhetoric and actions (both state-sponsored and on the streets) currently proliferating in the United States and some European countries, where people who may have been local for years (even centuries) are being told (once again) that they do not belong, or others who may wish to become local are being turned away. The travel apps themselves are implicated in exclusions around the local, seen, for example, in the problems that Airbnb has had with discriminatory hosts (Benner, 2016) or with the displacement of residents by taking possible long-term rental housing off the market ("New Airbnb"). Such concerns point to racial, class- and religion-based aspects to localism. So that when the WithLocals app promises "over 1200 things to do and food experiences with *verified* locals" (Withlocals.com, emphasis added), this calls into question not only that company's specific verification process but what such a process—and subjectivity—even means about the local, the global, and its increasing conflation through mobility and social networks.

Notes

1 Zuelow (2016) pointed out that in response to the backlash against mass tourism, the tourism industry responded quickly "by generating a global playground of 'cool' attractions"; however, he noted, "the catch is that what is cool one minute is passé the next" (p. 174).
2 In fact, the rise of popular photography has been linked to the rise of modern mass tourism and the middle classes (e.g. Sontag, 1977), and Larsen (2014) noted that "middle-class family albums are packed with tourist snaps" (p. 90), shown to visitors and proudly displayed in the home.
3 To avoid validating and reproducing the discursive distinction between "traveler" and "tourist," I use the terms interchangeably in this chapter unless referring directly to their different usage.
4 www.vayable.com/

5 www.withlocals.com/app/
6 www.vizeat.com
7 www.airbnb.com/s/experiences
8 Much is at stake in the economy of living local. As with other products sought after by the consumer classes, travel and its associated experiences have become valuable commodities; the World Travel & Tourism Council claims the growing industry currently represents 10.2% of world GDP (US$7.6 trillion), and accounts for 1 in 10 jobs on the planet ("Economic impact," 2016).

References

[*Airbnb*]. (2016). *Don't go there. Live there*. April 19. Video file. www.youtube.com/watch?v=B_1itDHomgE

Andersson, T.D. (2007). The tourist in the experience economy. *Scandinavian Journal of Hospitality and Tourism*, 7(1), 46–58.

Azariah, D.R. (2016). "The traveler as author: Examining self-presentation and discourse in the (self) published travel blog. *Media, Culture, and Society*, 38(6), 934–945.

Azariah, D.R. (2017). *Tourism, travel, and blogging: A discursive analysis of online travel narratives*. New York: Routledge.

Become an experience host. (n.d.) *Airbnb*. www.airbnb.com/host/experiences

Benner, K. (2016). Airbnb adopts rules to fight discrimination by its hosts. *New York Times*, Sept. 8. www.nytimes.com/2016/09/09/technology/airbnb-anti-discrimination-rules.html

Bourdieu, P. (1984). *Distinction: A social critique of the judgement of taste*. Cambridge, MA: Harvard University Press.

Bourdieu, P. (1987). What makes a social class? On the theoretical and practical existence of groups. *Berkeley Journal of Sociology*, 32, 1–18.

Brown, S. (2005). Traveling with a purpose: Understanding the motives and benefits of volunteer vacations. *Current Issues in Tourism*, 8(6), 479–496.

Bruner, E.M. & Kirshenblatt-Gimblett, B. (1994). Maasai on the lawn: Tourist realism in East Africa. *Cultural Anthropology*, 9(4), 435–470.

Chafkin, M. & Newcomer, E. (2016). Airbnb faces growing pains as it passes 100 million guests. *Bloomberg Business Week*, July 11. www.bloomberg.com/news/articles/2016-07-11/airbnb-faces-growing-pains-as-it-passes-100-million-users

Coldwell, W. (2017, Aug. 10). First Venice and Barcelona: Now anti-tourism marches spread across Europe. *The Guardian*. www.theguardian.com/travel/2017/aug/10/anti-tourism-marches-spread-across-europe-venice-barcelona?CMP=share_btn_link

Dinhopl, A. & Gretzel, U. (2016). Selfie-taking as touristic looking. *Annals of Tourism Research*, 57, 126–139.

Economic impact analysis. (2016). *World Travel & Tourism Council*. www.wttc.org/research/economic-research/economic-impact-analysis/

Germann Molz, J. (2012). *Travel connections: Tourism, technology and togetherness in a mobile world*. London: Routledge.

Hewitt, E. (2010). How to blend in with the locals: 20 tips. *Independent Traveler*. www.independenttraveler.com/travel-tips/travelers-ed/how-to-blend-in-with-the-locals-20-tips

Hoeller, S.C. (2015). 10 travel apps that will make you feel like a local. *Time*, Sept. 4. http://time.com/4023144/travel-apps-feel-local/

How this works. (n.d.). *Vayable*. www.vayable.com/how_this_works

Iyer, P. (2000). Why we travel. *Salon*, March 18. www.salon.com/2000/03/18/why/

Jansson, A. (2007). A sense of tourism: New media and the dialectic of encapsulation/ decapsulation. *Tourist Studies*, 7(1), 5–24.

Kersten, L. (2015). Been there done that—Fake your way around the world. Oct. 15. Web log post. http://mastersofmedia.hum.uva.nl/blog/2015/10/15/fake-your-way-around-the-world/

Kim, J. & Tussyadiah, I. P. (2013). Social networking and social support in tourism experience: The moderating role of online self-presentation strategies. *Journal of Travel & Tourism Marketing*, 30, 78–92.

Klein, B. (2016). How to travel like a local. *Life Hack*, Sept. 18. Web log article. www. lifehack.org/articles/lifestyle/how-travel-like-local.html

Larsen, J. (2008). De-exoticizing tourist travel: Everyday life and sociality on the move. *Leisure Studies*, 27(1), 21–34.

Larsen, J. (2014). The (im)mobile life of digital photographs: The case of tourist photography. In J. and M. Sandbye (Eds.), *Digital snaps: The new face of photography* (pp. 90–125). London: I. B. Tauris.

Lepore, E. (2017). Doing it for the gram: A semester abroad according to Instagram. March 26. Web log post. https://themodernfeministweb.wordpress.com/2017/03/26/doing-it-for-the-gram-a-semester-abroad-according-to-instagram/

Leung, D., Law, R., van Hoof, H., & Buhalis, D. (2013). Social media in tourism and hospitality: A literature review. *Journal of Travel & Tourism Marketing*, 30, 2–22.

Litvin, S. W., Goldsmith, R. E., & Pan, B. (2008). Electronic word-of-mouth in hospitality and tourism management. *Tourism Management*, 29(3), 458–468.

Lofgren, O. (1999). *On holiday: A history of vacationing.* Berkeley: University of California Press.

MacCannell, D. (1976). *The tourist: A new theory of the leisure class.* New York: Schocken Books.

MacCannell, D. (1999). *The tourist: A new theory of the leisure class.* Rev. edn. Berkeley, CA: University of California Press.

Munt, I. (1994). The "other" postmodern tourism: Culture, travel and the new middle classes. *Theory, Culture & Society*, 11, 101–123.

New Airbnb study questions underpinnings of another "gig economy" company (2017). *Seattle City Council Insight.* March 17. https://sccinsight.com/2017/03/17/new-airbnb-study-questions-underpinnings-another-gig-economy-company/

Padykula, J. (2015). 10 ways to travel like a local anywhere. *Urban Adventures Blog*, February 18. www.urbanadventures.com/blog/10-ways-travel-like-local-anywhere.html

Papacharissi, Z. (2011). Conclusion: A networked self. In Z. Papacharissi (Ed.), *A networked self: Identity, community and culture on social network sites* (pp. 304–318). New York: Routledge.

Paris, C. M. & Pietschnig, J. (2015). "But first, let me take a selfie": Personality traits as predictors of travel selfie taking and sharing behaviors. *Tourism Travel and Research Association: Advancing Tourism Research Globally*, 1.

Polson, E. (2016). *Privileged mobilities: Professional migration, geo-social media, and a new global middle class.* New York: Peter Lang.

Pons, P. (2003). Being-in-tourism: Tourist dwelling, bodies and places. *Tourist Studies*, 3(3), 47–66.

Quadri-Felitti, D. & Fiore, A. M. (2012). Experience economy constructs as a framework for understanding wine tourism. *Journal of Vacation Marketing*, 18(1), 13–15.

Rojek, C. (1993). *Ways of escape: Modern transformations in leisure and travel.* Lanham, MD: Rowman & Littlefield.

Rosen, D., Lafontaine, P. R., & Hendrickson, B. (2011). Couchsurfing: Belonging and trust in a globally cooperative online social network. *New Media & Society*, 13(6), 981–998.

Rubinstein, D. & Sluis, K. (2008). A life more photographic. *Photographies*, 1(1), 9–28.

Schnell, S. M. (2011). The local traveler: Farming, food, and place in state and provincial tourism guides, 1993–2008. *Journal of Cultural Geography*, 28(2), 281–309.

Schwartz, R. & Halegoua, G. (2015). The spatial self: Location-based identity performance on social media. *New Media & Society*, 17(10), 1643–1660.

Silverman, J. (2015). "Pics or it didn't happen": The mantra of the Instagram era. *The Guardian*, Feb. 26. www.theguardian.com/news/2015/feb/26/pics-or-it-didnt-happen-mantra-instagram-era-facebook-twitter

Simpson, K. (2004). "Doing development": The gap year, volunteer-tourists and a popular practice of development. *Journal of International Development*, 16, 681–692.

Sims, R. (2009). Food, place and authenticity: Local food and the sustainable tourism experience. *Journal of Sustainable Tourism*, 17(3), 321–336.

Soica, S. (2016). Tourism as practice of making meaning. *Annals of Tourism Research*, 61, 96–110.

Sontag, S. (1977). *On photography*. New York: Farrar, Strauss & Giroux.

Uriely, N. (2005). The tourist experience: Conceptual developments. *Annals of Tourism Research*, 32(1), 199–216.

Urry, J. (1990). *The tourist gaze: Leisure and travel in contemporary societies*. London: Sage.

Urry, J. & Larsen, J. (2011). *The tourist gaze, 3.0*. London: Sage.

Walker, A. (1989). *Living by the word: Selected writings, 1973–1987*. New York: Harvest Books.

Watson, M. (2015). Instagram Analysis Reports: August 2015. *Get Chute*. 15 October. http://blog.getchute.com/insights-outlook/instagram-analysis-reports-august-2015/

Withlocals.com. (n.d.). www.withlocals.com/

Zuelow, E. G. E. (2016). *A history of modern tourism*. London: Palgrave.

12

THE NETWORKED SELF AND DEFENSE OF PRIVACY

Reading Surveillance Fiction in the Wake of the Snowden Revelations

Adrienne Russell and Risto Kunelius

Since Edward Snowden revealed the National Security Agency's colossal technological and bureaucratic snooping program, awareness has notched up among network publics about new-level threats to privacy posed by government and corporate interests. The once secret program enables the NSA and its partner organizations to oversee and analyze most communications taking place on digital networks, including Internet traffic and telephone calls. These revelations mark a crucial moment in our collective awareness not only of this overreach of power but also, and perhaps more shockingly, of the prevalence and scale of tracking, profiling, personalization, and snooping that characterizes our digitalized everyday life.

Discussion has followed about the relationship between privacy and the networked self—how receding privacy is an important force shaping our sense of self. As surveillance increases so too does everyday awareness and cultural resistance. A 2016 Pew survey reports that 91% of American consumers feel they have lost control of their personal information, and 86% reported that they were "taking steps" to remove or mask their digital footprints (Rainie, 2016).

Responses to this loss of control and of privacy vary. Some choose to trust the motives of intelligence professionals. Some resort to cynicism, noting that there is nothing new in states spying on their citizens. Some respond with detached irony. Others adopt the naive and self-righteous credo, *If you have nothing to hide, you have nothing to fear* (Solove, 2011). Still others mitigate their anxiety by taking practical steps to protect their privacy. There has been a steady rise, for example, in the development and use of encryption tools (Finley, 2014) and a decrease in the use of search for both personally sensitive and government-sensitive search terms (Marthews & Tucker, 2015).

Indeed, the practical task of developing tools and strategies for protecting online privacy is closely linked to more conceptual changes that the revelations about surveillance have set in motion. In the ongoing critical discussion about political and commercial surveillance, privacy emerges as a core value to be defended, and privacy takes on various meanings. The crafting and negotiation of meanings takes place in different public platforms and genres. Such heated political debates offer rich material to explore the struggle over interpretations of privacy and surveillance (Kunelius et al., 2017; Hintz et al., 2017). At the same time, in the broader realm of public culture, the future of privacy, and by extension the nature of the networked self, is being questioned and re-crafted. This chapter examines how several recent popular novels address pressing contemporary issues related to privacy in the networked media landscape.

In particular, this chapter examines how privacy is treated in Dave Eggers's *The Circle* (2014), Suzanne Collins' *The Hunger Games* (2010, 2013, 2014), Jonathan Franzen's *Purity* (2016), Patrick Flanery's *I Am No One* (2017), and Cory Doctorow's *Little Brother* (2010) and *Homeland* (2014). All of these novels address distinct visions of the relationship between privacy and the networked self. We use George Orwell's dystopian classic *1984* (1961) as a point of comparison. First published almost seventy years ago, its sales skyrocketed after the Snowden Revelations (Riley, 2013) and again more recently with the rise in concern over Trump era "alternative facts" (de Freytas-Tamura, 2017). This selection of work serves up a sampling of emergent narratives and themes that attempt to make sense of how new networked social and political arrangements shift the way we perform the self. They are examples of texts used in thinking through our collective understanding of the forces at work and the stakes involved in current developments. They capture and dramatize shifts we have all somehow experienced but, caught up in the rush of change, have had limited perspective to interpret. All these works are propelled by anxiety about privacy and ultimately seem to defend a normative notion that sees privacy as a necessary condition for both personal well-being and public efficacy. At the same time, they point to a key set of questions about the different aspects of the self that are supported and threatened in contemporary networked surveillance societies.

The rise of the novel, as a genre, and its popular spin-offs are historically tied to the construction of modern privacy, depicting the experience of individuals and often offering readers imagined access to the privacy of others. Drawing its narrative power from glimpses into the inner worlds of specific characters, such narratives move readers to reflect on their own individuality. In our reading of this collection of works, we identify three distinct but overlapping representations of the networked self that raise issues related to privacy. First, surveillance fiction highlights how, by handing over a constant stream of personal data, the self becomes both complicit in and a target of corporate and government surveillance systems. This aspect is addressed in the novels primarily through cautionary tales about the dangers of excessive transparency. Second, the narratives point to how our knowledge that we are being watched changes our relationship with ourselves, which has dramatic consequences on how we relate socially and politically to one another. This fundamental link between the protection of an imagined inner self and the ability to feel solidarity is demonstrated throughout the literature. Finally, a kind of third self appears as an agent who acts in defense of privacy. Most prominently and explicitly this takes place in the two novels written by Cory Doctorow, a vociferous advocate of online civil liberties whose novels are populated with young hackers who create and use technology that is compatible with rather than anathema to democracy. By examining these distinct elements of selfhood as they are depicted in popular fiction, this chapter takes stock of some key fronts on which privacy is being negotiated, elaborating the potential opportunities and limits of the discourse, and in some cases echoing long-held modern notions of privacy.

The Fine Line Between Transparency and Surveillance

Economies of connective media engage the individual as both a networked laborer and a consumer (Andrejevic, 2011, p. 82). That is, the data produced and shared by networked publics are what constitute the very network. Without the active participation of network users—their content choices, linking practices, likes, and other tracked activities—the system would not function. This participation creates a rich source for both commercial and government surveillance. As Amy Webb (2017) put it, "Data is the new oil and we humans are the wells."

In the process of going about our days online—shopping, working, completing school assignments, booking travel, socializing, and so on—we both contribute to and become subject to the data collection and surveillance apparatus that pervades contemporary society—we expose ourselves to its manipulations (Sandvig, 2014), information silos, and encroachments on privacy (Turow, 2012), that characterize contemporary transnational information/network capitalism (Fuchs, 2008). With more critical research—and revelations like Snowden's—we are more and more aware of the double-edged sword of connectivity. José Van Dijck (2013) uses the term *connective media* in order to reference both the frontend (of the internet), where users are social, and the backend, where automated systems engineer and manipulate connections and then track, code, and commodify them. In contrast, the term *social media* implies that platforms like Facebook, Twitter, and YouTube are user-centered and primarily concerned with participation and collaboration.

On one hand, the power of surveillance relies on the idea that those who are surveilled do not know they are seen and tracked. On the other hand, the panoptic power of surveillance, and its diffuse political and social effects, lies also in the awareness of this gaze, the realization that you *might* be being watched. In this sense, the public exposure, the "spectacle of surveillance" (Andrejevic, 2017), has enhanced its psychological effect: Being forced to look at oneself through the eyes of power means being simultaneously a subject and an object.

This two-sided interactivity, one's own complicity in the system of control, is a key theme of surveillance fiction. In Orwell's *1984*, Winston Smith, agent of the party propaganda machinery, slaves dutifully away at the task of manipulating the historical record. The panoptic gaze of the state with which he is intimately familiar, leaves him hopeless throughout the story—despite his growing desire to resist, he is sure any such efforts would be futile. Yet Winston's slow transformation from a confused but obedient agent of the system to small-scale revolutionary is one of the instructive plotlines of the book. Through simply recording his thoughts in a diary, he grows into a self-conscious, defiant actor—and individual—but with no avenue to assert himself. In the end, state control is unbreakable because it is based not on any ideology but rather on only the desire for power.

The Circle, a retelling of Orwell's cautionary tale, updates these themes with distinct twists. In Eggers's version, Mae, an ordinary young woman, quickly works her way from an entry-level consumer feedback staffer to a celebrity who embodies the total transparency ideology of the global internet company she works for. The book depicts the way the seduction of technology can turn people into agents of their own surveillance, and cogs in the workings of the system. Mae's story shows her voluntary transformation into a company brand icon and model subject of the new elite, and how she step-by-step comes to embrace the logic of total transparency—the mythical "completion of the circle"—as a cure for social ills. Both Orwell's Winston and Eggers's Mae end up losing their humanity, one through political torture, the other through voluntary submission to a new corporate logic: "Freedom is Slavery" is updated to "Privacy is Theft." Orwell's torturer is a cruel, ruthless, cold, and intelligent Party boss, Eggers's is a benign, fatherly, and deceivingly soft-spoken CEO.

The wildly popular *Hunger Games* trilogy by Suzanne Collins also echoes Orwell. The *Hunger Games* novels and films depict a fictional autocratic nation, Panem, in which the government elite hoards all of the resources and the public lives in squalor in districts outside the capitol. The power of Panem is maintained by subjecting the people to constant surveillance. Katniss Everdeen, the protagonist, learns to hold her tongue so that "no one could ever read her thoughts" (p. 6). She also learns to avoid the Jabberjays birds created in the capitol labs to spy on enemies and rebels through their ability to memorize and repeat entire human conversations. Everyday spying is complemented by the annual Hunger Games, gladiator-like reality television contests, where children are forced to fight to the death. Central to the games' power is the fact that they are broadcast to audiences throughout the districts who enthusiastically root for their favorite contestant. The spectacle helps maintain social order by reminding citizens of state power over the life and death of children, and by inciting a degrading pleasure that renders spectators powerless to organize and resist (Horning, 2012). The series, like *1984* and *The Circle*, is ultimately a commentary on the effects of living under constant surveillance, suggesting that we play along to both work around and win favor from those who control the unseen eye. In the games, contestants compete for the support of sponsors who donate money that can be used to buy supplies for them when they are in the arena. Katniss becomes a master at the game, a kickass warrior and media darling and at the same time a rising symbol of rebellion against the capitol. The series is perhaps so popular among young audiences because they too struggle with the knowledge that they are being watched and need to decide how much to perform for the unseen eye (Horning, 2012).

In Patrick Flanery's novel *I am No One*, an academic expert on East German surveillance history learns that his digital life has been tracked for years, leading him to internalize the gaze of the surveiller and begin to suspect himself of wrongdoing. In describing his befuddlement over why he would be the target of surveillance, he echoes the sentiment that commonly drives networked publics' feeling of security in the face of surveillance, telling his daughter, "But I am no one." Indeed, crucial to all of these narratives is the fluctuation the characters experience between being seemingly ordinary (no one) and extraordinary (someone). The oft-repeated narrative sees the protagonist gain privileged insight into the workings of the system by becoming a target of that system. The loss of humanity that they experience from becoming the target of and participant in the loss of privacy leads them to question the normative value of transparency.

The Link between Our Private and Public Selves

While participation in and subjection to surveillance—be it commercial or state— is a recurring theme in popular narratives, these narratives also highlight ways the knowledge of being watched can change our relationship to ourselves and how we relate socially and politically to one another.

Scholars concerned with the impact of ubiquitous surveillance question the very premise of *the social* online. Nick Couldry (2014) cautions against the myth of "us" created by these industry platforms and business practices, which, he writes, encourage "us to believe that our gatherings on connective media platforms are a natural form of expressive collectivity, even though it is exactly that belief that is the basis of such platforms' creation of economic value." Yet at the same time there is little doubt that our social lives are largely played out online and that this environment supports a particular type of sociability. Zizi Papacharissi (2011) calls this a form of networked sociability in which people constantly traverse private and public spheres. As she puts it, "Networked and remixed sociabilities emerge and are practiced over multiplied places and audiences that do not necessarily collapse one's sense of place, but afford a sense of place reflexivity" (p. 331). The notion of the privacy paradox (Hargittai and Marwick, 2016) also suggests a sort of reflexivity, where connective media users at the same time take steps to protect their privacy and reveal themselves online in order to sustain social connections and gather information (Stutzman et al., 2012). Given the sophistication of data collection tools and their centrality to business models and law enforcement practices, however, users face an overwhelming structural disadvantage.[1] The commodification of our social interactions distorts them by transforming relationships into data points that are used to manipulate online space to benefit political projects as well as government and commercial interests. What makes the digital environment historically and qualitatively different is the fact that surveillance has become more efficient and its logic broadened from monitoring what we are doing now to predicting what we will be doing in the future. The monitorial, panoptical presence of surveillance is complemented with an assumed predictive knowledge of the self (Andrejevic, 2017).

It is not just our relations with others that are altered by invasions of privacy; our relationship with ourselves, too, is intimately influenced by technologies of surveillance. As Michael P. Lynch put it in a *New York Times* opinion piece published just after the 2013 Snowden leaks, what gives us ownership over our own thoughts is "privileged access":

> This means at least two things. First, you access them in a way I can't. Even if I could walk a mile in your shoes, I can't know what you feel in *the same way* you can: you see it from the inside so to speak. Second, you can, at least sometimes, control what I know about your thoughts. You can hide your true feelings from me, or let me have the key to your heart.

Lynch argues that privacy is a necessary condition of autonomy; which begins with the privileged access to oneself—dreams, beliefs, concerns, and so on.

Despite the popular emphasis on totalitarian "newspeak" and manipulation of history, the importance of privacy to the personal and social elements of one's identity is key to Orwell's *1984*. Winston's tragic narrative illustrates two sources of hope: the social world of human relations and the distinct sense of one's own particularity and value, the relational and intimate dynamics of the self. The love affair between Julia and Winston is a curious mix of revolutionary hopes and escapism. In it, Julia dramaturgically functions as reflective surface where Winston can see himself as a distinct, self-sufficient, and authentic subject, because her motivation for being with him is not ultimately or distinctly political. Another reflective surface is his diary. Jotting down seemingly haphazard notes about a party propaganda film featuring a mother and her dying child, Winston stumbles on a chain of associations that lead to memories of his own mother:

> She had not been an unusual woman, yet she had possessed some kind of nobility, a kind of purity, simply because the standards she obeyed were private ones . . . It would have not occurred to her that an action that is ineffectual thereby becomes meaningless, if you loved one, you loved one and when you had nothing else to give, you still gave him love.

These insights lead Winston to a new understanding of the state, and how it maintains power not through the strong bonds of shared ideology but through destroying primary loyalties—the "proles" he looks down on in the beginning of the narrative suddenly are exposed as having something that Winston has lost: "not loyal to a party or a country or an idea, they were loyal to one another." Such trains of thought make the random traces on the page of a diary—material acts of privacy—dangerous to the state. It is not what he writes, but rather, *that* he writes; writing helps him gain himself and become a threat to the Party.

Orwell's almost romantic link between privacy, self-esteem, and loyalty can seem outdated. But *The Circle* presents similar notions of privacy in large part through a series of cautionary tales about the cost of digital life and its corresponding eclipse of privacy. Mae's zealous embrace of transparency is outstandingly destructive—she interrupts her parents having sex and, because she wears a recording device that broadcasts her life in real-time to millions of viewers, violates their privacy in the most humiliating way. Her ex-boyfriend crashes his car and is killed while trying to get away from Mae and her millions of viewers. And perhaps most tellingly, when her secret lover comes to her with a plan to undercut the metastasizing reach of the company, she betrays him, maintaining instead her dedication to The Circle. Eggers is arguing that, without privacy, intimacy becomes impossible and hence so too does true personal or political solidarity.

In *The Hunger Games*, Collins explores the relationships with others and with the self by examining the way Katniss performs intimacy in order to win the games. Despite her reluctance, Katniss realizes that she needs to perform a romance with another competitor from her district, Peeta, in order to get sponsorship and thus resources to support her performance in the games—things like weapons and other survival supplies. To have any chance at survival, a player must cater to the vicarious needs of the audience by exposing their feelings in a compelling and convincing way. "I want to draw away, to close those shutters again, but I know I can't," Katniss thinks. The contestants of the Hunger Games essentially trade on affective labor, performing a faux intimacy in order to survive (Horning, 2012).

Jonathan Franzen's *Purity* is a novel of secrets and lies. It exposes the link between personal identity and public exposure through its main character Purity (or Pip), and her quest, quite literally, to find herself. Her eccentric mother will not tell Pip her real name or the identity of her father. At 23, struggling with student loan debt, a dead-end job, and life in a squatter house in Oakland, Pip is sure that if she can uncover her own history her problems will abate. This quest to discover her backstory spurs Pip to join the Sunlight Project, a clearing house for leaks or what Pip refers to as a revenge-porn site, run by an East German Julian Assange-like character, Andreas Wolf. Unlike *The Circle*, which is told through a narrator, and the first-person narration of *I am No One*, *Purity* is divided into sections, each delivered from the point of view of a different character. For the reader, this gives the effect of eavesdropping on characters as they talk to each other, making us privy to the tension between secrets and transparency in Franzen's characters. In the case of Wolf, for example, we learn that he secretly hates the internet as much as he hates the state socialism he grew up in, because they are both "impossible to opt out of." He also preaches transparency while harboring the secret of a murder he committed in his youth. By embracing the principle of transparency, he gains power and celebrity; however, when he tries to apply transparency to private relations by revealing his secret to Pip, he ends up destroyed by his own secrets. At one level then, the message of the novel is similar to that of *The Circle*: imposing the idea of transparency on intimate social relations is destructive, a form of violence.

While varied in terms of genre, plot, and narrative approaches, these novels all tend to put forth a classic modernist take on privacy as related to the self, the social, and the political. Privacy in each work is primarily about developing a sense of self, the right to individuality, a sense of difference from others. Robbing people of their privacy is tantamount to denying them even the possibility of self-esteem. The opportunity to appreciate and cultivate one's sense of self demands that space exist where one can be alone. Only such distinct selfhood, the authors suggest, affords people the opportunity to develop and cultivate mutual social relations. This secondary level of privacy is the terrain where people can learn to recognize their own value through the eyes of others. Appreciating others and identifying with others' appreciation is not possible without the sense of self. It is in such horizontal relations that democratic politics—the will of people or the wills of different kinds of people—become imaginable. Thus, without privacy to support a sense of the self, and connections to others, people cannot create the shared vocabularies and articulate shared interests that drive the workings of democracy. Protection of privacy, in this light, is essential to democracy and a democratic right.

These articulated links between the self, the social, and the political are largely a creation of the Enlightenment and have led to a set of self-understandings, practices, and mutual expectations that give people a sense of things in common, what Charles Taylor (2004) calls a modern social imaginary. While the consistent cultural strength of such vocabularies is well illustrated in the creative imagination of the novelists, the argument about their contingent, historical roots also begs a difficult question. Given the pace and scope of change, can we effectively defend privacy through such normative and fundamentally moral modern discourses of individuality? Or, put another way, do digital systems present such a radical change of material conditions that such modern notions of privacy and its defense do not suffice?

Self Defense in the Face of Complex Surveillance Systems

The literature reviewed so far tends to reflect modernist notions of privacy, but it also suggests what is new in the reality of surveillance-based digital environments is the scale of surveillance—our complicity in our own loss of privacy, and the complexity of the workings and uses of surveillance. Indeed, the scale of government and corporate surveillance is so vast that it is increasingly difficult to imagine anything that falls outside its purview. And as we become an essential part of surveillance structures, complicit in their workings, our ability to function in digital societies becomes more and more tied to the loss of privacy.

While scale and complicity are key themes in the literature and useful in thinking through the consequences of our altered state of privacy, another significant difference in digital-era surveillance is its complexity, the often-invisible ways that surveillance operates through ubiquitous points of data collection and invisible algorithms that sort, refine, and use personal data—and predict our behavior in addition to merely tracking it. While *The Circle, Purity, The Hunger Games,* and *I am No One* each deliver a welcome challenge to the idea that technology is neutral, they do little to help us imagine ways technology might be enlisted in efforts to resist the loss of privacy. More broadly, they steer away from asking how values can be incorporated—through conscious design—in technologies and how technology designers and producers can take values into consideration. For such ideas, we need to turn to the practices and narratives of those who see new technology as a powerful mechanism or tool for asserting social, political, and moral values that can also run counter to the dominant logic of surveillance.

Issues of access and security, for example, have long been central to the work of technology activists. Freenet lets you chat, anonymously share files, browse, and contribute to forums without vulnerability to censorship. The Tor (The Onion Router) bounces communication around distributed networks of relays run by volunteers all around the world in order to prevent anyone from tracking and blocking sites. Virtual private networks (VPN) mask your IP address with the address of the VPN server. To make these tools more accessible and widely adopted by those outside the tech community, several guides and packages have been created through collaboration among NGOs, advocacy groups, and technology developers. One of the most commonly used suites of tools among journalists, The Amnesic Incognito Live System (Tails), is a live operating system, a sort of uber mobile computer that you install on a portable memory drive (DVD, USB stick, or SD card) independent of a computer's original operating system. Using a suite of existing free software tools, like Tor or Linux, optimized for anonymity, Tails comes with several built-in applications that are pre-configured to offer the most security: web browser, instant messaging client, email client, office suite, image and sound editor, and so on. It is particularly useful for journalists who can use Tails to chat off the record, browse the Web anonymously, and share sensitive documents. Most famously, it was used by Edward Snowden and the journalists most involved in his initial leaks: Glen Greenwald, Laura Poitras, and Barton Gellman. Embedded in all of these tools are values that privilege collaboration, privacy, and free speech. And their widespread development and use signal a growing understanding of the need for protection.

Such technological approaches have been celebrated in popular TV shows like *Mr. Robot,* where the protagonist Elliot worked in corporate cybersecurity by day and used hacker skills by night to change the world—eliminating everyone's debt by wiping out the pertinent data. Cory Doctorow's young adult novels *Homeland* and *Little Brother*, in turn, are both Internet civil rights crime thrillers and practical handbooks of digital self-defense. In *Little Brother* teenage hackers caught up in the aftermath of a 9/11-like terror attack use Xbox game consoles to create protected mesh networks over which to coordinate a large-scale youth-led defense of civil rights. The plot is driven by the idea that we need to improve our relationship to information technology by creating alternatives to the existing uses and platforms. As Marcus Yarrow, the book's central character, put it: "My technology was working for me, serving me, protecting me. It wasn't spying on me. This is why I love technology: if you use it right, it could give you power and privacy" (Doctorow, 2010, p. 88). Because he has built his own technology to embody his own values—privacy, security, people power—it is a force of good. *Homeland* picks up when Marcus is a few years older. At the annual Nevada desert art festival Burning Man, he receives a USB drive full of leaks that would embarrass government and corporate elites. While *Little Brother* is about terrorism and violations of civil rights in the name of security, *Homeland* explores how citizens ought to respond to a world where more and more information about them is available to the state. In addition to being optimistic and uplifting novels, both works are how-to manuals that provide practical information on secure communication storage and sharing. And both are calls to learn to control rather than be controlled by technology. As Doctorow put it: "Even if you only write code for one day, one afternoon, you have to do it. Computers can control you or they can lighten your work—if you want to be in charge of your machines you have to learn to write code" (2010, pp. 142–143). In a review of *Little Brother* Austin Grossman (2008) suggests that the book is a call for nerds to save democracy:

> The framers of the American Constitution were in a sense a bunch of political science nerds too, pulling all-nighters to hack together code for a government without tyranny. Little Brother argues that unless you are passably technologically literate, you are not fully in command of those constitutionally guaranteed freedoms—that in fact it's your patriotic duty as an American to be a little more nerdy.

These heroes of tech resistance and the alternative tools and networks they use in the battle for online civil liberties place modern discourses of privacy into an active role and create an imaginary that is informing and inspiring technological solutions. By doing so, they also reflect on the way human values—conscious and subconscious—shape our technological environment and resist what Amy Webb calls "the real horror show on the horizon."

This "horror show" consists of the black box systems whereby invisible algorithms are created by humans with biases; that is, the infrastructure of the future is being built by computer scientists, network engineers, and security experts who do not recognize and correct for their own biases, encoding major flaws into the structure of the system, as each iteration will be "just a little off," compounding the problem (Webb, 2017). Webb explains that black box systems amount to power without accountability, and that we can see evidence all around us:

> Just as we are seeing a step function increase in the spread of AI [Artificial Intelligence], something else is happening: the rise of ultra-nationalism, rightwing authoritarianism and fascism. All of these movements have shared characteristics, including the desire to centralize power, track populations, demonize outsiders and claim authority and neutrality without being account-able. Machine intelligence can be a powerful part of the power playbook.

The fictional treatments of privacy in the novels examined here demonstrate the threats to privacy that have the potential to severely inhibit the networked self and the need to resist corporate and government surveillance or the false notion that, as Facebook CEO Mark Zuckerberg claimed, privacy is no longer a social norm (Johnson, 2010). In these narratives, we see glimpses of how networking tools and platforms can be used in defense of privacy, and that the struggle for privacy is both psychological and technological. It is psychological in the classic modern sense that we need it to be ourselves and thus to participate in public life. It is technological in the sense that, if we continue to depend on tools that are built to serve as data collectors we will be subject to increasingly trampled privacy rights.

In an Afterward to *Homeland*, internet activist and star coder Aaron Swartz wrote "The system is changing. Thanks to the internet, everyday people can learn about and organize around an issue even if the system is determined to ignore it. Now, maybe we won't win every time—this is real life, after all—but we finally have a chance" (Doctorow, 2014). The book was published a month after Swartz killed himself under the threat of prosecution for downloading mil-lions of academic journal articles in the hopes of making them freely available. Doctorow and Swartz were friends. The characters in *Little Brother* and *Homeland*—tech-savvy kids deeply suspicious of technologically sophisticated corporate and government power—embody the same ethos Swartz was known for. His message at the end of the book reminds us that the battle for online civil liberties depicted in all of the contemporary fiction discussed here has real casualties (Sleight, 2013). It should also remind us that it is crucial to think about what it means in the digital era to put our faith not in companies nor in the systems they create, but in the collective ability of the public to generate knowledge and make the best decisions for the common good.

Note

1 See, for example, *The Guardian* coverage of the Snowden revelations for a comprehen-sive account of U.S. and U.K. government surveillance and Joseph Turow's *The Daily You* (2012) for more on corporate data collection.

References

Andrejevic, M. (2011). Social network exploitation. In Z. Papacharissi (Ed.), *A networked self: Identity, community, and culture on social network sites* (pp. 82–101). New York: Routledge.

Andrejevic, M. (2017). To preempt a thief. *International Journal of Communication*, 11, 879–896. doi: 1932–8036/20170005

Collins, S. (2010). *The hunger games.* New York: Scholastic Press.

Collins, S. (2013). *Mockingjay.* New York: Scholastic Press.

Collins, S. (2014). *Catching fire.* New York: Scholastic Press.

Couldry, N. (2014). The myth of "us": Digital networks, political change and the production of collectivity. *Information, Communication & Society*, 18(6), 608–626.

de Freytas-Tamura, K. (2017). George Orwell's "1984" is suddenly a best-seller. *New York Times, 25 Jan.* www.nytimes.com/2017/01/25/books/1984-george-orwell-donald-trump.html?_r=0

Doctorow, C. (2010). *Little brother.* New York: Titan Books.

Doctorow, C. (2014). *Homeland.* New York: Titan Books.

Eggers, D. (2014). *The circle.* New York: Vintage.

Finley, K. (2014). Encrypted web traffic more than doubles after NSA revelations. *Wired*, May 14. www.wired.com/2014/05/sandvine-report/

Flanery, P. (2017*). I am no one.* New York: Tim Duggan Books.

Franzen, J. (2016). *Purity.* New York: Picador.

Fuchs, C. (2008). *Internet and society.* New York: Routledge.

Grossman, A. (2008). Nerd activist. *New York Times Sunday Book Review*, 12 September.

Hargittai, E. & Marwick, A. (2016). "What can I really do?" Explaining the privacy paradox with online apathy. *International Journal of Communication*, 10, 3737–3757.

Hintz, A., Dencik, L., & Wahl-Jorgensen, K. (2017). Digital citizenship and surveillance society. *International Journal of Communication*, 11, 731–739. http://ijoc.org/index.php/ijoc/article/view/5521/1929

Horning, R. (2012).Value-seeking surveillance and The Hunger Games. *The New Inquiry*, March 26. https://thenewinquiry.com/blog/value-seeking-surveillance-and-the-hunger-games/

Johnson, B. (2010). Privacy no longer a social norm, says Facebook founder. *The Guardian*, Jan. 10. www.theguardian.com/technology/2010/jan/11/facebook-privacy

Kunelius, R., Heikkilä, H., Russell, A., & Yagodin, D. (2017). *Journalism and the NSA revelations: Privacy, security and the press.* Oxford: Reuters Institute/I.B. Tauris.

Lynch, M.P. (2013). Privacy and the threat to the self. *New York Times*, June 22.

Marthews, A. & Tucker, C.E. (2017). Government surveillance and internet search behavior. http://dx.doi.org/10.2139/ssrn.2412564

Orwell, G. (1961). *1984.* New York: Signet Classic.

Papacharissi, Z. (2011). *A networked self: Identity, community, and culture on social network sites.* New York: Routledge.

Rainie, L. (2016). The state of privacy in post-Snowden America. Pew Research Center, September 21. www.pewresearch.org/fact-tank/2016/09/21/the-state-of-privacy-in-america/

Riley, C. (2013). Sales of Orwell's "1984" spike after NSA leak. *CNN Money.* http://money.cnn.com/2013/06/12/news/1984-nsa-snowden/

Sandvig, C. (2014). Corrupt personalization, social media collective. June 26. https://socialmediacollective.org/2014/06/26/corrupt-personalization/

Sleight, G. (2013). "Homeland" by Cory Doctorow. *Washington Post*, February 1. www. washingtonpost.com/entertainment/books/homeland-by-cory doctorow/2013/02/01/ 59ea6af0–67ec-11e2–9e1b-07db1d2ccd5b_story.html?utm_term=.95a04b16da0e

Solove, D. (2011). *Nothing to hide: The false trade-off between privacy and security*. New Haven: Yale University Press.

Stutzman, F., Gross, R., & Acquisti, A. (2012). Silent listeners: The evolution of privacy and disclosure on Facebook. *Journal of Privacy and Confidentiality*, 4(2), 7–41.

Taylor, C. (2004). *Modern social imaginaries*. Durham, NC: Duke University Press.

Turow, J. (2012). *The daily you: How the new advertising industry is defining your identity and your worth*. New Haven and London: Yale University Press.

Webb, A. (2017). Opposing views on what to do about the data we create. *New York Times Book Review*, March 15. www.nytimes.com/2017/03/15/books/review/data-for-the-people-andreas-weigend.html

Van Dijck, J. (2013). *The culture of connectivity: A critical history of social media*. Oxford: Oxford University Press.

13

MOBILE MEDIA STORIES AND THE PROCESS OF DESIGNING CONTESTED LANDSCAPES

Jason Farman

In the predawn hours of August 16, 2017, city workers in Baltimore, Maryland took down statues honoring Confederate soldiers of the American Civil War. The previous weekend, a rally called "Unite the Right" had gathered in Charlottesville, Virginia to protest the removal of a Confederate statue. For the rally organizers, the statue represented the culture and traditions of the American South as well as neo-Nazi ideologies of white dominance; for the counter-protestors, the statues and the rally's participants represented the continued racism and violence against African Americans stemming from slavery to contemporary killings enacted by police. The rally turned violent, as conflicts broke out between neo-Nazis and the anti-racist/anti-fascist protestors, resulting in the death of one person and over a dozen injured. The scene looked similar to the Bronze Night in Estonia that happened a decade earlier, when the relocation of a statue honoring Soviet World War II soldiers resulted in violent conflicts between the Russian community and ethnic Estonians, who saw the statue as a symbol of Soviet occupation, repression, and the killing of many Estonians who resisted Soviet rule.

These conflicts over statues represent a growing awareness of the relationship between space, symbolism, and cultural identity. That is, space is produced through the ways stories are told about that space and these stories come to represent the ways that certain cultures link with that space or are removed entirely. As Denson (2017) argues, the erecting of monuments is a place-making practice that claims authority over the right to tell the story of a place. As such, monuments are an "act of possession. When we create a place through public history, we frequently take it as our own, identifying its past as the cultural patrimony of our specific community or population" (p. 12). Site-specific narratives and the media through which they are told are practices of place making that connect the signifiers used to the histories that best represent the people who lay claim to a space. The ways spatial stories are communicated come through a range of media, from statues to plaques, from graffiti to billboards, and from public screens to individual mobile devices. Together, these form a media ecology of storytelling platforms that form the basis for what I call contested landscapes. In this chapter, I seek to understand how space is produced through storytelling media in the digital age, as technologies such as mobile devices work alongside previous media forms to tell varied and wide-ranging stories of a location's meaning. The result is a polyvocality that demonstrates that no single story can—or should—dominate a space (Adichie, 2009; Marino, 2014); instead, spaces are produced through the range of narratives told about that site. I then go on to detail the considerations that must be accounted for when designing mobile media storytelling projects. In order to create work that allows for spatial polyvocality—for the many voices and stories to be told at a site through mobile technologies—designers must contend with a range of considerations such as medium specificity, content creation, participant motivation, materiality of the space and device, as well as the temporal aspects of mobile storytelling. This chapter thus seeks to combine a theoretical analysis of spatial production through narrative with the applied media studies approach to knowledge-through-practice (Ostherr, 2017).

This chapter begins by drawing on the theories of spatial production proposed by Henri Lefebvre (1991) as well as the scholarly literature on locative media (de Souza e Silva, 2006; Farman, 2012; Wilken & Goggin, 2014; Liao & Humphreys, 2015; Frith, 2015) and spatial narratives (Ruston, 2010; Cooley, 2014; Farman, 2015). Contemporary studies of spatial, digital narratives build on the scholarship of the fields of digital storytelling (Burgess, 2006; Couldry, 2008; Bassett, 2014; Alexander, 2017) and electronic literature (Montfort, 2005; Hayles, 2008; Emerson, 2014).

Ultimately, this chapter will discuss the range of perspectives on contested landscapes, analyzing the advantages of polyvocality for spatial production as well as the potential pitfalls and challenges created by these contested landscapes. I will discuss the ways in which practitioners have produced locative stories for mobile devices and the ways in which these narrative projects extend the storytelling potential for places. This chapter thus links the theories of spatial production to the applied media studies approach for analyzing these theories through the designs of locative storytellers and cultural landscapes.

At stake is an advocacy for the role that digital media play in the dynamic production of physical space. Rather than being distinct from physicality, digital media are vital elements for how spaces are produced in the age of mobile media. With the rise of mobile technologies, especially with the launch of smartphones and app stores in the mid-2000s, there has been a backlash that argues that these digital media pull users from their location, whether it is the dinner table, the office, or in outdoor spaces (Turkle, 2015). Technology is often seen as distracting and distinct from the places in which users are located. However, digital technology, and especially mobile technology, is perpetually producing and shaping the spaces and the places of the user. From practices such as spatial search (Frith, 2017) to affiliated notions such as "code/space" as theorized by Kitchin and Dodge (2011), the mobile age is increasingly defined by the interrelationship between digital content and the spaces in which it is accessed. Code/space, in this regard, is defined as the moments when "software and the spatiality of everyday life become mutually constituted, that is, produced through one another" (Kitchin & Dodge, 2011, p. 16). Code/space continues the theoretical trajectory established by de Souza e Silva (2006) in her coining of the term "hybrid space," defined by the deep interrelationship between physical space and data (especially data conveyed over a mobile device).

This relationship between spatial production and digital media is perhaps best seen in site-specific storytelling, in which the digital and physical come together to create compelling narratives and expand a user's everyday encounter with a place. Mobile storytelling projects can radically shift a user's understanding of everyday experience through new perspectives and new methods of interaction. Storytelling is a lens into the many ways a space can be understood, and mobile storytelling projects highlight the many ways that narratives continually redefine a location. For the fields of design and cultural heritage, then, it is key to have a deep understanding of how to create these narratives to tell alternative stories about a space and push the boundaries of site-specific storytelling and digital technology.

Concepts of Spatial Production

In his seminal work, *The Production of Space*, Lefebvre (1991) argued that space and embodiment are mutually constituted. For Lefebvre, space was not simply a container that people entered; instead, space took on its significance based on how bodies produced that space. These bodies—their cultures, relationships, ideologies, and different levels of status and power—shape the meaning of a space through the practice of everyday life.

In theorizing how space is produced alongside bodies, Lefebvre argued for a conceptual triad for understanding the emergence of spatial meaning: spatial practice, representations of space, and representational spaces (p. 33). *Spatial practices*, at their core, are concerned with the social formation of space that creates cohesion for the people producing this space. Here, the everyday is enacted through practices of production (and reproduction). *Representations of space*, the second element of the spatial triad, are the systems of signs that shape these spatial practices. City planners and architects, imposing an order of signs and pathways that form the shape of the space, typically enact Lefebvre's representations of space. Finally, *representational spaces* are tactical responses to these imposed spaces, creating new forms of symbolism that are "linked to the clandestine or underground side of social life" as well as those spaces produced by artists (p. 33). Here, representational space "overlays physical space, making symbolic use of its objects" (p. 39). These three elements of Lefebvre's spatial triad connect to another triad brought up in his work: spaces that are perceived, conceived, and lived (p. 39).

For the study of mobile storytelling, I am primarily concerned with the overlapping nature of these three concepts as they map onto spatial narratives. It is vital to recognize the ways that stories influence all portions of this spatial triad. Spaces take on meaning through the stories that are told about them. The significance of a space is communicated through narrative means, as exemplified through important historical events that took place in a location or the more mundane stories of two people falling in love at a particular place.

People often encounter these stories in ways that take place in the realm of the cognitive unconscious rather than in the realm of cognitive awareness (Kihlstrom, 1987). That is, many of the stories are so embedded in the daily practices of a culture that they rarely draw attention to themselves and instead are encountered as common sense. Here, these stories thus connect the sphere of *spatial practice* to the sphere of *representations of space*: the common sense of spatial stories is how those in positions of power (including city planners and officials) can enact the practices that best fit with the dominant views of that space. By making the stories of a space common sense and unquestioned, people enact the hegemony without the need for direct coercion. Power—communicated through the common sense, spatial stories—defines a space through dominating the narratives that shape this space. This power is often exerted through the media that communicate these narratives such as plaques, statues, street and building names, and epigraphy (or the writing on the surfaces of buildings). These media typically require either extensive wealth or infrastructure, limiting the participation of the everyday person in these kinds of narratives. These spatial stories are also defined in the ways they get embedded into a space as part of the everyday; that is, they are often unremarkable and exert their influence in implicit rather than explicit ways. These media often enjoy the "prestige of neutrality and objectivity," as cultural geographer Craib (2000, p. 8) has noted. He continues, "The most oppressive and dangerous of all cultural artifacts may be the ones so naturalized and presumably commonsensical as to avoid critique."

Interceding in the common sense of representations of space are the tactical media of Lefebvre's representational spaces. Raley (2009) notes that tactical media are alternative artistic practices that counter dominant narratives through a "micropolitics of disruption, intervention, and education" (p. 1). In sum, the tactical media of representational spaces seek to make these common sense narratives visible through disrupting or defamiliarizing the accepted narratives of these spaces. For example, the Monument Lab project—run through Mural Arts Philadelphia—launched a series in early fall of 2017 that brought a critical perspective to the monuments in the city. The project's goal was to ask, "Where are the women? Where are the people of color? Where are the monuments to the city's heroes of civil rights, its champions of the downtrodden? In fact, where are the downtrodden?" (Salisbury, 2017). Among these new pieces that critique the stories offered by the city of Philadelphia's monuments and statues is Sharon Hayes's work *If They Should Ask*. This piece, located in Rittenhouse Square, is comprises six concrete bases on which statues would stand; however, there are not any statues present. Instead, the bases are inscribed with the names of women who contributed to Philadelphia's public life. Participants can contribute other names through the website companion to the piece. Ultimately, the lack of women standing on Hayes's pedestals brings light to the lack of women represented on monuments throughout the city.

Within this sphere of tactical, representational spaces are alternative modes of spatial storytelling, including mobile media storytelling. The mobile narratives that have been produced should not be understood as existing in distinct ways from projects like the Philadelphia Monument Lab; instead, mobile media in their very nature are encountered in lived, public spaces in which a wide range of media form the understanding of that site. Within this media ecology arises what Schwartz and Halegoua (2015) have termed the "spatial self," an identity formulated through practices with spatial media. Identities utilize their relationships with media in lived environments in order to take shape through everyday practices. As I seek to understand the range of ways this happens, it is key to explore how each medium uniquely conveys the spatial stories that shape notions of identity, community, and inclusion.

Designing Contested Landscapes through Mobile Storytelling

As designers, artists, and cultural heritage practitioners have utilized mobile and location-aware technologies to tell the stories of a place (since at least 2002 with the creation of *34 North, 118 West* by Jeff Knowlton, Jeremy Hight, and Naomi Spellman), they have sought to bring alternative stories to participants. These narratives often speak directly to the existing narrative infrastructures and monuments in order to tell alternative stories. These modes of "urban markup," as termed by McCullough (2008), tell the stories of a space using a range of media from the durable to the ephemeral. As I have argued elsewhere (Farman, 2014, 2015) the stories of a place are often told through durable media (statues, plaques, epigraphy) that limit the narrative scope of a place. These durable media are often expensive, require collaborations between city or state departments and officials, and have limited space to tell their story. The results are narratives that tend to reiterate the dominant ideologies of those in power and present a truncated, uncomplicated version of the history of a site.

Mobile media, in contrast, are able to present multiple stories on a single spot utilizing both durable and ephemeral forms. These technologies layer stories, allowing many voices to be heard. While this can lead to an enabling of marginalized voices that have been silenced by those in power, it can also lead to alternative narratives that seek to reestablish voices that have historically silenced others (as in the case of the neo-Nazi rally organizers in Charlottesville, Virginia). To advocate for contested landscapes may be to advocate for the confrontation of voices intentionally silenced due to their violent and racist histories. As one scholar noted to me, he feared alternative stories told on mobile devices about sites related to the Holocaust; alternative stories are not an advantage at some places. This point resonates deeply at a time when people are confronting the legacies of racism, sexism, and homophobia in significant ways.

Within this context, this chapter advocates for the creation of contested landscapes in order to demonstrate the ways that those in power have often silenced the voices of the marginalized in order to maintain the status quo. That is to say, silencing voices and the narratives that present a coherent, singular version of history tend to function as means to further marginalize those who already lack a voice and agency within a culture: the oppressed, the victimized, the marginalized, and the stigmatized in a culture. By advocating for contested landscapes, I advocate for a disruption of the notion of a single, grand narrative of a place. Instead, places are always formed by multiple narratives that can often contrast and contradict each other. This is the power of a place rather than a flaw in the practices of spatial production. Multiple actors and cultural contexts produce a site's meaning. This allows for the status quo to be challenged and the hegemonic narratives of common sense to be contested.

With this as the aim, the remainder of this chapter looks at ways that narrative production using mobile technologies can effectively approach the challenges faced by this medium. Mobile storytelling confronts many unique hurdles as a narrative platform and designers often impose other expectations drawn from different narrative platforms onto mobile devices. In order to engage polyvocality and design for contested landscapes, mobile storytellers must deal with issues of medium specificity, participant motivation, and temporal considerations.

Medium Specificity

While it is important to understand site-specific storytelling through the holistic lenses of media ecology or transmedia storytelling, it is essential to also look at these narratives through the lens of medium specificity. Initially coined by Hayles (2004), a "media specific analysis" recognizes that the nature of the medium will always impact the ways in which content is communicated. Building on McLuhan's (1964) work on the relationship between mediation and content, a medium-specific approach looks at the ways storytelling is shaped around the media through which it is conveyed. People do not simply experience content; instead, content is experienced through a medium that deeply influences the ways that the narrative is understood. While many narratologists position content as the goal and focus of analysis that is conveyed through a range of media

(Murray, 1997), a medium-specific analysis always considers the content as part-and-parcel of the medium itself. The two are never distinct and must be understood simultaneously. Thus, the materiality of site-specific storytelling is key to doing any analysis of these narratives. Though viewed holistically, understanding the medium and its spatial context are key sites of analysis. This study thus seeks to move between the macro level of analysis that studies these narratives within their broad cultural contexts and histories, as well as zooming into the micro scale of analysis that looks at the specificities of a single mobile device and how those affordances create and shape the content.

Designers of mobile storytelling projects confront this challenge frequently, as they seek to make tactical narratives that tell a unique story (or stories) of a site. For mobile storytellers, it becomes crucial to think in very granular terms about the medium that they are using. A notable distinction must be drawn between the established traditions of digital storytelling (typically utilizing modes of web design) and mobile storytelling, both of which require different thinking and utilize different conventions of narrative. Similarly, as a medium-specific analysis moves along in its granularity, designing for a tablet is different than designing for a smartphone, which is different than designing for a desktop computer. Recognizing these differences is crucial to crafting site-specific stories, because this process demands a deep understanding of the affordances of these technologies. While smartphones are highly versatile and well suited to location-based experiences, desktop computers prevent users from moving through different locations to connect to a story. Similarly, because a tablet is not pocket-sized or easily maneuverable with one hand, it poses a problem for certain location-based activities. This is not meant to discount the possibilities that tablets, desktop computers, and other more static technologies present for site-specific storytelling. The mobility of a mobile device is, however, one of its key affordances that should be designed for in unique ways compared to browser-based narratives for laptops or desktop computers.

When storytellers ignore the materiality of their medium, they ignore the massive impact that medium has on their narrative, likely leading to poor design. Hayles (2004, p. 87) notes that with the rise of digital technology comes a shift in the production of text, and that "the immateriality of the text has ceased to be a useful or even a viable fiction." Norman (2002) discusses similar ideas when he focuses on how the design of objects signifies their capabilities to users. He notes that a technology's affordances are primarily drawn from the human perception of what a technology can do, while its constraints are drawn from the perception of what a technology cannot do. Designers must think about the perspective of their audiences as well as the abilities and limitations of the technologies. In mobile storytelling projects, constraints should *not* always be viewed as limitations. Constraints can often be enabling, and propel a project forward. As Orson Welles is famously noted for saying, "The absence of limitations is the enemy of art." Thus, designing for a technology is not an inherently restricting process, but is instead a strategic bounding of the project's goals in order to design well for the specificities of a medium.

One example of this tension is found in the Curatescape platform that is used to create mobile and web projects for cultural heritage such as *Explore Baltimore Heritage* and *Cleveland Historical*. This mobile framework takes historical content about a site, such as photographs and narrative histories, and layers these media onto a map of the city. As people "explore Baltimore"—as the title of the project suggests they do—they are encouraged to pull up the app and access historical information and content about the place at which the participant is standing. For example, in Baltimore, if a participant walks along North Avenue, just west of the 83 expressway, they will encounter the monument to Colonel William Watson and those who fought in the Mexican-American War. As they load the app, they are given the history of the monument's unveiling in 1903 with veterans present who fought in the war. Those engaging this history through the *Explore Baltimore Heritage* app will also learn of the contested nature of the monument in a time when many in Baltimore were anti-imperialist and saw the war as the United States's move into imperial conquests. There are also a range of media such as historic photographs of the monument.

However, most people who access this history do so on a web browser on a personal computer at home rather than on their mobile devices at the site. According to the designers of these Curatescape apps, it is far more common for the histories to be accessed remotely rather than at the site related to the narratives (M. Tebeau and L. Cebula, personal communication, April 17, 2017). For the goals of Curatescape—to serve as a digital and public history repository, accessible to a broad audience—this usage does not conflict with its mission. Broad accessibility is key for Curatescape, so allowing for what has been termed a "site agnostic" (as opposed to a site-specific) accessibility affords the widest possible audience.

However, such an approach conflicts with the idea of mobile medium specificity. While it affords the broadest audience and reach far beyond the specific locales, it ultimately leads to people not using the mobile app in favor of web browsers on personal computers. It is thus more of a web-based project than a mobile framework (as it terms itself). One problem with this outcome—that people do not access these histories *in situ*—is that the content of these histories is not simply textual or photographic; instead, a vital element of these histories is the place itself. Standing at the site has significance and offers information that cannot be conveyed by other means. Thus, as users engage *Explore Baltimore Heritage* on their laptops instead of their mobile devices, they are deprived of important data that can only be accessed at the site itself. The place is part of the content, and most users of these apps are not receiving a vital element of the historical scope of the sites. Curatescape was designed with the idea that content can be easily transferred across devices, meaning that the content, once published, can be accessed from either with the same effect upon the viewer. However, the outcome of this thinking is a disconnect between the content and the platform; users are no longer linking the stories they experience to the location they are in. Ignoring the specific affordances and constraints of a device is to imagine that content is not deeply affected by the medium through which is conveyed.

When it comes to site-specific storytelling design, creators must understand that location is a primary component of their project's content. If place is removed from a project, then the project begins to deviate from its goals as a mobile platform for storytelling. This leads to a poverty of experience. Storytellers can only incorporate location into the content of a project with a thorough understanding of how users are accessing that content and the ways that a mobile device is a part of the content itself.

Different technologies have different affordances and constraints that offer them different abilities for storytelling projects. To imply that content on one technology can be transferred without alteration to another is ignoring how that content has been crafted for a specific medium. As content moves across platforms, from laptop to mobile or mobile to laptop, the very nature of the content shifts in dramatic ways because the location shifts as the user gains or loses mobility. If a participant is less mobile, or less able to go to a location, they are going to experience the story in a drastically different way, often outside of the storyteller's initial design or intention. The content of a site-specific storytelling project is not only the medium used to tell story, but also the location and the journey to that location.

Participant Motivation

From the perspective of medium specificity, getting participants to engage these narratives at the site corresponding to the story is necessary for the creation of contested landscapes; however, getting people to walk or move to these locations presents one of the key challenges of mobile storytelling. As Ritchie (2014) argues, keeping readers engaged with a story requires that the participant be willing to cross the "narrative value threshold," or the perceived payoff that a reader will get by reading through the story such as the denouement of a narrative thread that readers seek to resolve. For reading a traditional text, the costs invested are typically time and minimal physical effort; these two costs are expanded as mobile stories ask participants to sometimes walk or journey miles and dedicate a significant amount of time to engaging their stories. These requirements also betray the typical usage of a mobile device, as users are accustomed to interstitial engagement that allows them to use the device during in between times while they wait for transportation or a friend to arrive for a lunch meeting. Mobile stories often ask users to invest their time and go out of their way to find these places that may be off the beaten path.

Ultimately, participants must perceive the "really nontrivial effort" (as Ritchie terms it) as valuable and worthwhile for engaging the story. Participants must view rewards as exceeding the perceived efforts required. Reading a story only requires the turn of a page to continue the narrative, but site-specific storytelling often requires a body to travel through space. This effort becomes physical, and sometimes economic and social, possibly demanding travel costs and public interaction. These costs, whether physical, monetary, or social, must be seen as worth it for the payoff of the journey and the narrative. This, as noted by Flanagan (2009, pp. 204–205), can reveal the class dynamics of these mobile narratives, since the leisure time required by them typically limits the experience to those who have the free time necessary to engage these stories.

Flanagan's work focuses on the relationship between games, spaces, and cultural analysis. Many of the mobile narratives employ game mechanics as a feature of encouraging participants to travel through space to a new location to experience a story. Drawing on the mechanics of gamification, while scorned by some (see Bogost, 2011), is seen by others as connecting to the embedded social instincts of all social beings, who use play as a means of socialization and environmental knowledge building (Huizinga, 1955). When a journey becomes playful or competitive, users are more likely to engage and continue their narrative.

Another technique, which is drawn from participatory theater and performance, is to start the project or story with a very small ask, whether that task is a distance traveled or the amount of time consumed by content. Following Ritchie's argument, accessing site-specific storytelling content is a non-trivial effort. Users must quickly see the reward for their non-trivial effort, or they will refuse to act. Presenting participants with large distances between content will discourage them from engaging. Small motivating factors act as inertia for the narrative that keeps the participant moving forward, and will likely keep them engaged. Thus, by encouraging participants through a small series of actions, storytellers can get participants to engage in a larger way. When it comes to distance traveling, it is possible that starting small may lead to more user retention and more engagement.

Other storytelling media have overcome the issue of non-trivial effort in interesting ways. Episodic television, for example, often relies on the cliffhanger to keep audiences engaged and interested until the next episode or season. By creating immersive narratives or mimicking episodic structure, storytellers can motivate participants to move to new locations and finish a narrative. Projects that showcase narratives as islands, with no links between stops or locations, encourage a stop-and-go participant, with little motivation to move on to individual stories. One of the strengths of mobile storytelling is its ability to literally immerse a user in a location. They are surrounded with the space of a story in a way in which other media cannot be, including virtual reality, which is built on recreating this experience. Users are immersed in the story not only through a compelling narrative, but also through the materiality of the story and the physical presence of a location.

These techniques for user motivation are employed in order to get participants at the site of the narrative, which is a key component of the content of these stories. Sites are contested landscapes in the ways they are practiced, and getting a location's stakeholders to engage the site is a foundational element for creating polyvocality at these places. For many stories to be told, the users must engage the site; for many stories to be experienced, participants should be present at the location since the place itself is a fundamental piece of the story.

Materiality

By getting participants to visit the location of these stories, mobile storytelling projects are countering the notion that mobile devices are pulling people away from a deep engagement with place and with the social life of the world around them. Thus, mobile stories should seek to find meaningful connections between the place and mobile device rather than relying solely on the screen as the site of content engagement. Placing emphasis on the content on the screen, as opposed to the materiality of a location, is ultimately a lost opportunity for site-specific storytellers. Encouraging users to engage with physical objects in a location brings together different aspects of the storytelling project to create a complete experience, driven by multiple layers. Instead of only engaging with the digital layer, usually consisting of audio or visual imagery, participants are now incorporating the physical layer of the story as well. These layers complement each other and add new context to the story. Layering is an important feature of these devices and links to the long history of the pleasure of visual media (from theater to augmented reality). "Seeing double" by creating dynamic interactions between a space and digital information affords users the complexity of these sites rather than the flatness of a grand narrative (see Farman, 2012, pp. 38–39).

One effective example of creating a meaningful link between the layers of the physical world and the mobile device is a project called *University of Death* (see Bunting, 2014). This storytelling project, which took place in Pullman, Washington, got users to enter new locations and engage with physical objects as key features of reading the fictional detective story. The designers did this by placing story content in geocache containers, library stacks at Washington State University, and holes in the walls of bathroom stalls. By hiding important information in physical locations, *University of Death* not only encouraged users to overcome the non-trivial effort to continue the story, but also immersed them by getting them to engage with the physical space in meaningful ways. *University of Death* notably required participants to touch objects such as archival documents that were clues to the next story elements readers needed to access, and asked participants to interact with a space beyond the screen.

Temporal Considerations

As locations develop and change throughout the years, so do the stories that correspond with them. Notably, for digital storytelling, the context of a story shifts when the location changes. What was once a church may years later be a bar, or a library, or an empty parking lot. The digital stories once associated with a location, while remaining unchanged in the digital layer, are understood differently when paired with an evolving location. Time, then, becomes an important element of a story's content; not only the length of the story, but also when the user chooses to access it.

An excellent example of this is a project called *[murmur]*, based in Toronto and placed in twelve cities around the world. The project placed green ear-shaped signs across these cities; on these signs was a phone number and code that participants could call and listen to an audio recording about that location. Each recording began with a slate, detailing the location the story took place in, and named objects or buildings in the scenery to focus attention on. This positions the viewer in the same way that the storyteller is positioned, directing them to view the correct objects in relation to the story. However, the cityscape is not static, and the objects mentioned by the storyteller had often changed or disappeared. The asynchronous nature of these stories adds an interesting level to this layered experience, as the recorded story becomes archival, and represents a reality that no longer exists. The story is no longer about what is, but what *was*. If designers plan ahead and craft content that can age while maintaining relevancy and accessibility, then site-specific stories can become ever-evolving without losing their effectiveness.

Utilizing a different approach, the project *These Pages Fall Like Ash*, based in the city of Bristol in the United Kingdom, created a story that could only be experienced for a short, two-week period of time. Rather than craft content that would be available for audiences at their convenience, *These Pages Fall Like Ash* capitalized on the culture of live performance and integrated it into digital storytelling. Participation in this event mirrored the value of rarity associated with concerts or theatre. Its ephemeral nature allowed only a select number of people to read and engage the work before it vanished. This format creates the feeling of being present for something rare and temporally limited. In this case, time became relevant to the content of the project not because of its effect on the location, but because of its limited nature. Similarly, as other projects become outdated or are no longer maintained, they also fade into history, and become inaccessible. Archiving site-specific storytelling is now part of the initial design process. Creators must plan ahead to decide whether their material will be permanent or temporary, and decide how to archive their app.

Conclusion

As a location's meaning and significance is produced through embodied actions in those spaces, stories remain vital to the ways a site becomes meaningful. Digital technology has certainly shifted the ways in which a space communicates its histories and significance. With the addition of the digital layer comes a plethora of new possibilities for storytelling, especially in the ways that a site can link to multiple stories. These stories can correspond or conflict, creating contested landscapes that demonstrate the ways that a single story should not dominate the meaning of a space. To capitalize on this potential, storytellers must understand the affordances and constraints of their medium and use those to propel their project forward. Location must be primary to the content of the project, and must be used beyond spectacle in meaningful ways that encourage participants to interact with the locations of their stories. As storytellers utilize mobile platforms for their projects, understanding the power of the material nature of these spaces and devices as they link with one another is key for effectively engaging a participant's body with the spatial narrative. In doing so, storytellers are able to communicate the ways that, as Ahmed (2006, p. 51) puts it, some spaces and objects "tend toward some bodies more than others. . . . So it is not simply that some bodies and tools *happen* to generate specific actions. Objects, as well as spaces, are made from some kinds of bodies more than others." By revealing the common sense narratives that shape these bodies and spaces, mobile storytelling projects allow for a polyvocality that contends with the narratives that reinforce the status quo of dominance and subjugation of those without power.

Acknowledgments

This chapter was drafted with the assistance of Joshua Hall and was sponsored by the University of Maryland Summer Scholars Program.

References

Adichie, C. N. (2009). The danger of a single story. *TEDGlobal*. www.ted.com/talks/chimamanda_adichie_the_danger_of_a_single_story

Ahmed, S. (2006). *Queer phenomenology: Orientations, objects, others*. Durham, NC: Duke University Press.

Alexander, B. (2017). *The new digital storytelling: Creating narratives with new media*. Santa Barbara, CA: Praeger.

Bassett, C. (2014). *The arc and the machine: Narrative and new media*. Manchester: Manchester University Press.

Bogost, I. (2011). Gamification is bullshit. *The Atlantic*, August 9. www.theatlantic.com/technology/archive/2011/08/gamification-is-bullshit/243338/

Bunting, B. (2014). The geocacher as placemaker: Remapping reality through location-based mobile gameplay. In J. Farman (Ed.), *The mobile story: Narrative practices with locative technologies* (pp. 161–174). New York: Routledge Press.

Burgess, J. (2006). Hearing ordinary voices: Cultural studies, vernacular creativity and digital storytelling. *Continuum: Journal of Media and Cultural Studies*, 20(2), 201–214.

Cooley, H. R. (2014). *Finding Augusta: Habits of mobility and governance in the digital era*. Hanover, NH: Dartmouth College Press.

Couldry, N. (2008). Mediatization or mediation? Alternative understandings of the emergent space of digital storytelling. *New Media & Society*, 10(3), 373–391.

Craib, R. B. (2000). Cartography and power in the conquest and creation of new Spain. *Latin American Research Review*, 35(1), 7–36.

De Souza e Silva, A. (2006). From cyber to hybrid: Mobile technologies as interfaces of hybrid spaces. *Space and Culture*, 9(3), 261–278.

Denson, A. (2017). *Monuments to absence: Cherokee removal and the contest over southern memory*. Chapel Hill, NC: University of North Carolina Press.

Emerson, L. (2014). *Reading writing interfaces: From the digital to the bookbound*. Minneapolis, MN: University of Minnesota Press.

Farman, J. (2012). *Mobile interface theory: Embodied space and locative media*. New York: Routledge Press.

Farman, J. (Ed.). (2014). *The mobile story: Narrative practices with locative technologies*. New York: Routledge Press.

Farman, J. (2015). Stories, spaces, and bodies: The production of embodied space through mobile media storytelling. *Communication Research and Practice*, 1(2), 101–116.

Flanagan, M. (2009). *Critical play: Radical game design*. Cambridge, MA: MIT Press.

Frith, J. (2015). *Smartphones as locative media*. Cambridge: Polity Press.

Frith, J. (2017). Invisibility through the interface: the social consequences of spatial search. *Media, Culture & Society*, 39(4), 536–551.

Hayles, N. K. (2004). Print is flat, code is deep: The importance of media-specific analysis. *Poetics Today*, 25(1), 67–90.

Hayles, N. K. (2008). *Electronic literature: New horizons for the literary*. Notre Dame, IN: University of Notre Dame Press.

Huizinga, J. (1955). *Homo ludens: A study of the play element in culture*. Boston: Beacon Press.

Kihlstrom, J. F. (1987). The cognitive unconscious. *Science*, 237, 1445–1452.

Kitchin, R. & Dodge, M. (2011). *Code/space: Software and everyday life*. Cambridge, MA: MIT Press.

Lefebvre, H. (1991). *The production of space*. Trans. D. Nicholson. Oxford: Blackwell.

Liao, T. & Humphreys, L. (2015). Layar-ed places: Using mobile augmented reality to tactically reengage, reproduce, and reappropriate public space. *New Media & Society*, 17(9), 1418–1435.

Marino, M. (2014). Mobilizing citizens: Alternative community storytelling. In J. Farman (Ed.), *The mobile story: Narrative practices with locative technologies* (pp. 290–303). New York: Routledge Press.

McCullough, M. (2008). Epigraphy and the public library. In A. Aurigi and F. de Cindio (Eds.), *Augmented urban space: Articulating the physical and electronic city* (pp. 61–72). Burlington, VT: Ashgate.

McLuhan, M. (1964). *Understanding media: The extensions of man*. London: Routledge.

Montfort, N. (2005). *Twisty little passages: An approach to interactive fiction*. Cambridge, MA: MIT Press.

Murray, J. (1997). *Hamlet on the holodeck: The future of narrative in cyberspace*. Cambridge, MA: MIT Press.

Norman, D. (2002). *The design of everyday things*. New York: Basic Books.

Ostherr, K. (2017). *Applied media studies*. New York: Routledge Press.

Raley, R. (2009). *Tactical media*. Minneapolis, MN: University of Minnesota Press.

Ritchie, J. (2014). The affordances and constraints of mobile locative narratives. In J. Farman (Ed.), *The mobile story: Narrative practices with locative technologies* (pp. 53–67). New York: Routledge Press.

Ruston, S. (2010). Storyworlds on the move: Mobile media and their implications for narrative. *StoryWorlds: A journal of narrative studies*, 2, 101–120.

Salisbury, Stephen. (2017). Philly's big new art project asks: Who deserves a monument anyway? *The Philadelphia Inquirer*, September 14. www.philly.com/philly/entertainment/arts/phillys-big-new-art-project-asks-who-deserves-a-monument-anyway-20170914.html

Schwartz, R. & Halegoua, G. (2015). The spatial self: Location-based identity performance on social media. *New Media & Society*, 17(10), 1643–1660.

Turkle, S. (2015). *Reclaiming conversation: The power of talk in the digital age*. New York: Penguin Books.

Wilken, R. & Goggin, G. (Eds.). (2014). *Locative media*. New York: Routledge Press.

INDEX

Note: index entries in the form 55n1 refer to page and endnote numbers.